PELTRIES OR PLANTATIONS

THE JOHNS HOPKINS UNIVERSITY STUDIES IN HISTORICAL AND POLITICAL SCIENCE

EIGHTY–SEVENTH SERIES (1969)

1. The Negro in Maryland Politics, 1870–1912
   BY MARGARET LAW CALLCOTT

2. Peltries or Plantations: The Economic Policies of the Dutch West India Company in New Netherland, 1623–1639
   BY VAN CLEAF BACHMAN

Peltries or Plantations

The Economic Policies
of the
Dutch West India Company in New Netherland
1623 - 1639

By

VAN CLEAF BACHMAN

THE JOHNS HOPKINS PRESS

BALTIMORE AND LONDON

338.974

B

The Johns Hopkins Press, Baltimore, Maryland 21218
The Johns Hopkins Press Ltd., London

Library of Congress Catalog Card Number   74–91336

Standard Book Number   8018–1064–7

CONTENTS

PREFACE vii

ABBREVIATIONS x

   I. THE " VOORCOMPAGNIEËN " 3
     i. The Technique of Trade 15

   II. THE WEST INDIA COMPANY 25
     i. The Operation of an Organizational Monster.... 37

   III. THE DECISION TO COLONIZE 44

   IV. THE EXPERIENCE OF THE EARLY YEARS 74

   V. THE PATROON SYSTEM 95
     i. Was the *Vryheden* Obtained by Fraud?........ 109

   VI. THE CAMPAIGN AGAINST THE PATROONS 120

   VII. THE PATH TO FREE TRADE 140

   VIII. SOME CONCLUDING OBSERVATIONS 154

APPENDIX I: Estimates, from Costs, of New Netherland
     Freight Rates in Relation to Baltic Freight Rates.... 157

APPENDIX II: Biographical Notes on Three Patroons:
     Blommaert, Coenrats, and de Laet 161

BIBLIOGRAPHY 168

INDEX 176

F'r te verdaenke

WOLFERT GERRITSZOON VAN KOUWENHOVEN

naabai Amersfoort (Pr. Utrecht) geboore,
" bouwmeester " van de West Indische Compagnie
op de Manhattes A° 1625
aen van Kiliaen van Rensselaer
en Rensselaerswyck A° 1630,
grontlaegster van de dur'p Nieuw Amersfoort
A° 1636,
aen die, en z'n leeve " Bestevaer " vernoemt deur z'n buure,
A° D° 1661, naa 'n lank aen vrugtbaar leeve,
uit dit werdelt es ferhuist,
ez dit skietnis deur z'n groot-grootkender
van de twaalvde geslogt
maet lievde aen eerebiet gesgreeve.

PREFACE

It is certainly a cruel twist of fate that defeat should be accompanied by oblivion, but the fact is that this ultimate demonstration of human insignificance all too often accompanies it. Who today, for example, amid the vociferous lamentations on behalf of this or that underprivileged group, bewails the lot of the Tasmanians, who have not only suffered indignities but have been exterminated from the face of the earth? In this and similar cases, the lack of a surviving population which identifies closely with the defeated party seems to make the obliteration of its memory from at least the popular consciousness a virtual certainty.

The descendants of the New Netherlanders have not, thankfully, met with physical extermination; but, in the nineteenth century, a flood of immigration from New England and Europe, industrialization with its many ramifications, and lack of control of government and schools combined with other, more subtle factors to break up the "Low Dutch" culture of New York and New Jersey and eradicate in the descendants of the New Netherlanders all but a sentimental identification with it. Today, therefore, the American descendant of the New Netherland pioneers is comfortably assimilated into the much maligned "wasp" segment of our population and shows little disposition to remember and honor his Dutch forbears, much less to defend his cultural identity to the point of riot and insurrection.

The group which stimulated, encouraged, and read Washington Irving and the more serious nineteenth-century historians of New Netherland, such as Brodhead and O'Callaghan, has thus been largely dissolved and with it the affectionate interest for New Netherland which once existed. Today colonial historians find little opposition when, like as not to cover over their ignorance, they dismiss New Netherland as an ephemeral surd in the mighty progress of English America.

The most recent serious book on New Netherland will hardly serve to jolt people out of this comfortable ignorance. "The Dutch years," we read on its jacket, "represent not a unique experience but rather a composite experience that reflects what was occurring elsewhere in the seventeenth century." Even more depressing is the statement in the same work that " the none too firmly rooted Dutch institutions were extirpated in 1664 and English ones substituted." [1] This not only ignores the vigorous continuation of the Reformed Church in the middle colonies but also carries the strong suggestion that 1664 brought the " extirpation " of noninstitutional aspects of Dutch culture as well.

 This, of course, is nonsense. I point out, to take only one of the most obvious facets of culture, namely language, that Low Dutch, the descendant of the language of the New Netherlanders, was surviving with considerable vigor in many rural areas *two hundred years* after the English conquest and that there are persons now living who can proudly claim that their grandparents knew not one word of English until they were sent to school.

In fact, a certain argument could be made that the very success of certain elements of Low Dutch culture has made us oblivious to their non-English origin. For example, how many of us know not only that Santa Claus came to us via New Netherland but also that our pronunciation of his name reproduces with considerable precision the vocalic peculiarities of the Low Dutch of the lower Hudson.

If a great deal of the culture of the Low Dutch has been obliterated by the nineteenth and twentieth centuries, so has most of the culture of Puritan New England. Where is the family farm, the pervading sense of the Creator's presence, the conscientious morality, the solidarity of the paternally dominated household? Not in Cambridge, Massachusetts or Greenwich, Connecticut.

Studies in the history of New Netherland are not less relevant to today's reader than studies of colonial history generally. Both give insight into a fascinating period of European expansion and, in uncovering a way of life radically different from our own, suggest meaningful perspectives on our own industrialized existence.

In many ways, a failure, such as New Netherland ultimately was, is no less productive of fruitful reflection than a success. Analysis of a defeat can lead us no less surely to the wellsprings of human behavior. And when that defeat is a product more of

1. Thomas J. Condon, *New York Beginnings: the Commercial Origins of New Netherland* (New York: New York University Press; London: University of London Press Ltd., 1968), p. viii.

slight miscalculations, bad luck, and powerful opposition than stupidity, moral laxness, or sheer laziness, it may give us pause to consider the slender threads on which our own fortunes hang.

The following pages deal with only a segment of New Nether-land's history, albeit a crucial and clearly delimited segment. Before 1638, the West India Company vacillated between two more or less contradictory methods of exploiting the region: concentration on the fur trade and agricultural colonization. After 1638, the Company was committed to the development of an agricultural colony in North America. The core of this study is an attempt to determine (1) exactly what were the Company's economic policies up to 1638 and (2) the reasons why the Company chose the courses it did.

Since only a small proportion of the West India Company's records for this period have survived, parts of this study are necessarily of a speculative nature; and it may strike some persons that the argument becomes at times unproductively hypothetical. I hope, however, that my approach of holding fast to what appeared to be the most significant course of inquiry, despite occasional shoals in the available evidence, has formulated new questions and that it is evident that researches which approach New Netherland and the Low Dutch with a rasp in the throat rather than a twang in the nose can still yield fruit.

I am particularly indebted to the unfailingly helpful advice of Professor Frederic C. Lane, formerly of The Johns Hopkins University, the kindness and generosity of Dr. Simon Hart of the Gemeente Archief of Amsterdam, and the patience and encouragement of my wife. Many thanks should also go to Professor Jack Greene of Johns Hopkins, without whose interest and encouragement the manuscript would certainly have mouldered away in the **cellar.**

ABBREVIATIONS

BMHG   *Bijdragen en mededeelingen van het Historisch Genootschap gevestigd te Utrecht* (1878 to date).

DCHNY   *Documents Relative to the Colonial History of the State of New York* . . . , edited by E. B. O'Callaghan and B. Fernow. 15 vols. Albany: Weed, Parsons and Company, 1856–87.

GAA   Gemeente Archief van Amsterdam (Municipal Archives of Amsterdam).

Hunt.   *Documents Relating to New Netherland, 1624–1626, in the Henry E. Huntington Library*, edited by A. J. F. van Laer. San Marino, California: 1924.

NNN   *Narratives of New Netherland 1609–1664*, edited by J. Franklin Jameson, Original Narratives of Early American History. New York: Charles Scribner's Sons, 1909.

VRBM   *Van Rensselaer Bowier Manuscripts, being the letters of Kiliaen van Rensselaer, 1630–1643, and other documents relating to the Colony of Rensselaerswyck*, edited by A. J. F. van Laer. Albany: University of the State of New York, 1908.

Wass.   Nicolaes van Wassenaer, *Historisch verhael alder ghedenck-weerdichste geschiedenissen die hier en daer in Europa, als in Duijtschlant, Vranckrijck, Enghelant, [Denemarcken,] Hungarijen, Polen, [Sweden, Moscovien,] Sevenbergen, Wallachien, Moldavien, Turckijen, [Zwitserland,] en Nederlant, [in Asia, . . .: in Africa, . . .: in America, . . .:] van den beginne des jaers 1621: [tot Octobri (1629)], voorgevallen syn*, 17 vols. Amsterdam: Jan Evertss. Cloppenburgh and Ian Iansz., 1622–1630.

A year beginning in July and ending in June will be designated by a slash: "1968/69," for example, means the year beginning July 1, 1968, and ending June 30, 1969.

CHAPTER ONE

THE *VOORCOMPAGNIEËN*

The growing prosperity of Western Europe in the sixteenth century expressed itself in a sharply increased demand for luxury products, among them fine furs. One reaction to this buoyant fur market was an intensification of fur hunting in Russia, the premier source of quality furs for Western Europe, and, as the Russian fur supply thinned, the penetration of Russian fur traders into Siberia toward the end of the sixteenth century.[1] A second reaction was the development of the French fur trade on the St. Lawrence from the second quarter of the sixteenth century. In 1610, when news of Henry Hudson's discovery of the future New Netherland reached the United Provinces, the Dutch had access to the Russian fur supply, especially through Archangel, but were firmly denied participation in the trade of New France.[2] Reports of a great river at 40° 45′ on the North American coast, inhabited in part by " friendly and polite people, who had an abundance of provisions, and many skins and peltries, martins, foxes, and many other commodities, . . ."[3] opened to the Dutch merchant the prospect of participation in the New World fur trade despite the French monopoly of Canada.

The first merchant really to appreciate the implications of Hudson's discovery seems to have been one Arnout Vogels of Amsterdam. Vogels was born in Antwerp about 1580 of Lutheran parents who settled in Amsterdam after the reduction of Antwerp by the

1. Raymond H. Fisher, *The Russian Fur Trade, 1550–1700*, pp. 16, 20-21. For specific cultural changes which tended to increase the demand for luxury goods, see Werner Sombart, *Luxus und Kapitalismus*.

2. Simon Hart, *The Prehistory of the New Netherland Company*, discusses Dutch relations with New France at this time, pp. 12-17.

3. Emanuel van Meteren, *Belgische ofte Nederlandtsche oorlogen ende gheschiedenissen, beginnende van 't jaer 1595 tot 1611* . . . (Schotlant buyten Danswyck: Hermes van Loven, 1611), in Henry C. Murphy, *Henry Hudson in Holland*, Appendix K.

3

Spaniards in 1585. As a young man, he was taken into the service of a trading partnership to which his father belonged and which, among other interests, was actively engaged in the fur trade; it is unknown, however, whether he stayed with this concern after his father's death in 1602.[4] On July 26, 1610, probably some time after the arrival of definite reports of Hudson's voyage in Holland, Vogels chartered the *Hoope* of about 100 lasts, skippered by Sijmen Lambertsz Mau from Monnikendam.[5] Mau contracted to convey " wares and merchandise " to the " West Indies, and nearby lands and places," and to trade here and there on the coast at the direction of the mate and supercargo, both of whom were appointed by the charterer. The only thing certain about the results of the voyage is that Mau survived it and sailed for the East Indies in December 1611.[6] It is possible that Vogels' objective was the smuggling trade in the Caribbean, but his subsequent interest in New Netherland suggests a conscious attempt to probe the fur resources of North America.[7]

4. Hart, *Prehistory*, pp. 41-42.

5. Charter party in GAA, Notarieel Archief No. 120, pp. 90–91. Receipt of information concerning Hudson's voyage in Holland did not follow immediately upon his return to Dartmouth, England on November 7, 1609. Contrary Channel winds prevented his employer, the Dutch East India Company, from obtaining prompt notification of Hudson's return, but, when informed, the Company ordered Hudson to return to Holland. However, in January 1610 he was prevented in this by the English government (van Meteren, *Belgische oorlogen*, in Murphy, *Hudson in Holland*, Appendix K). Evidently the explorer never reported personally before his Dutch employers (for a contemporary Spanish source which tends to confirm this, see F. C. Wieder, *Onderzoek naar de oudste kaarten van de omgeving van New York*, p. 5 and 5n.); but information concerning the voyage undoubtedly reached Holland through Dutch members of his crew, one of whom, the mate, probably showed van Meteren, the Dutch consul in London, his own journal of the voyage early in 1610 (NNN, p. 5).

6. Hart, *Prehistory*, p. 42n.

7. In his *Nieuwe Wereldt ofte Beschrijvinghe van West-Indien* . . . (Leyden: Isaack Elzevier, 1625), Johannes de Laet wrote that " in the year 1610 some merchants again sent a ship thither [to the Hudson]," and the 1633 and 1640 editions call them " merchants of Amsterdam." (Extracts translated in NNN, p. 38 and 38n.) In 1625 de Laet was a director of the West India Company, then the administrator of New Netherland, and it is possible that he was using a doubtful or fictitious 1610 voyage to bolster Dutch claims by demonstrating continuous navigation to the region since Hudson's voyage.

In 1632 the West India Company briefed the States General on its claims to New Netherland in connection with an English challenge to the Company's rights there. Perhaps borrowing from de Laet, the Company pointed out that " after some of your inhabitants had resorted thither, in the year 1610 and following years, your High Mightinesses had finally, in the year 1615, granted some of your inhabitants a charter. . . ." (DCHNY, I, p. 51).

The following year, 1611, Vogels sought to circumvent the French near-monopoly of the North American fur trade in two ways. One was through a partnership with two French merchants to trade with Canada, which, since the lapse of de Monts' patent in January 1609 was open to all Frenchmen.[8] The other disdained such surreptitious means. On May 19th, in company with Francoijs and Leonnaert Pelgrom, he chartered the *St. Pieter* of 60 lasts, skipper Cornelis Ryser of Amsterdam.[9] The charter party stipulated that Ryser was to carry "wares and merchandise" and three supercargoes to Terra Nova (Newfoundland) and trade there for two months "in all such places as shall please the merchants, or supercargos." If trade was unsuccessful during these two months, the crew was required to help with fishing.

The mention of Cornelis Ryser as skipper suggests that this voyage is the same as the Christiaensz-Block voyage recorded some fourteen years later in Nicolaes Wassenaer's *Historisch Verhael*.[10] Wassenaer related that Hendrick Christiaensz from Cleves (not Hudson) was the first to sail to the Hudson River:

> When he had made a voyage to the West Indies, he happened near there. But as his vessel was laden and a ship of Monickendam had been lost in the vicinity, he dared not approach that land, desiring to make that attempt at another time. It so happened that he with the honorable Adriaen Block chartered a ship with the skipper *Ryser* and accomplished his voyage thither, bringing back two sons of the principal person there.[11]

Although not dated by Wassenaer, this first voyage of Christiaensz and Block probably occurred no later than 1611, for a declaration of two of Block's crew on his 1612/13 voyage reveals that Block had made two previous voyages to "Virginia."[12] Thus a probable chronological agreement as well as the coincident appearance of skipper Ryser, who is otherwise unknown in connection with New Netherland, tends to confirm that Wassenaer was reporting the *St. Pieter's* 1611 voyage for Vogels and his

---

8. Hart, *Prehistory*, pp. 15-16.
9. Charter party in GAA, Not. Arch. No. 125, pp. 64v–65v.
10. Hart has pointed this out: *Prehistory*, pp. 18–21.
11. Wass., VIII, p. 85.
12. GAA, Not. Arch. 197, pp. 614v–615, in Hart, *Prehistory*, Appendix 3.

partners and that Christiaensz and Block were the supercargos, who, according to the charter party, were to direct the skipper to places of trade.

Ryser's voyage must have reaped either profits or encouraging prospects, for it is very likely that Vogels *cum suis* invested in a ship for their new trade shortly after Ryser's return. On January 17, 1612, Adriaen Block, having returned to Amsterdam, purchased the *Fortuyn*, a 55 last *spiegelschip*.[13] This purchase was almost certainly made for the account of the Vogels partnership, and presumably Block made his second voyage to Virginia as skipper of this vessel in 1612.[14] Something about the results can be inferred from a letter from Vogels' partner, Francoijs Pelgrom, to his wife, dated July 30, 1613. The succeeding voyage of 1612/13 was good, he wrote, "yes, a better voyage even than last year."[15]

Block's scantily known 1612 voyage was the last unclouded by competition. He was dispatched again by the Vogels group in 1613, but seven weeks after his arrival in the Hudson, he was unexpectedly joined by skipper Thijs Mossel, who had been sent out by a second Amsterdam partnership.[16] Mossel sought to discredit Block before his aboriginal clientele by offering up to three times as many goods per beaver as Block,[17] and, before sailing for home, left on the river a mulatto from San Domingo with a supply

13. Van Dale's *Groot woordenboek der Nederlandse taal*, p. 1871, describes the *spiegelschip* as a ship with a long beak head, high rising aft, and flat stern. Hart states that Block bought the *Fortuyn* for his shipowners, "the Van Tweenhuysen Company" (*Prehistory*, p. 50), and in another place he describes the company which "sent Block on his voyages" as consisting of Arnout Vogels, Francoijs, Leonnard, Paulus, and Steffen Pelgrom, Hans Hunger, and Lambert van Tweenhuysen (p. 22). In reality the notification of the sale of the *Fortuyn*, dated January 17, 1612, says nothing about Block's shipowners, and there is no evidence that any of the last four persons mentioned had any connection with New Netherland ventures before the 1613/14 voyage.

14. A *Fortuyn* served the Vogels partnership in 1613/14 (DCHNY, I, p. 11), and in 1617 two members of the New Netherland Company, into which the Vogels partnership had merged, sold a ship of similar name and tonnage (Hart, *Prehistory*, pp. 50–51).

15. Letter book of Francoys Pelgroms Geerartsen (July 9, 1613–March 7, 1616), GAA, Not. Arch. 373; extract in Hart, *Prehistory*, appendix 2.

16. Hart, *Prehistory*, pp. 22–23. Hart gives the names of these partners (p. 23), but he is assuming that the partners in the succeeding voyages also participated in this first voyage. The only certain participants were Jan Holscher and Gerrit Allertsz Ruyll, who sold Mossel's ship October 1, 1613 (*ibid.*, p. 22n).

17. GAA, Not. Arch. 197, pp. 614v–615, in Hart, *Prehistory*, Appendix 3.

of hatchets and knives to continue trade until his return the following winter. Although Mossel pretended that the mulatto had
simply jumped ship, Block, undeceived, and probably unable to
recruit from his own crew a candidate for a half year's stint in the
wilderness, made an unsuccessful attempt to kidnap this first factor
in New Netherland.[18]

After the return of their ships from the "Virginias," the two
partnerships continued their bitter competition by more subtle
means. By August 1613 Vogels and his associates, who about this
time began styling themselves "the Company of lands situate
between Virginia and Nova Francia," [19] had obtained some sort
of patent or authorization from the *Stadhouder*, Prince Maurits,
for their Virginia trade, and in that month Block pretended that
it empowered him to protect their monopoly by force in a con-
versation with a prospective competitor. Mossel's principals pro-
tested the granting of the patent, and by his letter of 23 September
1613, Prince Maurits nullified the privilege and admonished both
parties to reach a settlement. The competitors met in the presence
of the learned geographer-dominie Petrus Plancius, but they could
agree neither to combine in one undertaking, nor to compensate
the other for withdrawal from the trade, nor to trade together
peacefully. Each side sent the other a notarized warning and statement of grievances, and the ships, two for the Vogels partnership
under Block and Christiaensz and one under Mossel for Vogels'
competitors, sailed away.[20]

18. This is the best interpretation of a declaration of two members of Block's
crews and one of Mossel's dated August 20, 1613, (*ibid.*) and a declaration of
nine members of Hendrick Christiaensz' crew on July 23, 1614 (GAA, Not. Arch.
198, pp. 97–98, in Hart, *Prehistory*, Appendix 7). Hart interprets these documents
differently, pp. 23 and 26.

19. They refer to themselves thus in a protest to Mossel's shipowners dated
September 30, 1613 (GAA, Not. Arch. 132, p. 197v; abstract in I. N. Phelps
Stokes, *The Iconography of Manhattan Island*, VI, pp. 4-5). The known partners
for the 1613–14 voyage were Arnout Vogels, Lambrecht van Tweenhuysen, and
Francoijs Pelgrom (GAA, Not. Arch. 197, p. 646v, in Hart, *Prehistory*, Appendix
4), Pauels Pelgrom (GAA, Not. Arch. 133, pp. 30–31, in Hart, Appendix 6),
and Hans Hongers (DCHNY, I, pp. 11-12).

20. For the dispute about the patent, see Hart, *Prehistory*, pp. 23–25, and
translations and abstracts of documents from the Notarial Archive of the GAA which
are given in Hart as Appendices 2, 6, and 11, and in Stokes, *Iconography*, VI, pp.
4–5.

The known participants in Mossel's second, 1613/14 voyage were Jan Holscher,
Wessel Schenck, Hans Claesz, Arnout van Liebergen, Jacob Bontenos, and Barent
Sweerts (GAA, Not. Arch. 456, no. 394; abstracted in Stokes, VI, pp. 4–5).

Adriaen Block arrived in the Hudson to find his fellow, Christiaensz, at loggerheads with Mossel. Perhaps Block, who sailed sometime after these two, brought word of a last minute agreement between the owners at home. In all events a cartel agreement was concluded between the rivals. According to a declaration of two members of Mossel's crew, this agreement provided that

> Block would profit by three skins out of five, and their skipper and supercargo the other two skins. Both parties agreed to this on condition that the said Block would depart from the river with his ship and leave the trade there to the ship of the witness and the ship of Hendrick Carstiaensz.[21]

This ⅗–⅖ partition must be interpreted as including the trade of Christiaensz and Mossel on the Hudson only, it being almost inconceivable that the representatives of the Vogels partnership, with their prior claim to the region and seemingly considerably larger investment in shipping, would have assented to any other terms. Doubtlessly, Block planned to scour the southern coast of New England for furs.

Not long after this accord, Block's ship was destroyed by fire. Mossel offered to take on one-half of Block's crew and pay their back wages in return for one-half of the trade, or even all of his crew for a larger share, but Block refused, probably relying on his sloop and his ability to construct a yacht to employ his crew and continue trading. On March 7, 1614, four or five weeks after the fire, the situation again changed dramatically when renegades from Block's crew seized Mossel's ship and sailed away to pirate in the West Indies. Mossel was able to continue trade in his sloop with some merchandise which the renegades in an inexplicable fit of generosity sent ashore after they seized his ship.[22]

The testimony concerning the capture of Mossel's ship mentions no other large vessel in the Hudson besides Christiaensz' *Fortuyn*. It is likely therefore that the two other vessels which reached the Hudson in 1613/14 arrived after this event. These new intruders were a second *Fortuyn*, skippered by Cornelis Jacobsz May and outfitted by a group of Hoorn merchants, and skipper Pieter Fransz' *Vos*, owned by the Amsterdam Admiralty but outfitted by

21. GAA, Not. Arch., 198, pp. 113v–115v, in Hart, *Prehistory*, Appendix 8.
22. For the events described in this paragraph, see Hart, *Prehistory*, pp. 28–30, and Appendices 8, 9, 11, and 17.

Simon Nooms, Jonas Witsen, and their partners. The baneful consequences of unbridled competition having become all too evident by this time, May and Fransz were included in a new trade cartel which granted a quarter of the furs traded to each of the four parties.[23]

While the fur traders in the "Virginias" were thus engaged, the States General promulgated a *Generael Octroy* (General Charter) on March 27, 1614, guaranteeing to discoverers of "new passages, havens, countries or places" a monopoly of the new navigation during a period sufficiently long to make four voyages thither. The charter applied only to discoveries "from now henceforward." If more than one company should make a given discovery "in or about one time or one year," the companies in question would conjointly enjoy the monopoly.[24]

Soon after the return of the ships in the summer of 1614, the four firms engaged in the Northern Virginia fur trade amalgamated into a single company. Their willingness to abandon unrestricted competition or simple cartel agreements probably derived primarily from the necessity of a united front in extracting a monopoly under the *Generael Octroy* from the governmental machinery. This must have been an exceedingly delicate task, because, strictly speaking, the Northern Virginias could not qualify as newly discovered in 1614: the East India Company, Vogels' partnership, and Mossel's principals had all had ships return from there before 1614, and at least Hudson's voyage had achieved a certain publicity through Emanuel van Meteren's *Belgische ofte Nederlantsche Oorlogen ende Geschiedenissen*, published in 1611.[25] A secondary motive for amalgamation was probably the prospect of reducing the redundancy of four ships and

23. Hart, *Prehistory*, p. 31; from GAA, Not. Arch. 198, pp. 113v–115v, in Hart, Appendix 8. Resolutions of the Amsterdam Admiralty, July 24, 1614, cited in S. Muller Fz., *Geschiedenis der Noordsche Compagnie*, p. 368.

24. *Groot Placaet-Boeck.* . . . I, cols. 563–66; English translation in DCHNY, I, pp. 5–6. Nellis M. Crouse says that the general charter was granted at the instance of the partnerships trading to New Netherland ("The White Man's Discoveries and Explorations," *History of the State of New York*, ed. Alexander C. Flick, I, p. 163), but there is absolutely no evidence that the "divers traders, inhabitants of the United Provinces" who had petitioned for such a monopoly were interested in New Netherland. O. van Rees suggests that Le Maire's Australian Company solicited the privilege (*Geschiedenis der Staathuishoudkunde in Nederland* . . . , II, p. 68).

25. Hart, *Prehistory*, p. 34, mentions the questionability of the New Netherland Company's claim.

crews to a more economical one or two and of setting up a single efficient organization of resident traders. These things a simple cartel agreement could not do.

October 11, 1614, the " United company of merchants who have discovered and found New Netherland " received exclusive per-mission to sail to the " newly discovered lands situate in America between New France and Virginia, whereof the sea coasts lie between the 40th and 45th degrees of latitude, now named New Netherland " for four voyages, to be made within three years beginning January 1, 1615. Infraction of this monopoly would incur confiscation of the delinquent vessel and cargo and a fine of 50,000 Netherland ducats for the benefit of the Company.[26]

Two weeks later the directors of the new " New Netherland Company " were obliged to serve notice upon Albert Gerritsz Ruyl and his associates, charging them to desist equipping a ship for New Netherland.[27] Ruyl's reply must have been highly discon-certing. He pointed out, quite correctly it would appear, that he " with his friends and shipowners have either been the first or certainly the second who have found, sailed to and visited the Virginias and tried to carry on trade and commerce there." [28] For this reason, and also because he had equipped his ship " before [the participants in the New Netherland Company] cunningly obtained the pretended charter," he declared his intention to go ahead with his voyage and prosecute for any damage done him. If the Company would pay him damages for the hindrance of his voyage according to arbitration, Ruyl would, however, sail else-where.[29]

That the New Netherland Company backed down and offered to purchase Ruyl's ship and merchandise according to an impartial appraisal (though not to pay damages for hindrance) would seem a tacit admission of the strength of Ruyl's claim; otherwise the Company would have simply threatened him with the penalties provided by the charter. Perhaps the directors feared that legal proceedings would call attention to the fraudulent claim that New Netherland was newly discovered in 1614. The conclusion of the

26. Charter translated in DCHNY, I, pp. 11–12.

27. Hart, *Prehistory*, pp. 34–35. GAA, Not. Arch. 119, p. 114; abstracted in Stokes, *Iconography*, IV, p. 42.

28. Ruyl's father was one of the owners of the ship in which Mossel made his first voyage to the Hudson River in 1612/13. See note 16.

29. GAA, Not. Arch. 137, pp. 117–18; in Hart, *Prehistory*, Appendix 15.

dispute is unknown. Ruyl refused the offer to purchase his ship
and reiterated his former demands, but the matter was probably
quietly adjusted shortly thereafter.[30] After the Ruyl episode the
stream of notarized statements and protests seems to cease, only
to reappear shortly after the termination of the New Netherland
Company's charter. This may indicate that the Company steered
clear of internal dissension and was not again threatened by Dutch
interlopers.

✶ The lasting contribution which the New Netherland Company
made to the economic development of New Netherland was the
establishment of a year round trading post. Thijs Mossel had left
his mulatto factor during the spring and fall of 1613, and Block
may have left a crew with his newly constructed yacht when he
and Hendrick Christiaensz sailed for Holland early in the summer
of 1614; but the initiative to set up a permanent factory came
from the New Netherland Company:

> . . . . their High Mightinesses the States General granted to
> these merchants the exclusive privilege of navigating to this
> river and trading there. For which purpose, in the year 1615,
> a redoubt or small fort was erected up the said river and
> occupied by a small garrison, ...[31]

30. Second offer of the New Netherland Company dated November 3, 1614;
GAA, Not. Arch. 119, p. 130; abstract in Stokes, *Iconography*, IV, p. 42.

31. De Laet, *Nieuwe Wereldt*, p. 84. In another place de Laet writes that the
fort was built in 1614 and that " Henderick Christiaensz first commanded there,
and in his absence Iaques Elckens, *on behalf of the Company which had obtained
the Charter in the aforesaid year 1614. . . .*" (*ibid.*, p. 88; italics mine). Despite
de Laet's highly plausible statements that the fort was built by the New Netherland
Company, some writers have assumed that Christiaensz built the post during his
1613/14 voyage (Crouse, in *History of the State of New York*, I, pp. 164–65;
Hart, *Prehistory*, p. 27). Of the three pieces of evidence which support this view,
two date from long after 1614: (1) an unsupported statement to the effect that
" one or two " forts were built in New Netherland before the year 1614, which
appears in a 1634 memorial of The Nineteen of the West India Company to the
States General (DCHNY, I, p. 94); and (2) the assertion that " two little forts "
were built on the Hudson and Delaware Rivers before the granting of the Charter
of 1614, which appears in a 1644/45 report of the West India Company's *Generale
Reeckenkamer* (DCHNY, I, p. 149). The latter statement is particularly suspect
since the Delaware was not discovered until 1615/16. The third possible support
for the early erection of Fort van Nassouwen rests on the highly questionable
assumption that a map upon which someone has written the dimensions of " Fort
van Nassouwen " was drawn early in 1614 *and not added to since*. Admittedly the
delineation of the lower Delaware River is so inaccurate as to suggest that the
trend of the coast was copied from a map dating from before the discovery of the
Delaware about 1615/16, but the seemingly rather accurate portrayal of the upper

The choice of the site for the fort, which, like remote Dutch out-posts in West Africa and South America, was patriotically named Fort Nassau, was basically sound. It was on an island in the Hudson several leagues south of the mouth of the Mohawk, thus near the junction of two great highways into the interior. At the same time it was still far enough downstream to be reachable by the transatlantic ships.

> This little fort was built in the form of a redoubt, surrounded by a moat eighteen feet wide; it was mounted with two cast iron pieces and eleven light cannon, and the garrison con-sisted of ten or twelve men.[32]

There is no evidence that the New Netherland Company had any other post of the size of Fort Nassau, although lodges may have been set up at strategic rendezvous, such as the mouth of the Hudson and, after its discovery about 1615/16, on the Delaware as well.

The charter expired on January 1, 1618, yet the Company made no move to renew it until the following October. Was this singu-larly tardy application prompted by the political revolution which had shortly before felled Oldenbarnevelt? Since the *Generael Octroy* contained no provision for renewal, and because the States General had turned down the Company's 1616 petition for a charter covering its discovery of the Delaware region, the Company's directors may not have cherished any hope of prolongation when the charter ran out. But when the resistance of Oldenbarnevelt and the States of Holland was finally broken by Prince Maurits and the Contraremonstrants towards the end of August 1618, the directors may have seen a faint chance for special favors. Gerrit Jacobsz Witsen, one of the most powerful men in the Amsterdam city council, was a zealous Contraremonstrant and supporter of Maurits. He and his nephew Jonas Witsen, also Contraremonstrant and also of the city council, were prominent members of the New

---

Delaware, which seems to reflect the findings of the explorer Kleynties about 1615, and the fact that the map, a copy of which appears between pp. 12 and 13 of DCHNY, I, was originally affixed to the New Netherland Company's 1616 petition for a monopoly of the Delaware lead me to reject unhesitatingly the view that the map in its entirety dates from 1614. Stokes argued that the map dated wholly from 1614 (*Iconography*, II, pp. 67 ff.) and he has generally been followed by other writers.

32. De Laet, *Nieuwe Wereldt*, p. 88.

Netherland Company.[33] It was possible, therefore, that the Company might get in on the spoils of Maurits' victory; and the directors may have acted upon this consideration in petitioning for prolongation of their charter on October 4th. Their attempt failed. Henrick Eelckens and Adriaen Jansz Engel, former participants in the Company, had already equipped a ship for New Netherland to carry on their own private trade there, and their petition that the States heed the expiration of the charter and permit them to sail unimpeded was sympathetically received.[34]

Henceforth free trade reigned in New Netherland until the West India Company undertook the exploitation of the region in 1623/24. Despite its lack of a charter and the defection of Eelckens and his associates and some or all of the Hoorn partners, the New Netherland Company seems to have remained the principal firm engaged in the New Netherland trade.[35] Other firms which traded to New Netherland in this period were the Eelckens partnership,[36] a Hoorn partnership containing at least one former member of the New Netherland Company,[37] and a Zeeland enterprise of Pieter Courten of Middelburg.[38] The spotty evidence which is available for these years reveals a predictable amount of discord, but no severe conflicts between the Dutch traders.[39] The only certain contact between the Dutch and foreigners occurred when Thomas Dermer, sailing in a pinnace from Virginia to New England, met some Dutch in the vicinity of the Hudson early in 1620. The meeting seems to have been entirely peaceable, though Sir Ferdinando Gorges, the indefatigable colonizer of New England, claimed years later that Dermer had pointed out the English right

33. For the political activities of Gerrit and Jonas Witsen see Johan E. Elias, *De Vroedschap van Amsterdam, 1578–1795*, I, especially pp. lv, lxvi–ii, lxxi, 167–68, 239–40.

34. The petition of the New Netherland Company and the counter-petition of Engel and Eelckens are translated in DCHNY, I, pp. 21–22.

35. I infer this from its having sent out two ships in both 1619/20 and 1621/22, whereas there is no record of any other firm sending out more than one yearly (DCHNY, I, pp. 22, 27. Hart, *Prehistory*, p. 43). The firm was still called the New Netherland Company in April 1620 (DCHNY, I, p. 24), but in its later years it probably dropped this pretentious title. I have retained it for the sake of convenience.

36. DCHNY, I, p. 26.

37. *Ibid.*

38. West-Indische Compagnie, Resolutions of The Nineteen, November 3, 1623, in F. C. Wieder, *De Stichting van New York in Juli 1625*, p. 11.

39. For notarial records of two disputes in this period see Stokes, *Iconography*, VI, pp. 5–6.

to the river.[40] Though this is the only record of contact with the English, the New Netherland Company was prompted by the threat of an English incursion to propose to the States General in February 1620 that New Netherland be secured to the United Provinces by the settlement there, under government auspices, of English Separatists from Leyden, the future Pilgrims.[41]

The inclusion of New Netherland in the charter of the West India Company, which took effect July 1, 1621, did not immediately end the activities of the *voorcompagnieën*, as the firms which operated in New Netherland prior to the West India Company will henceforth be designated. Three of these were granted permission by the States General to make one more voyage there in 1621/22 to wind up their affairs.[42]

Although the West India Company was still being organized a year later, the States General did not renew the privilege for 1622/23. Nevertheless, several firms traded in New Netherland that year, perhaps after having paid a recognition to the Company,

40. The peaceable nature of the meeting is indicated in Ferdinando Gorges, *A briefe relation of the discovery and plantation of New England: and of svndry accidents therein occvring, from the yeere of our Lord M.DC.VII. to this present MDCXXII. . . .* (London: John Haviland, 1622), in *Sir Ferdinando Gorges and his province of Maine*, ed. James Phinney Baxter, I, pp. 216–17. Gorges' *A briefe narration of the originall undertakings of the advancement of plantations into the parts of America. Especially, shewing the beginning, progress and continuence of that New-England* (London: E. Brudenell, for Nath. Brook, 1658), *ibid.*, II, p. 45, states that Dermer pointed out the English right to the river.
41. DCHNY, I, pp. 22–24. Writing many years later, William Bradford related that while the Leyden congregation was "perplexed with the proseedings of the Virginia Company . . . some Dutchmen made them faire offers aboute goeing with them" (*Bradford's History of Plymouth Plantation 1606–1646*, ed. William T. Davis, p. 64). Edward Winslow was more specific in his 1646 "Brief Narration (occasioned by certain aspersions) of the true grounds or cause of the first planting of New England." While attempting to prove that the emigration to Plymouth was not occasioned by disagreement within the church at Leyden, he mentions "large offers the Dutch offered to us, either to have removed into Zealand and there live with them, or, if we would go on such adventures, to go under them to Hudson's river, . . . and how they would freely have transported us, and furnished every farm with cattle, &c." (*Chronicles of the Pilgrim Fathers of the Colony of Plymouth, from 1602 to 1625*, ed. Alexander Young, p. 385). The New Netherland Company's petitions to the States General made no mention of such offers, and it seems improbable that a single, charterless *voorcompagnie* would have been willing to undertake colonization. Perhaps Winslow is referring to surmises as to an eventual agreement with the not yet formed, but already actively discussed, West India Company; or perhaps the passage of years had in Winslow's mind amplified and made into definite proposals vague feelers or off-hand comments which did in fact emanate from the New Netherland Company.
42. DCHNY, I, pp. 26–27.

but more likely simply on the assumption that the inability of the Company " to continue the trade " that year was ample excuse. The ships of the New Netherland Company and the Eelckens partnership seem to have left New Netherland for good in the fall of 1623,[43] but Willem Snellen, a Zeeland merchant, still had his skipper there in early 1624. By this time, however, the West India Company was itself equipping the first colonizing expedition to New Netherland, and the Company, in no mood to overlook continued interloping, directed the officers of their New Netherland bound vessel to lodge formal protest with Snellen's skipper so that the ship could be arrested on its return.[44] With the departure of Snellen's ship, the era of the *voorcompagnieën* seems to have been finally closed.

The Technique of Trade

Four basic technical problems faced by the *voorcompagnieën* were (1) to establish transatlantic communications with New Netherland, (2) to contact the Indians over as wide a territory as possible, (3) to induce them to hunt and trade furs, and (4) to sell the furs in Europe.

The trade winds offered two possible routes to New Netherland. The more direct northern route ran from the English Channel to the Newfoundland Bank and then skirted the coast to the Hudson. This course, in essence that followed by Henry Hudson in 1609, involved bucking the prevailing southwesterly winds and also, until the southwest moving Labrador current was reached off Newfoundland, the Gulf Stream.[45] This was primarily a summer route, since drift ice and fierce westerly gales made it dangerous and

43. For the return of the ships of the New Netherland Company and the Eelckens partnership, see David Pietersz de Vries, *Korte Historiael, ende Journaels-Aenteyckening e van verscheyden Voyagiens* . . . , ed. H. T. Colenbrander, p. xix; from the Resolutions of The Nineteen of the West India Company; and Hart, *Prehistory*, p. 69. The firm of Pieter Courten, a Zeelander, was thought to still have goods, sloops, and men in New Netherland in November 1623 (West-Indische Compagnie, Resolutions of The Nineteen, November 3, 1623; in Wieder, *Stichting*, p. 11). When these returned is uncertain. It is conceivable that Courten was Snellen's partner. Both were Zeelanders.

44. Resolution of The Nineteen of March 29, 1624, in Stokes, *Iconography*, IV, pp. 56–57.

45. Hudson, having first attempted a northeast passage to the East, crossed the Atlantic from the Faeroes. His mate's journal of the 1609 voyage is printed in Samuel Purchas, *Hakluytus Posthumus or Purchas his pilgrimes*, XIII.

difficult in winter.[46] The second route followed the north-east trades in a wide swing to the south before heading for the Hudson; but, since a ship could sail before the wind much of the way, it was not necessarily much longer than the northern route. Equally practicable in winter or summer, this latter route was that generally used by the *Nieu Nederlandtvaerders*. Wassenaer, writing in 1624 of the experience of the *voorcompagnieën*, explained that

> This country, now called New Netherland, is usually reached in seven or eight weeks from hence. The course usually lies toward the Canary Islands; thence to the savage islands, then towards the mainland of Virginia, crossing over, in fourteen days, leaving the Bahamas Channel on the left and the Bermudas on the right hand, between which the winds are variable with which the land is made.[47]

Seven to eight weeks was probably an exceptionally good voyage, however, and crossings of double this length, even for the light ships used by the *voorcompagnieën*, may not have been unusual.[48]

The return voyage was more direct, following the Westerlies across the North Atlantic to the Channel, and Wassenaer reports that it was often made in thirty days.[49] Again, thirty days was probably more the ideal than the usual, for a ship could be held

46. The northern route was frequently, perhaps mostly, followed by the Puritan immigrants to New England. For journals of Puritan voyages to New England by this route, see John Winthrop, *Winthrop's Journal, 1630–1649*, ed. by James Kendall Hosmer, I, pp. 23–51; and *Chronicles of the first planters of the colony of Massachusetts Bay from 1623 to 1636*, ed. Alexander Young, pp. 213–238 and 445–481.

47. Wass., VI, p. 144v.

48. The passage time of two 40 last ships, the *Witte Duyf* in 1619 and the *Meeuwken* in 1626 are known, and the two winter crossings probably represent a random selection. The former crossed from Texel to the Hudson in 13 weeks and 4 or 5 days, and the latter in 16 weeks and 3 or 4 days or a little less (Hart, *Prehistory*, p. 39; Wass., in NNN, pp. 87, 88; for the lastage of the *Meeuwken*, see Ioannes de Laet, *Historie ofte Iaerlijck Verhael van de verrichtingen der Geoctroyeerde West-Indische Compagnie*, Appendix, p. 4).

49. Wass., cited in NNN, p. 71. Wassenaer also states that the ships returning from New Netherland caught the West wind for the Bermudas and then proceeded to the Channel (*ibid.*, p. 76). Since in the summer, when the ships of the *voorcompagnieën* typically returned to Holland, this course would be against the prevailing winds, and since on a short voyage there would be no need to provision at the Bermudas, I assume that Wassenaer meant the Azores. In 1633 de Vries, leaving the Hudson, steered southeast to 40° in order to clear Long Island, and then east " to run in sight of Corvo " (de Vries, *Verscheyden voyagiens*, p. 179).

up for weeks by contrary winds in the Channel. The *Rensselaers-wyck*, for example, a small ship of unknown tonnage, made Plymouth, England in seven weeks five days in August and September 1637, but unfavorable weather delayed her return to Holland for over five weeks more.[50]

In the days of the *voorcompagnieën*, the ships usually sailed from Holland in the fall and returned in the summer.[51] This sailing pattern, which virtually precluded the choice of the northern route to New Netherland, probably finds its primary explanation in the seasonality of the fur " crop." Not only was the traditional hunting season of the Indians the winter months, but the heavy coats of animals caught at this time were much preferred by the European trader.[52] Trade, therefore, began in the late winter or very early spring, depending on the severity of the weather.[53] If

50. VRBM, pp. 355–89. The fastest passage from New Netherland to Texel of which I have found record was made in October 1627 by the West India Company's 60-last yacht *Bruynvisch* in just 3 weeks 5 days (de Laet, *Historie ofte Iaerlijck Verhael*, 1644, p. 119 and Appendix, p. 3).

51. I have found records of 19 voyages to New Netherland undertaken by various of the *voorcompagnieën* through 1622/23, not including the voyages of Hudson in 1609, Ryser–Block–Christiaensz in 1611, Mossel in 1612/13, and May and Fransz–de Wit in 1613/14, all of which were exploratory. Of the 19 voyages only two seem to have left Holland in the early spring, Block's *Fortuyn* in 1612 and an unidentified ship which was icebound in Amsterdam in mid-February 1622. Twelve ships either definitely or very probably sailed for New Netherland in the fall, however. The sailing date of the others is not at all certain.

Of ten ships which I have identified as returning from normal, non-exploratory voyages through 1620/21 (I am excluding the exploratory voyages mentioned above and the unusual voyage of the *Swarte Beer* of 1618/19), two certainly and one probably arrived in Holland by July 30, one arrived before August 14, two arrived before September 13, two arrived before September 25, and the arrival dates of the other two are entirely unknown. The States General granted four ships permission to make the 1621/22 voyage on condition that they be back by July 1, 1622. (DCHNY, I, pp. 26–27). The ships on the 1622/23 voyage probably extended their stay in New Netherland as long as possible. Of three ships I have discovered on that voyage, one arrived in Holland "in the fall," one left New Netherland about September, and one was still in New Netherland when the preceding ship left there.

52. "Le Castor neuf, qu'on appelle aussi Castor d'Hyver, . . . est le Castor qui provient de la chasse que les Sauvages [de Canada] font pendant l'hyver. Il est le meilleur, & le plus propre pour les belles fourroures; parce qu'il n'a rien perdu de son poil par la muë" (Jacques Savary des Bruslons, *Dictionaire Universel de Commerce*, I, col. 588). For the Indian hunting season, see Allen W. Trelease, *Indian Affairs in Colonial New York: The Seventeenth Century*, pp. 11, 17.

53. Block, Christiaensz, and Mossel were actively trading on the lower Hudson as early as the first week in March, 1614, despite drift ice (GAA, Not. Arch, 198, pp. 99–101v, in Hart, *Prehistory*, Appendix 9). Van Rensselaer wrote in 1635 that " it has been a very hard winter and therefore the skins could not arrive before the latter part of March " (VRBM, p. 315).

a firm lacked factors in New Netherland, arrival there much after this time probably meant losing the cream of the fur harvest to its competitors; and even if it possessed a resident staff, a fresh lot of trading truck and the services of the transatlantic ship and its crew were highly desirable in the peak trading season. Since a ship might be icebound in Holland during January and February, it would have to sail in the fall to be sure to be in New Netherland in March and April.[54]

The ships employed by the *voorcompagnieën* were generally small. When the English ambassador investigated Dutch activities in New Netherland early in 1622, he found that the ships sent there were " of 30 and 40 lasts at the most," and meager evidence from other sources confirms his observation. The largest ship employed in the trade after the exploratory voyages, of which I have found record, was the *Fortuyn*, a *spiegelschip* of 55 lasts, bought in 1612 for the Vogels partnership. The *Witte Duyf*, which made four voyages for Eelckens' partners from 1619/20 to 1622/23, was of about 40 lasts, and the first ship of that partnership, the *Schiltpadde*, bought in 1618, was only 22 lasts. By comparison, the average Dutch ship in the Baltic trade, which provided bulky cargos, was from 100 to 110 lasts at this time. Small size was possible because the New Netherland cargos were not bulky, and desirable because a shallow draft vessel was able to penetrate further up the rivers and kills in quest of trade.[55]

The probably fairly even distribution of beaver and otter throughout New Netherland in the early years of the Dutch trade, the slight development of commerce between economically virtually self-sufficient Indian bands, and the commerce inhibiting effects of general political fragmentation, combined to compel the *voorcompagnieën* to seek out the fur hunters over a wide territory.[56] The transatlantic ship was itself a mobile trading post and

54. For ice conditions in Holland, see DCHNY, III, pp. 7–8.

55. The Dutch ship's last was a measure of weight, 1,976 kg. (Frederic C. Lane, " Tonnages, medieval and modern," *Economic History Review*, 2d ser. XVII (1964), p. 224). For the findings of the English ambassador, see DCHNY, III, pp. 7–8. The lastages of the *Fortuyn, Witte Duyf*, and *Schiltpadde* are found (respectively) in Hart, *Prehistory*, p. 50; DCHNY, I, p. 26; and Hart, p. 36n. For the average size of Dutch Baltic traders, see A. E. Christensen, *Dutch Trade in the Baltic about 1600*, pp. 95–96, 100.

56. Trelease (*Indian Affairs*, pp. 11 and 31), notes the wide distribution of furs and the effect of relative self-sufficiency on inter-tribal commerce. Writing of the general problems of the New Netherland fur trade in 1633, Van Rensselaer stated that " the savages are at enmity with each other almost everywhere and do not allow each other to pass to and fro " (VRBM, p. 245).

could contact many tribes from the break-up of the ice in the spring to its departure for Holland; but maximization of profit depended on making as many additional contacts as possible. The earliest method of extending the territory covered by the trans-atlantic ship was simply to dispatch some of the crew on separate trading expeditions in small open boats which could be propelled by either oars or sails. These craft, called " sloops " or " Biscayan shallops," were carried over on the transatlantic ships, probably after having been knocked down in some way.[57] In 1613/14, the last year before the establishment of a permanent factory, at least three of the five skippers on the Hudson were expanding their trade through the use of these small boats. Christiaensz and Block had at least one sloop each, and Thijs Mossel manned two sloops with his supercargo and seventeen of his crew.[58]

After the introduction of a year-round trading staff, exploration and trade could be extended throughout the summer and fall. Though the animals actually caught in these months had inferior pelts, the fine weather enabled the trader to contact remote tribes, obtain their better furs, and encourage them to take more pelts in the future. For long expeditions along the coasts when the trans-atlantic ships were absent, the resident traders required a larger vessel than a sloop. The need was provided by light yachts, the known examples of which ranged between eight and sixteen lasts. Some or all of these were constructed in New Netherland, and in one of them Cornelis Hendricksz discovered the Delaware about 1615/16.[59]

57. The two boat types are distinguished in lists of the craft of the Eelckens partnership (GAA, Not. Arch. 440, pp. 176v–178, mentioned in Hart, *Prehistory*, p. 38n; GAA, Not. Arch., Portfolio 256, Reg. 61, p. 331, in Stokes, *Iconography*, VI, p. 13), but they were probably often lumped together as " sloepen." Skipper David de Vries was able to carry two " Bosscheysse-Sloepen " besides his ship's boat on the *Walvisch* in 1632 (de Vries, *Verscheyden voyagiens*, p. 149).

William A. Baker, *Colonial Vessels: Some Seventeenth Century Sailing Craft*, pp. 36–51, notes that a number of early English expeditions to North America carried shallops over the ocean in cut up or otherwise dismantled form. Shallops of the early seventeenth century often had a single-masted fore-and-aft rig, but the Biscayan variety had both a mainmast carrying a single large square sail and a foremast close to the bow, which carried a much smaller square sail (*ibid.*, p. 63).

58. GAA, Not. Arch. 198, pp. 97–98, 113v–115v, and 99–101v, in Hart, *Prehistory*, Appendices 7–9.

59. The *Onrust* was built by Adriaen Block when his ship burned early in 1614 (de Laet, *Nieuwe Wereldt*, in NNN, p. 50); it is probably the same as the New Netherland Company's 8-last yacht which discovered the Delaware about 1615/16 (DCHNY, I, p. 12). The Eelckens partnership had two yachts at the termination

Besides serving as a base from which the Dutch could launch trading expeditions in the summer and fall, the year-round trading post encouraged the Indian to come to the trader. Assured of a market, some of the local " savages " soon demonstrated a certain commercial sophistication, as, buying up furs in the interior and reselling them at the post, they began to act as middlemen. At the advent of the West India Company, these native middlemen were an established institution, and the low prices they offered their correspondents in the interior frequently impelled the latter to make the long journey to the posts themselves.[60] Some inlanders traveled thirty days and more to trade directly with the Dutch; others came from even further and " make mention of great waves that wash their land; so that what many think may be true, that Hudson's Strait runs through to the South Sea." [61] Sometimes Indians arrived from Quebec and Tadoussac, indicating that the Dutch were already beginning to tap the St. Lawrence, hitherto monopolized by the French.[62]

It is possible that timber, Indian tobacco, and Cape Cod or Newfoundland fish may have been included in some of the return cargoes of the *voorcompagnieën*; but there is no evidence that they sought or obtained anything but peltries. From the beginning, beavers seem to have far outweighed all the other furs traded, and, judging from the first years of the West India Company's operations in New Netherland, beavers must have outnumbered otters, the next most popular skin, by fully eight to one.[63] Other

of its activities in 1623: the 8-last *Rooduyf* and the 16-last *Omvallende Nooteboom*. The latter, constructed in New Netherland about 1621/22, " had sailed to the South and to the North, along the entire coast" (GAA, Not. Arch., Portfolio 256, Reg. 61, p. 331, in Stokes, *Iconography*, VI, p. 13; GAA, Not. Arch. 441, p. 155v, in Albert Eekhof, *Jonas Michaelius, Founder of the Church in New Netherland; His Life and Work*, pp. 96–97; Hart, *Prehistory*, p. 38n).

60. Wass., in NNN, p. 70.

61. Wass., VI, p. 145v.

62. De Laet, *Nieuwe Wereldt*, in NNN, p. 47.

63. The predominance of beavers on the 1612/13 voyage is implied in a statement that Thijs Mossel sought to spoil Adriaen Block's trade by offering twice as many goods "for a beaver" (GAA, Not. Arch. 197, pp. 614v–615; in Hart, *Prehistory*, Appendix 3). After the 1613/14 voyage the Amsterdam Admiralty heard that Hendrick Christiaensz had " some beaver skins," which were traded on the joint account of the four partnerships in New Netherland (Resolutions of the Amsterdam Admiralty, July 24, 1614, in Muller, *Noordsche Compagnie*, p. 368).

In the years 1624 and 1625 the West India Company obtained about 9,295 beavers to about 1,136 otters (de Laet, *Historie ofte Iaerlijck Verhael*, [1644] Appendix, pp. 29–30).

skins traded were foxes, minks, wild cats, martins, and bear; but,
again inferring from the early experience of the West India Company, these were probably but an insignificant smattering.[64]

To induce the Indians to hunt and trade furs, the agents of the
voorcompagnieën offered a variety of manufactures. Wassenaer
lists " beads, with which they decorate their persons; knives, adzes,
axes, chopping knives, kettles, and all sorts of iron work which
they require for housekeeping," [65] and all these items, except
chopping knives, appear in a variety of other sources for the
period. Surprisingly, there is no certain evidence of trade in
duffels, a foremost article of exchange in the early years of the
West India Company.[66] A single piece of evidence relating to
liquor suggests it was used more to create good will than as a
genuine article of trade,[67] and fire arms, essential to the precarious
balance of power between trader and Indian, were certainly not
traded. During the years of the voorcompagnieën, the Indians'
demand for European manufactures, and hence their industry in
fur hunting undoubtedly increased as their familiarity with the
Dutch and their wares grew. The permanent trading post, where
the wonders of civilization could be continually dangled before
the savages, was an important agent in this process. Where the
Dutch had no post and maintained only occasional contact with
the natives, trade was sometimes disappointing. On the Housatonic
River " many beavers are caught; but it is necessary for the people
[the Quiripeys] to get into the habit of trade, otherwise they are
too lazy to go hunt the beavers." [68]

By their last years the voorcompagnieën seem to have discovered

64. De Laet, Nieuwe Wereldt, cited in NNN, p. 48. Wass., ibid., p. 83. GAA,
Not. Arch. 198, pp. 97–98, in Hart, Prehistory, Appendix 7. A breakdown of the
cargo of the Wapen van Amsterdam in 1626 gives 7,246 beavers, 853½ otters,
81 minks, 36 wild cats, and 34 rats [muskrats?] (DCHNY, I, p. 37).

65. Wass., cited in NNN, p. 71.

66. The Fransz—de Wit expedition of 1613/14 freighted, among other trading
truck, "woolen cloths" and "five English cloths prepared here," but the hostility
of the natives prevented their being traded. In August 1614, the participants in
the voyage, who very shortly thereafter merged into the New Netherland Company,
petitioned the Amsterdam Admiralty for exemption from export duties on these
goods when they were sent a second time to the Hudson (Resolutions of the
Amsterdam Admiralty, August 13 and 14, 1614, in Muller, Noordsche Compagnie,
pp. 368–69).

67. Wassenaer, speaking of the authority of the Indian chief, says "he comes
forward to beg a draft of brandy along with the rest" (NNN, p. 77).

68. De Laet, Nieuwe Wereldt, p. 86.

the profitability of the entirely internal trade in _sewan._ Sewan, beads made from a kind of shell found along the coasts of New Netherland, was the money of the Northeast Indians. It was possible for the Dutch to buy up large quantities on the coast, transport it inland, and exchange it for furs at advantageous prices. Jacob or Jaques Eelckens, member of Christiaensz' crew in 1613/14, second in command at the New Netherland Company's Fort Nassau, and finally supercargo for the partnership of Hendrick Eelckens, seems to have understood the economics of this trade by 1622. In that year he visited the Sickenames, a tribe in the _sewan_ producing region, imprisoned its chief aboard his yacht, and, threatening to cut off the sachem's head, obtained a ransom of 140 fathoms of the beads.[69]

It would be extremely interesting to trace the changes in the terms of trade, that is, the value of merchandise given per fur, as severe competition between the Dutch traders alternated with monopolistic conditions and as the Indians grew in commercial sophistication. There is, however, no scrap of evidence relating to the _voorcompagnieën_ which permits any inference, and we can only assume that exchange between very nearly furless Holland and neolithic America was generally profitable to both parties.

The final problem of the _voorcompagnieën_ was advantageous disposal of their furs. The single known piece of evidence regarding the marketing problems of the _voorcompagnieën_ indicates that the ultimate market of many of their furs was Germany and that New Netherland and Russian furs were in direct competition. On September 25, 1620, the heirs of Arnout Vogels, who at his death on May 16 had possessed a one-tenth share in the New Netherland Company, were seeking to delay the immediate sale of furs brought over on two of the Company's ships. The other partners insisted on immediate sale,

> since at present the opportunity presents itself to dispose of the aforesaid goods and can suffer no longer delay, as the ships from Muscovy, which are bringing a great quantity of the aforesaid goods, are expected at any hour and [the goods] will immediately sharply fall off [in price] as a result. Also, because of the great plague and mortality in Danzig and

69. Wass., in NNN, p. 86. Eelckens' various positions are noted respectively in (1) GAA, Not. Arch. 198, pp. 97–98, in Hart, _Prehistory_, Appendix 7; (2) de Laet, _Nieuwe Wereldt_, in NNN, p. 47; and (3) Hart, p. 37.

Königsberg and the war in Germany, the goods will decline in price more and more.[70]

The European fur market of the early seventeenth century has not been the subject of detailed investigation, but the very patchy picture of this market I have been able to assemble confirms the above observations. France, generously supplied with Canadian furs of the same variety of species, was probably not a dependable market for the pelts of the *voorcompagnieën*. In fact, in 1624 the French invaded the Dutch market by sending a large quantity of excellent otter skins to Amsterdam.[71] Some furs were, of course, used in the Netherlands, and some may have been exported to England or the South of Europe; but many of the furs which Dutch merchants obtained in Russia were sent to Germany and Poland,[72] and Leipzig was the premier fur market of Western Europe.[73] It is thus entirely believable that the plague and warfare in various parts of Germany would have dampened the prospects of New Netherland furs in September 1620.

Perhaps a 1626 statement of Isaac de Rasieres, at that time the chief commercial agent of the West India Company in New Netherland, attests to the advantage of selling New Netherland furs before the arrival of shipments from Russia. He described the Amsterdam *Kerckmisse*, a September fair commencing on the Sunday after the feast of St. Lambert, thus, presumably, before the onslaught of competition from Russian furs, as the "proper" market for New Netherland furs and predicted that each good otter sold at this fair would bring two or three guilders more than at the Frankfurt or Leipzig fairs.[74]

*

When the West India Company took over the New Netherland fur trade in 1623/24, the *voorcompagnieën* had already worked

---

70. GAA, Not. Arch. 164, pp. 70v-72. Hart, *Prehistory*, pp. 43–44.

71. Wass., in NNN, pp. 76–77. Yet some sorts of peltries were imported into France from Germany: "for many years it has been customary for tallow [" talck "], potash, and peltries to be sent directly from Hamburg to Calais and Rouen. . . ." ("Koopmansadviezen aangaande het plan tot oprichting eener compagnie van assurantie, 1629–1635," ed. P. J. Blok, BMHG, XXI [1900], p. 75).

72. *Ibid.*, p. 66.

73. Fisher, *Russian Fur Trade*, p. 196.

74. Isaacq de Raziere to the Directors of the West India Company, September 23, 1626, in Hunt., pp. F30, 231. Van Laer gives the date of the fair *ibid.*, p. 275.

out many of the problems of the trade. Besides accumulating a large store of geographical knowledge and practical experience of the humors of the natives, they had adopted more or less consistent sailing patterns, discovered the most vendible merchandise, and, through their permanent trading establishments, promoted the " commercialization " of the Indians. Presumably the trade was profitable, for some individuals continued to invest in it year after year for nearly a decade; and it could have been made even more profitable if the heavy competition could have been checked. The question faced by the West India Company was whether to continue and extend, under the protection of its monopoly, the system of exploiting New Netherland worked out by the *voorcompagnieën*, or to use its enormous resources to strike out in new directions.

CHAPTER TWO

THE WEST INDIA COMPANY

Unlike the East India Company or the relatively diminutive New Netherland Company, the West India Company was not the product of a merger of previously existing firms. Instead, it was created by a government edict, the *Octroy* or Charter of 1621.[1] This charter granted the West India Company extensive privileges, imposed certain obligations, and established its organizational framework. Some knowledge of the document is essential to an understanding of the Company's operations.

The most important privilege granted the as yet incorporeal company was an extensive trade monopoly for twenty-four years. This monopoly comprised (1) the "coasts and lands" of West Africa from the Tropic of Cancer to the Cape of Good Hope, (2) the "lands of America or West Indies," including the coasts south of Newfoundland on the Atlantic and the entire Pacific coast, with the single exception of the great salt pan at Puncto del Rey (Venezuela), (3) the islands on either side of America, and (4) the vaguely conceived "Australian or South Lands" which lay between the meridians of the east end of New Guinea on the west and the Cape of Good Hope on the east. Within these limits, the Company was empowered to "do everything that the service of this country and the profit and increase of trade shall require," from the pacific colonization of fertile and uninhabited places to open warfare if "a powerful and continued obstruction" of the Company's trade and navigation so required. To enable it to pursue such extensive and aggressive commercial policies, the Company was delegated certain normally sovereign rights: in the

---

1. "Octroy, by de Hooge Mogende Heeren Staten Generael, verleent aende West-Indische Compagnie, in date den derden Iunij 1621." This document appears in many places, but I have used primarily the Dutch text and English translation appearing in VRBM, pp. 86–115.

name of the States General and on obligation to make report to that body, it could make alliances with the inhabitants, appoint governors, administer justice, and maintain armies and fortresses. By way of subsidy the government made unconditional grants of (1) freedom from *Convoyen*, an import and export duty, for at least eight years and (2) the sum of ƒ 1,000,000, one-half a gift and one-half risked as an investment.[2]

Although the preamble of the Charter stated that the States General's purpose in granting such generous privileges was the promotion of the trade and navigation of its subjects, the government also saw in a West India company a painless means of extracting a naval war against Spain from the pockets of its business community. Though hostilities between the Company and the Spanish Crown were almost inevitable given that monarch's claim to virtually the entire area of the Company's charter, the States General seems to have been concerned lest sooner or later commercial considerations lead to a flagging of the Atlantic offensive against the national enemy. At any rate the charter granted by their High Mightinesses contained a variety of provisions which tended either (1) to encourage directly the prosecution of vigorous warfare, or (2) to bind the Company to an arbitrary level of military activity undetermined by commercial prospects, or (3) to insure the influence of the government within the Company's councils. The first class comprised the promise of a subsidy if the Company's operations should materially lessen the military pressure on the Republic and the offer of sixteen (unmanned) warships and four large yachts on condition that the Company maintain an equal number.[3] The second class was represented by the stipulation that the proceeds from all prizes be ploughed back into warfare and not paid out in dividends, unless, as happened after Piet Heyn's capture of the Silver Fleet in 1628, the proceeds were so great as to permit a distribution without weakening the war

2. The geographical limits of the *Octroy* are specified in Article I. The general authorization quoted and the authorization to plant colonies appears in Article II of the *Octroy*. The authorization to wage war is not stated directly but is implied in the States General's promise that " if by a powerful and continued obstruction in the aforewritten navigation and trade the affairs in the limits of this Company should be brought to an open war," the government would offer certain military assistance (Art. XL).

Article II delegates the sovereign rights mentioned, while the grant of subsidies is made by Articles X and XXXIX.

3. Arts. XLI and XL.

effort.[4] Direct influence within the Company's councils was obtained primarily by a government seat in the Assembly of the Nineteen, the supreme governing body of the Company; but other stipulations tended to the same result. Disagreements within The Nineteen were subject to the binding decision of the States General. Resolutions on military affairs required the States General's approbation; and, if the Company accepted the government's offer of twenty unmanned warships, the Company's war fleet and any accompanying merchantmen would be placed under an admiral appointed by the States General " after previous advice " of The Nineteen and would be bound to follow the commands of the States General as well as the instructions of the Company.[5] By these means the state assured itself of a considerably stronger influence on the West India Company than it had obtained at the organization of the East India Company in 1602.[6]

The inherent bias towards warfare which was created by the above conditions was extremely dangerous to the Company, not because warfare was intrinsically unprofitable, but because a bias toward it made it exceedingly difficult to preserve the fine and essential distinction between commercially justifiable and unjustifiable wars. Perhaps to calm the fears of prospective investors on this count, the Charter contained a few provisions which could tend to check ruinous involvement in war. These were not, however, particularly efficacious. The principal provision of this sort stipulated that separate accounts be kept for war and trade. This device could have been effective in curbing warfare *per se*, but it would actually tend to confuse rather than facilitate distinctions between commercially justifiable and unjustifiable military operations. Another provision, which may in fact have remained a dead letter, prescribed payment of a dividend whenever the trade account showed a profit of ten percent. This stipulation would work to protect the Company's commercial profits but not its capital from being expended in warfare.[7]

4. Art. XLII.

5. The decisive role of the States General in disputes and the necessity of its approval in military matters are stipulated in Articles XXIII and XIX, respectively. The subordination of the Company's fleet to an appointee of the States General is specified in Article XL. For further discussion of the Assembly of the Nineteen, see below, pp. 29 and 37 ff.

6. S. van Brakel, *De Hollandsche handelscompagnieën der zeventiende eeuw: hun ontstaan—hunne inrichting*, p. 80.

7. Article XVI provides for separate accounts, as well as for the payment of

The appallingly decentralized political organization of the United Provinces in the seventeenth century encouraged the prescription of a like decentralization for the nation's greatest business organizations, the East and West India Companies. The West India Company's charter divided the Company into five branches or chambers (*cameren*), located in Amsterdam, Zeeland, the Maes cities, the Noorderquartier, and Friesland and Groningen. These chambers were called upon to administer a specified portion of the Company's capital (Amsterdam 4/9, Zeeland 2/9, and the rest 1/9 each) in accordance with the general directives of the Company's central coordinating body, The Nineteen.[8] The *raison d'être* for the chambers, which should be conceived as branches of a single firm rather than participants in a cartel, lay primarily in the equitable distribution of the Company's business over the maritime cities of the Republic.[9] Unless such a distribution were assured, the inhabitants of the smaller economic centers might baulk at investing in a company which would bring rival cities business. As a contemporary put it,

dividends out of the trade account. The directors' disregard of this obligation is indicated in a letter of the Utrecht shareholders to the States of Utrecht of about 1637 ("Stukken betreffende den vrijen handel op Brazilië, 1637," *Kroniek van het Historisch Genootschap*, XXV, 1869, p. 199). Willem Usselincx, who takes credit for conceiving the West India Company, though many of his specific suggestions were not put into practice, thought that this provision was inserted "to make a good mouth" [Corte aenwysinge van de voornaemste verschillen tusschen 't concept van octroy op West Indien dat . . . de Staten Generael inde maent van Februario aen de respective Provincien is gesonden ende tgene daerna by de Gecommitteerde uit de groote Zee Steden van Hollandt ende West-Vrieslandt is beraemt 1620] (in van Rees, *Geschiedenis der staathuishoudkunde*, II, p. 424).

8. The assignment of the administration of capital appears in Article XI of the "Octroy"; the obligation of the chambers to follow the directives of The Nineteen in Article XX.

9. For the *raison d'être* of the system, see van Brakel, *Hollandsche handelscompagnieën*, p. 81. That the chambers were branches of a single firm rather than participants in a cartel is not made explicit in the *Octroy*, but it is implicit in several of its provisions. Most indicative is the provision which fixed the amount of the Company's capital that each chamber might administer irrespective of the capital actually subscribed at each chamber (Art. XI). Two other articles indicate the basic unity of the Company: Article XXVI, which stipulates that if the chambers were unequally provided with returns of merchandise the unprovided chambers were to receive merchandise from the others, and Article XXVIII, which made the basis for the remuneration of the directors of the various chambers the equipments and returns of the entire company, rather than the respective chambers. Van Brakel (*Hollandsche handelscompagnieën*, p. 71) points out that the practice of distributing dividends to shareholders irrespective of the chamber where their shares were registered confirms the evidence from the *Octroy* that the chambers were branches of a single firm.

What reason would one be able to give wherefore people, who have ample capacity for the equipment of ships and for trade in their own cities, should take their money elsewhere in order, to the ruin of their own cities, to transport the trade elsewhere and rob themselves of it? [10]

Central direction over this well dispersed undertaking was vested in a "general assembly" of representatives from the various chambers, each of which was allowed two representatives for each one-ninth part of the capital it administered. To these eighteen delegates was added a delegate from the States General, making nineteen seats in all, and the assembly was usually referred to as the "Assembly of the XIX" or simply "The XIX." This body was empowered to consider and decide "all matters concerning this Company," and no chamber was at liberty to deviate from its directives. The meeting place of The Nineteen was to be alternately six years in Amsterdam and two in Zeeland.[11]

When the East India Company was incorporated in 1602, the management of its chambers had been entrusted to directors who were virtually independent of the will of the shareholders. These directors held office for life, shared with the Provincial States or municipal corporations the responsibility of selecting replacements to vacated directorships, and were obliged to render account of their stewardship to the shareholders only every decennium.[12] Perhaps in part because of the mounting opposition to this system by many East India Company shareholders and in part because the profit prospects of the West India Company were not so rosy as to render such an arrangement palatable, the framers of the West India Company's charter introduced a somewhat more liberal arrangement. By the new plan the term of office of the West India directors was fixed at six years, the larger shareholders were granted a muffled voice in the choice of new directors, and a general accounting every six years was made obligatory.

Since the directors (*bewindhebberen*) were the persons upon

10. Willem Usselincx, "Corte aenwysinge van de voornaemste verschillen . . . ," printed in van Rees, *Geschiedenis der staathuishoudkunde*, II, pp. 417–18, cited by van Brakel, *Hollandsche handelscompagnieën*, p. 81.

11. Articles XVIII to XXI define the composition, authority, and meeting place of The Nineteen.

12. Charles de Lannoy and Herman van der Linden, *Histoire de l'expansion coloniale des peuples européens*, II, pp. 164–66.

whom the administration of the West India Company principally devolved, a fuller explanation of the complex method of their election is necessary. The Charter fixed the number of directors at twenty for the Amsterdam Chamber, twelve for Zeeland, and fourteen for each of the other chambers, plus an unspecified number of "supernumerary" directors, one of whom might be appointed by a chamberless province to any chamber in which its inhabitants invested ƒ 100,000. Personal eligibility for the chambers' directorates depended on the investment of ƒ 6,000 in Amsterdam and ƒ 4,000 in the other chambers. The procedure by which the first directors were to be chosen was left to the discretion of the provinces, who were thus in a position to retain, if they so desired, sole control over the selection of the first directors or to delegate such control to the municipal corporations. If this option was indeed exercised, the dominance within the first directorate of the regents, the merchant aristocrats who controlled the political life of the Republic, was virtually assured. However, the first directors could not, by the terms of the Charter, remain in office indefinitely. After six years and every two years thereafter, one-third of the directors was required to retire, and the nomination of successors was entrusted to assemblies at each chamber of the remaining and retiring directors together with the inevitably much larger number of *hoofdparticipanten*, shareholders who possessed enough shares to be themselves eligible to be directors. Three persons were to be nominated for each vacant place, and the final selection from these nominees was left to the respective provinces or city councils.[13]

The Charter granted the directors a remuneration of one percent of the Company's equipments and returns, but out of this the bookkeepers and cashiers had to be paid. Several provisions were designed to protect the shareholders from directoral maladministration. The directors were responsible for the actions of the bookkeepers and cashiers as well as for their own, and, if a director "could not make good what was entrusted to him for his administration," the loss to the Company might be charged against his investment. Conflict of interest was reduced by a prohibition of sales to or purchases from the Company by the directors. Every six years a general and public accounting was required, in default

13. "The number, qualifications, and method of selection of the directors are prescribed in Articles XI to XIV."

of which the directors forfeited their remunerations. Finally, the
Charter demanded from each director a solemn oath enjoining
faithful administration and constant regard for the greatest profit
for the Company.[14]

The Charter, which had been primarily framed by various government committees, was first subjected to the approval of the
ordinary investor when the five month term for subscription began
on July 1, 1621.[15] The States General, the provinces, and many
city governments launched a vigorous subscription drive, in which
an effort was made to play on every prospect of profit and sentiment of patriotism; but the purses of the investors remained shut,
and the Company received only a thin trickle of subscriptions.[16]

There was, of course, a whole complex of reasons for the
public's indifference, but the fundamental reason seems to have
been the doubtfulness of the Company's financial prospects. Willem Usselincx, who had been the first to conceive a West India
Company and who remained its indefatigable propagandist, reported the general sentiment about a year before the Charter was
finally promulgated:

> It is obvious then that if one wants to get money, something
> has to be proposed to the people which will move them to
> invest. To this end the glory of God will help with some,
> harm to Spain with others, with some the welfare of the
> Fatherland; but the principal and most powerful inducement
> will be the profit that each can make for himself, which profit

14. For the remuneration of the directors and the bookkeepers and cashiers,
see Articles XXVIII to XXX. The provisions designed to prevent maladministration may be found in Articles XVI, XXXI, XXXIII, XXXIV, and XLIV.

15. The terms of subscription were regulated by Article XXIV of the "Octroy."
Willem Usselincx, who first began propagandizing for a West India Company
around 1600, gave the government plentiful advice on the Company's formation,
but many, perhaps most, of his ideas were not accepted by the government. For
summaries of the long and involved history of the drafting of the Charter, see van
Rees, *Geschiedenis der staathuishoudkunde*, II, 72–124; J. Franklin Jameson, "Willem Usselinx, founder of the Dutch and Swedish West India Companies," *Papers
of the American Historical Association*, II (1887), pp. 28–75; and Catharina
Ligtenberg, *Willem Usselinx*, pp. 16–27 and 32-34.

16. W. E. J. Berg van Dussen Muilkerk, "Bijdragen tot de geschiedenis onzer
kolonisatie in Noord-Amerika," *De Gids* (1849), pp. 713–14. Ligtenberg, *Willem
Usselinx*, pp. 37–38. For a history of the struggles of the Rotterdam branch of
the Maes Chamber to obtain capital, see R. Bijlsma, "Rotterdams Amerika-Vaart
in de eerste helft der zeventiende eeuw," *Bijdragen voor vaderlandsche geschiedenis
en oudheidkunde*, 5th series, III (1916), pp. 105–109.

is perceived by few people . . . yes, they are so far from having
great desire for this that I can say in truth, that I . . . have
found no one who has not disagreed with me in the matter
of profits. That harm can be done to the King of Spain they
admit readily, but there is all too much difference between
harming another and making one's own profit.[17]

This uncertainty over the Company's profit prospects was com-
pounded by a fear that the Company would be solely a vehicle
for the government's military designs. An enthusiastic supporter
of the Company reported to the States General in October 1622
that

> some persons fear and pretend, but in secret, that an entirely
> political matter will be made of it [the Company], excusing
> themselves in public with one or another frivolous excuse to
> avoid subscription.[18]

As a means to relieve the suspicions of these people, he recommended that the States General take care that in its acts and
resolutions

> the profit of the Company, the welfare of the Republic, and
> the damage to the King of Spain be together promoted and
> held in recommendation, and not the one without the other.[19]

Perhaps the second most important objection to the new Company concerned the feebleness of the shareholders' influence on
the directors. It was unfortunate for the West India Company
that feeling on this matter was greatly exacerbated by events in
the East India Company. The East India directors' flat refusal to
give a second decennial accounting in 1622 had provoked a bitter
controversy over the directors' management. Among the allegations which the malcontent East India Company shareholders
publicized and which were not specifically denied by the counter-
blasts of the directors were charges that the East India directors

---

17. "Corte aenwysinge van de verovering van Brazilië door de West-Indische
Compagnie [1622]," *Kroniek van het Historisch Genootschap, gevestigd te Utrecht,*
XXVII (1871), p. 231.
18. "Advies tot aanbeveling van de verovering van Brazilië door de West-
Indische Compagnie [1622]," *Kroniek van het Historisch Genootschap,* XXVII
(1871), p. 231.
19. *Ibid.,* p. 232.

had published false information and paid dividends out of borrowed money to further their own stock speculations, equipped needlessly large fleets and purchased excessive cargoes in the East to increase their commissions, and, what was particularly scandalous, bought from and sold to the Company at ridiculous prices.[20] Little wonder that, as reported to the States General in October 1622,

> Some people pretend that the points on which this Company [the West India Company] was formed will not be maintained, especially in the matter of paying dividends and rendering accounts; but [they] will be altered and lessened as the directors think fit; and as an example for this view is alleged the East India Company.[21]

Faced by the extensive reluctance of the investing public, the States General was forced to amplify the Charter. Considering perhaps that organizational objections could be readily overcome by prospects of profit, the States General overrode the fierce opposition of the North Holland salt traders and included the Puncto del Rey salt trade in the *Octroy* in June 1622.[22] This great salt pan provided a place where otherwise unsuccessful privateers or merchantmen in the Company could be sure of obtaining a valuable return cargo, and its inclusion encouraged the first heavy investment in the Company.[23]

About the time of the salt concession, the States of Holland, to which was delegated the responsibility of regulating the choice of the first directors in three of the chambers, moved to dispel the common objections that

20. Van Brakel, *Hollandsche handelscompagnieën*, p. 133.
21. "Advies tot aanbeveling . . . ," *Kroniek van het Historisch Genootschap*, XXVII, p. 232. *Derde discours by forma van missive, daer in kortelijck en grondich vertoont wort/ de nootwendicheyt des Oost ende West-Indische navigatie/ . . . ,* (1622), states that "most all the principal people" were waiting to see whether the "reasonable request" of the East India Company participants would be accepted before investing in the West India Company (pp. 1, 3).
22. "Extract uyt het Placaet van den thienden Iunij 1622," prefacing de Laet's *Iaerlijck Verhael.*
23. The stimulus to investment which followed the inclusion of the salt pan in the *Octroy* is mentioned in "Ampliatie van 't Octroy: Waer inne de zout-vaert op Puncto del Rey buyten de Compagnie verboden wert: Mede den tijdt van inleggen geprolongeert, &c. In date den 10 Iunij 1622 [dated Feb. 16, 1623]," in Dutch and English in VRBM, pp. 120–21.

they are now turning their back on them [the *hoofdpartici-panten*] and [the *hoofdparticipanten*] are being recognized in nothing. . . .[24]

and that

nothing else is or will be sought, than the helping of some needy friends to profitable offices, without considering whether the same are capable or not; by which means the profits will in part be lost.[25]

The plan of the States of Holland granted the *hoofdpartici-panten* the right to nominate three of their number for each directorship, the final choice from these nominees being reserved to the municipal corporations.[26] Whether this plan was put into effect in the Noorderquartier and on the Maes is unknown, but it was at Amsterdam in October 1622, with the result that the regents failed to dominate the composition of that city's chamber.[27] Eight of the twenty new directors were closely associated with the municipal oligarchies, but at least ten were emigrés from the Southern Netherlands more or less outside the local regents' group.[28] In Zeeland a plan similar to that introduced in Amsterdam was adopted, so that at least two-thirds of the Company in

24. *Derde Discours*, pp. 1–2.

25. "Advies tot aanbeveling . . . ," *Kroniek van het Historisch Genootschap*, XXVII, p. 230. *Derde discours* also mentions the same objection (p. 2).

26. The States General granted its approval to the plan of the States of Holland, while leaving the other provinces free to adopt other courses, by "Ampliatie van 't Octroy, in date den derthienden Februarij sestien-hondert drie-en-twintich," in Dutch and English in VRBM, pp. 122–25.

27. Samuel Blommaert, one of the first directors, states explicitly that the first directors were nominated by the *hoofdparticipanten* in his "Memorie-boeck van ons geslachten," a manuscript now in the GAA.

28. W. J. van Hoboken, "The Dutch West India Company; the political background of its rise and decline," *Britain and the Netherlands. Papers delivered to the Oxford-Netherlands Historical Conference*, pp. 50-51. Elias, *Vroedschap*, mentions six regents among the first directors (I, pp. lxix-lxx). The lists of directors upon which van Hoboken's and Elias' compilations are based are found in Samuel Blommaert's "Memorie-boeck" and in Wass., IV, p. 20. The municipal oligarchs were more successful in some other cities. All four of the first directors from Hoorn (Noorderquartier Chamber) were regents (Theodorus Velius, *Chronijk van Hoorn*, . . . , 4th edition annotated by Sebastiaan Centen, p. 609 and appendices), as were all five of the first directors from Delft, Maes Chamber (C. te Lintum, "De Kamer der West-Indische Compagnie te Delft," *Bijdragen tot de Taal-, Land- en Volkenkunde van Nederlandsch-Indië*, 7th successive series, vol. IX [vol. LXIII of the complete series], 1910, p. 97.

point of capital administered permitted the larger investors a voice in the selection of the first directorate.[29]

An initial voice in the choice of the directors did not imply that the chief participants would maintain a continuing and effective surveillance over the directors' activities. Realizing this fact, the Amsterdam *hoofdparticipanten*, after several bargaining sessions with the new directors of their chamber, induced the States General to summon deputies from the directors and *hoofdparticipanten* of all the chambers to discuss additional assurances. The fruit of this gathering was an " *accoordt* " between the two groups. This agreement, promulgated by the States General as an amplification of the Charter on June 21, 1623, provided important safeguards for the chief participants and, indirectly, for the minor shareholders as well.[30] In each chamber, the *hoofdparticipanten* were empowered to elect from their ranks a board of surveillance which would have access to the chamber's books and reports; and though bound to keep secret what the directors were required to keep secret, the board members could make general report of their findings to their principals. Thus informed, the *hoofdparticipanten* of all the chambers were permitted a direct voice in the Company's government on several important matters. Changes, extensions, and the interpretation of the Charter as well as the borrowing of money at interest became subject to the approval of a joint meeting of the directors and *hoofdparticipanten*; and lawsuits against the Company which could not be amicably settled were to be handled according to the advice of both groups. In addition, the *hoofdparticipanten* in three chambers were permitted indirect participation on the boards of directors through their chosen representatives. The first two vacant seats in Amsterdam and Zeeland and the first vacant seat on the Maes were allotted to directors who, though participating in the chambers' administration as other directors, were elected and subject to recall by direct vote of the *hoofdparticipanten* and specially charged with the protection of the chief participants' rights.[31] One of these special directors from

29. For the Zeeland arrangement, see van Brakel, *Hollandsche handelscompagnieën*, pp. 82–83.

30. " Accoordt tusschen de bewinthebberen ende hooft-participanten vande West-Indische Compagnie, met approbatie vande Ho: ende Mog: Heeren Staten Generael ghemaeckt. In date den 21 Junij 1623," printed in Dutch and English in VRBM, pp. 126–35.

31. J. Spinoza Catella Jessurun's *Kiliaen van Rensselaer van 1623 tot 1636* errs in asserting that the right of the *hoofdparticipanten* to elect directors directly was

Amsterdam and one from Zeeland were granted seats in the General Assembly of the Nineteen. Other important articles of the *Accoordt* designated specific dates for the first general accounting and the first change of one-third of the directors, prohibited East India Company directors or their near relatives from serving henceforth as directors of the West India Company, and prolonged the period for subscription to the last of August 1623 for inhabitants of the United Provinces and the end of October for foreigners.

The inclusion of the salt trade, the liberal disposition of the provinces of Holland and Zeeland in the matter of selecting the first directors, and the *Accoordt* of June 1623 succeeded in loosening the investors' purse strings. By the end of October 1623, the capital subscribed amounted to ƒ 7,108,161:10. This sum was furnished by the government and chambers as follows: [32]

The States General	ƒ 500,000
Chamber Amsterdam	2,846,582
Chamber Zeeland	1,379,775
Chamber Maes	1,039,202:10
Chamber Groningen-Friesland	836,975
Chamber Noorderquartier	505,627
	ƒ 7,108,161:10

Although the *Accoordt* had stipulated that no person was to be admitted to the Company after October 31, 1623, the Amsterdam Chamber accepted an investment of about ƒ 100,000 from the burghers of Deventer in the spring of 1624.[33] The Zeeland Chamber seems also to have obtained nearly ƒ 100,000 additional,

not maintained beyond the first such election (p. 23n). The list of directors prefacing de Laet's *Iaerlijck verhael* indicates that by 1636 the Amsterdam Chamber had had fully five directors elected by the *hoofdparticipanten*.

32. Velius, *Chronijk van Hoorn*, p. 607n. [Jacques Accarias de Serionne], *Hollands Rijkdom, behelzende den oorsprong van den koophandel, en van de magt van dezen staat; . . .*, rev. Elias Luzac, I, p. 318.

33. J. Acquoy, *Deventer's participatie in de West-Indische Compagnie*, pp. 7–9. Among the Dutch West India Company Papers at the Historical Society of Pennsylvania is a manuscript with the heading "Besoingnes van Guinea," composed of pp. 104–50 of a ledger book. On p. 139, "the old capital of Amsterdam" is given under the heading "Capitael Actien op de boecken van Amsterdam staende." The sum mentioned is ƒ 2,944,946:10:–, which probably represents the chamber's capital when the subscription campaign was finally ended c. 1624.

and the States General increased its investment by ƒ 250,000.[34] The total capital of the Company was brought therefore to something over seven and one-half million guilders, over a million guilders more than that of the East India Company.[35]

The Operation of an Organizational Monster

Failure breeds criticism; success escapes it. Had the West India Company enjoyed considerable financial success, its organizational inefficiencies might have gone largely unnoticed. As it was, from the early 1640's, the conspicuous decline of the Company, which was primarily due to a non-organizational cause, the ruinous Brazil war, reduced tolerance of inefficiency and maladministration to a very low level. We should remember, therefore, in evaluating the criticism contemporaries leveled on the Company's organization in its declining years, that the criticism was the product of an unusually close scrutiny.

The Nineteen, the only central coordinating body of the West India Company, was not a continuously functioning authority capable of initiating decrees independently of the advice of the chambers; instead it was an occasional assembly of deputies provided with specific instructions from their principals. Several times

34. "Besoingnes van Guinea," p. 138v, lists the "Cappitale penningen Anno 1643." The capital for Amsterdam and Zeeland is separated into the original capital and the capital increases of the 1630s, viz.:

Amsd	ƒ 2944946.10.–
Item verhoocht.......	ƒ 3567692. 5.–
Zelandia	ƒ 1472473. 4.–
Item verhoocht........	ƒ 1894966. 3. 8

Since ƒ 2944946:10 is designated "the old capital of Amsterdam" on p. 139, it is reasonable to suppose that ƒ 1472473:4 represents the old capital of Zeeland and that the latter chamber therefore received a substantial increment to its capital soon after the first reckoning at the end of October 1623.

The increase of the States General's participation is indicated on a small paper entitled "Sommier der eerst ingeleijde Capitael inde west Jndische Compe.," which is inserted between pp. 138v and 139 of the same manuscript, "Besoingnes van Guinea."

35. A notation of the "Capitael vande Comp̄: " on p. 138 of "Besoingnes van Guinea" gives the "eerst inlech" (first investment) as 75 tons of gold, i. e., ƒ 7,500,000. The figures for the old capital of Amsterdam and Zeeland plus the increase of the States General mentioned on this page would place the total at slightly over seven and one-half million guilders, namely ƒ 7,549,224:4. Whether the smaller chambers also received additional subscriptions soon after October 31, 1623, is unknown to me.

The East India Company capital was ƒ 6,459,840 (Lannoy and van der Linden, *Histoire de l'expansion coloniale*, II, p. 46).

each year the presiding chamber, either Amsterdam or Zeeland depending on where The Nineteen was to convene, issued to the several chambers *Poincten van beschrijvinge* (points of convocation), consisting of the list of subjects the delegates were to come prepared to discuss.[36] The various chambers then deliberated on the points and issued instructions to their delegations, who were manned in turn by all the directors.[37] At The Nineteen the delegates expressed the viewpoint of their chambers as contained in their instructions. Probably they were unable to deviate from these instructions: at least this was the case in the organizationally similar East India Company.[38] What prevented The Nineteen from degenerating into a mere sounding board for the ideas of independent ambassadors was the provision that a decision of the majority was binding on all.[39]

This process of decision making could be exceedingly cumbersome and slow. In a 1647 report to the States General, the Company's own Board of Audit admitted that The Nineteen " has not for a considerable time, had such speedy dispatch and expedition as the Company's service indeed required." The Board gave as reasons the frequent omission of important subjects from the *poincten van beschrijvinge* and the common failure of the delegates to arrive at the appointed time and furnished with adequate instructions. In addition, " on proceeding to business, the points are not finally disposed of, but frequently referred to the next meeting; incidental matters and disputes consume the most of the time." [40]

36. " Considerations of the Board of Audit of the West India Company regarding the reform of said Company, drawn up pursuant to the order of the High and Mighty Lords States General of the United Netherlands and delivered to their High Mightinesses' Commissioners at the Hague, the 27 May, 1647 " (DCHNY, I, p. 239). For an example of the *poincten*, see BMHG, III (1880), pp. 354–57.

37. For the practice of instructing delegates, see " Considerations of the Board of Audit " (DCHNY, I, p. 239). For the directors' practice of representing their chamber at The Nineteen by turn, see *Ooghen-Salve tot verlichtinghe van alle participanten, so vande Oost, ende West-Indische Compagnien*, . . . , p. 9. The one Amsterdam and one Zeeland delegate named by the *hoofdparticipanten* were, of course, outside of this system of rotation.

38. The East India Company practice is mentioned in Lannoy and van der Linden, *Histoire de l'expansion coloniale*, II, p. 164.

39. " Advice of the Deputies of Holland 1647 " (DCHNY, I, p. 232) proposes that " in matters of taxation, &c., conflicting with the charter there shall be no plurality voting," which proposal indicates that plurality voting was the usual mode. This was also the practice of the East India Company (Lannoy and van der Linden, *Histoire de l'expansion coloniale*, II, p. 164).

40. " Considerations of the Board of Audit," in DCHNY, I, p. 239.

That the Company continued to function despite these grave inefficiencies was undoubtedly because much of the Company's business was handled at the cameral level. Not only were the instructions of The Nineteen in regard to equipment of ships and disposal of returns executed by the chambers, but the administration of many of the Company's minor colonies and trading posts was eventually delegated to the particular chambers under the only very general supervision of The Nineteen. One of the colonies so delegated was New Netherland, which was throughout its history administered by the Amsterdam Chamber.[41]

Perhaps more serious than the slowness with which The Nineteen's decisions were made was the negligence with which the decisions were executed by the various chambers. According to a seemingly well informed pamphleteer in 1651, The Nineteen had often made very good resolutions concerning the equipment of ships and dispatch of merchandise, but

> it has been often and repeatedly found that the individual chambers have neither agreed to nor followed the same [the resolutions], or they have not understood each other correctly; or else, if something was indeed done, the same has been done piecemeal and by halves, also sometimes after passage of time, after the market and after the season, also sometimes completely neglected.
>
> Such, that from this has frequently resulted that instead of obtaining rich returns, they have been fishing behind the net.[42]

This lamentable state of affairs is confirmed in the previously quoted report of the Company's Board of Audit in 1647.[43]

The difficulty of coordinating the activities of the chambers was complicated by the splitting up of the Maes and Noorderquartier chambers into three and two chambers respectively. Soon after the

41. Amsterdam also administered Curaçao; the Guiana colonies were under Zeeland (Lannoy and van der Linden, *Histoire de l'expansion coloniale*, p. 187). In 1628 an agreement was made whereby Amsterdam was granted the trade to Cape Verde, Zeeland the trade to Argijn (West Africa), and the Rotterdam subchamber to Sierra Leone (van Brakel, *Hollandsche handelscompagnieën*, p. 73n). Presumably the trading posts at these places were administered by the respective chambers.

42. *Vertoogh, over den toestand der West-Indische Compagnie, in haer begin, midden, ende eynde, met een remedie tot redres van deselve*, p. 5.

43. "Considerations of the Board of Audit," in DCHNY, I, p. 239.

promulgation of the Charter, the principal Maes cities, Dordrecht, Rotterdam, and Delft, agreed to divide the directors and business allotted the Maes Chamber equally between them.[44] This partition agreement led eventually to the erection of three separate chambers. As the Board of Audit reported in 1647, each of these subchambers on the Maes, as well as the two subchambers of the Noorderquartier at Hoorn and Enckhuysen,

> has its separate government, with little direct communication with the others; each in practice hath, also, its own Bookkeepers, Cashiers, storekeepers, houses, yards, stores and whatever else appertains thereunto, not without confusion and burthensomeness to the Company.[45]

In Zeeland intermunicipal jealousy did not lead to a total dissolution of the province's chamber; but it did lead to a potentially inefficient partition of the chamber's allotted business. After repeated intercession of " neutral " cities, an accord was reached between Middelburg, Vlissingen, and Veere, whereby Middelburg received two-thirds of the Zeeland Chamber's equipments and the storage and sale of its goods. This accord was followed in turn by an agreement between Vlissingen and Veere, which divided the concession obtained from Middelburg. By virtue of these settlements the Zeeland Chamber was obliged to distribute its business between the three cities in the proportions two-thirds (Middelburg), two-ninths (Vlissingen), and one-ninth (Veere).[46]

Although, as has been pointed out, the chambers were really branches of a single firm, they often acted more like business rivals. Though the Charter specifically forbade chambers to maintain their own factors where another chamber was able to handle their affairs, most of the " outer " chambers maintained their own factors in Amsterdam.[47] The above quoted pamphleteer of 1651 reported that, when cargoes for the account of two or more chambers were sent back to the Netherlands,

> then it will be found, and it is indeed true, that the chamber where the ship or ships have arrived have played *prima mihi*

---

44. Bijlsma, *Bijdragen voor vaderlandsche geschiedenis en oudheidkunde*, 5th series, III, p. 104.
45. " Considerations of the Board of Audit," in DCHNY, I, pp. 237–38.
46. Van Brakel, *Hollandsche handelscompagnieën*, pp. 82–83.
47. " Considerations of the Board of Audit," in DCHNY, I, p. 241.

and kept the freighted goods as booty wholly for itself, leaving the other chambers without the means to make new equipments.

The result of these practices was that by 1651

Hooren has no current debt; Enckhuysen much. Rotterdam is not behind; Dort and Delft are up to their necks in debts. Zeelandt is keeping even; Amsterdam is way behind.[48]

The individual chambers undoubtedly operated more efficiently than the Company as a whole. At Amsterdam, the entire director-ate met at least once and often twice a week. Eleven committees of from three to seven directors each managed different aspects of the affairs of this chamber, such as equipment of ships, pro-visions, munitions, and the treasury.[49] Since Amsterdam was soon delegated the administration of New Netherland, one of these committees handled New Netherland affairs. The members of this committee, the *commissarissen van Nieu Nederlandt*, were normally the intermediaries between the Company and the colonial government, and their special knowledge of New Netherland affairs probably often gave them a decisive voice in the formulation of New Netherland policy. Thanks to this small compact com-mittee, the progress of New Netherland was saved from perpetual ensnarlment in the cogs of an unwieldy and diffuse organization.

Probably the most serious organizational inefficiency of the individual chambers was the rapid turnover of the directors. The Charter limited the directors to a six-year term of office, and this limitation was interpreted as to prohibit retiring directors from succeeding themselves immediately. A 1644 pamphlet discerned a fundamental disadvantage of the system:

48. *Vertoogh, over den toestand der West-Indische Compagnie*, p. 5. The state of intercameral relations as portrayed by the Board of Audit in 1647 was no better. In speaking of the "troubles and canker of jealousy among the chambers," the Board recounted that "the one chamber does its business without communi-cating with the other; each pays more attention to his own chamber's profit than to that of the general body; yea, endeavors to defraud the latter" ("Considerations," DCHNY, I, p. 240).

49. Jessurun, *Kiliaen van Rensselaer* (p. 24), explains the committee structure and also the practice of meeting once or twice a week. "The weekly meeting" of the chambers is also mentioned in "Considerations of the Board of Audit," DCHNY, I, p. 238.

A director needs at least two years to learn anything, to know and understand the maxims, regulations, and order of government, [so] that he can be of some service. He needs this time just to become thoroughly acquainted with the affairs of his own committee . . . ; but he needs more time to grasp the state and entire administration of the Company from the convocations . . . of the XIX, where he seldom has a turn. . . . If then he has learned well the first two years, then in the two following years, say three, the Company will obtain service from him. . . . But let him come in the fifth or sixth year, then he loses all his industry and desire and lets the affairs of the Company go as they will or can.[50]

Another disadvantage of the frequent changes of directors was the tendency of Company policy to vacillate as factions holding differing views alternated in power. As will be seen, the consistency of the Company's New Netherland policy suffered severely from this cause in the early 1630's.

Though the West India Company directors by no means entirely escaped allegations of fraudulent behavior, they were never charged with the multiplicity of misdeeds ascribed to the first directors of the East India Company. Part of the explanation for this healthy state of affairs may lie in the relatively close supervision by the States General or even in the directors' appreciation of their patriotic duty as administrators of a powerful weapon in the war against Spain. But credit is probably also due the effective surveillance and control exercised by the *hoofdparticipanten*. Quite contrary to the development in the East India Company, where the supervisory committees of *hoofdparticipanten* erected by that Company's second charter in 1623 were soon made entirely subservient to the directors, the rights of the West India Company *hoofdparticipanten* of at least the Amsterdam and Zeeland Chamber were not only scrupulously maintained, but even extended.[51] Probably as an outgrowth of their direct voice in the Company's borrowing policy, the West India *hoofdparticipanten* came to have an important influence on the formation of the Company's commercial, colonial, and military policies as well.[52] In 1633, for example,

50. *Ooghen-Salve*, p. 9. See also "Considerations of the Board of Audit," DCHNY, I, p. 237.

51. Van Brakel summarizes developments in the East India Company, *Hollandsche handelscompagnieën*, pp. 146–47.

52. Lannoy and van der Linden, *Histoire de l'expansion coloniale*, II, p. 186.

we find the Zeeland Chamber resolving upon the necessity of sending a contingent of troops to Brazil, " but on the advice and with the assistance of the *hoofdparticipanten*." In 1634 we see the Zeeland *hoofdparticipanten* deliberating on the advisability of continuing to occupy the island of Curaçao and hear that some ex-directors in Amsterdam are trying to bring about a change in New Netherland policy through the *hoofdparticipanten* of Amsterdam.[53]

*

The Charter and its amplifications subjected the West India Company to the rather close supervision of the States General, provided enticements and strictures biasing the Company towards aggressive warfare, saddled it with a cumbersome, decentralized organization, and granted its principal shareholders the means to exercise effective control over the directors. These characteristics, combined with the great power of an immense capital, determined the " personality " of the giant organization. Our next concern will be to sketch the giant's environment, the territory of its *Octroy*.

---

53. The 1633 decision of the Zeeland Chamber and the 1634 deliberation on Curaçao are recorded in J. H. J. Hamelberg, *Documenten behoorende bij " Nederlanders op de West-Indische Eilanden,"* pp. 15 and 42. For the New Netherland maneuvers, see VRBM, p. 270.

CHAPTER THREE

THE DECISION TO COLONIZE

The first directors of the West India Company faced a problem of exceptional breadth and complexity. The legal and geographical limits of the *Octroy* contained a very large number of possibilities, some well known, others only hazily suspected, some promising attractive rewards, others but dubious advantages. The task of the directors was to make a selection from these possibilities according to their ends and the resources of the Company. In so doing, the merits of a particular project, colonization in New Netherland, for example, would have to be assessed in the light of the alternatives. Our attempt to understand the Company's decision to colonize New Netherland must begin therefore with this question: what opportunities seemed to present themselves to The Nineteen in the fall of 1623 when that decision was made?

*

A hostile Spanish-Portuguese colonial empire sprawled across nearly the entire area of the *Octroy*. The Company was therefore faced with three basic alternatives. It could (1) tap the economic arteries of that empire through privateering, (2) trade or colonize in areas unoccupied by the Iberians, or (3) conquer some part of the economic heartland of the empire.

Dierick Ruiters' *Toortse der Zeevaert*, published in 1623, indicates the extent of Dutch knowledge of the West Indies trade at the time the West India Company was just getting under way.[1] Ruiters distinguished three principal avenues of the East-West trade between Spain and her colonies. The most important, fol-

---

1. Ed. S. P. L'Honoré Naber, pp. 39 ff. Ruiters' *Toortse* seems to have been used by one of the very first fleets sent out by the West India Company, that of Philips van Zuylen which left Texel in September 1623 (de Laet, *Iaerlijck Verhael*, ed. S. P. L'Honoré Naber, I, p. 12). L'Honoré Naber describes the book as the former " seaman's Baedeker of the South Atlantic " (*ibid.*, p. 12 n).

lowing the northeast trade winds from Cadiz to the Caribbean, was sailed by a " General Fleet," laden primarily with various European manufactures. The other two led to the Caribbean via the Canary Islands and the West African coast, where the ships loaded wine and Negroes respectively.[2] The far more alluring eastbound trade from New Spain was gathered yearly into a single mighty convoy at Havana.[3] Composed as it was of the treasure fleets from Mexico and Panama, the " Silver Fleet " was the dream of every privateer and pirate of Northern Europe, but as yet it had never been captured. Spain's dependence on this fleet was revealed to the Dutch early in 1623. In September 1622 a great storm had in part destroyed and in part forced back to Havana the 1622 fleet carrying over eleven million *reals* in goods. According to Wassenaer, this loss and delay

is causing there [in Spain] great dearth and bad trade. All payments have been postponed six months by the King. The workers are utterly idle. . . . This [the Fleet] is his [the King's] great artery; if it is once stuck, most of his life is taken from him.[4]

Less glamorous but still lucrative results might be obtained from plundering the trade between Spain's satellite, Portugal, and Brazil. Brazil's imports, like those of New Spain, consisted largely of manufactures, wine, and slaves, and necessarily arrived by different routes. Her exports, principally sugar, were carried to Portugal in great fleets, " sometimes forty, fifty, and sixty sails strong," which sailed northwest, close-hauled, to the Sargasso Sea, and then caught the Westerlies for the transatlantic crossing. These Brazil fleets were not well armed convoys such as the " Silver Fleets," and they were easy prey for privateers. Of the thirty vessels which left Pernambuco in November 1623, all but three were taken by the Turks or " adventurers " from the Netherlands.[5]

Privateering was exceedingly risky: it could bring fabulous windfalls or squander huge sums of money. If, as happened re-

2. Ruiters, *Toortse*, p. 40.
3. De Laet, *Nieuwe Wereldt*, pp. 20–21.
4. Wass., IV, p. 124.
5. Ruiters (*Toortse*, pp. 9–11 and 29) describes Brazilian imports and exports and the size and course of the fleets which returned from Brazil. C. R. Boxer (*The Dutch in Brazil, 1624–1654*, p. 33) mentions the poor armament of the Brazil fleets; and Wass. (IV, p. 124) records the disastrous 1623 voyage.

peatedly in the subsequent history of the Company, slow and unreliable communications, the vastness of the ocean or inadequate naval strength prevented the regular tapping of the principal arteries of the Iberian imperial system, vessels might spend months or even years devouring thousands of guilders in wages, stores, and worm-eaten and weather-beaten ships with no greater results than the seizure of a few barks plying the coastal trade. Willem Usselincx warned of these dangers in a memorial to the States General in 1620 and pointed out that

> those who understand the outfitting of ships know well that there is no weaker power than sea power, because it consumes not only itself but also its masters, if there are no resulting profits to maintain that power.[6]

Just as the most important trade routes were the best defended, the most valuable provinces of the Iberian empire were generally the most solidly occupied. Besides New Netherland, only Chile and Guiana, among the still unoccupied regions of the New World, offered any real economic potential. Chile, remote and vaguely known, exerted a peculiar fascination, because there the Dutch would find successful brothers in arms against Spanish tyranny. As early as 1609, an alliance with the Chileans was recommended to Oldenbarnevelt in order to

> infest the whole coast of Peru, New Spain [Mexico], and many islands lying in the Pacific . . . and consequently not only to prevent and cut off the King of Spain's trade routes but also the gathering of his gold and silver.[7]

In his *Nieuwe Wereldt*, Johannes de Laet, one of the first directors of the West India Company, stressed the insecurity of the Spanish in Chile and the remarkable military capability of the natives:

> These Indians do not fight as other wild people and bar-barians, but keep very good order in all their attempts, throw

---

6. "Corte aenwysinge van de voornaemste verschillen . . . ," in van Rees, *Geschiedenis der staathuishoudkunde*, II, pp. 419–20. For the riskiness of priva-teering, see also Ralph Davis, *The Rise of the English Shipping Industry in the Seventeenth and Eighteenth Centuries*, p. 333.

7. Isaac le Maire, Remonstrance to Oldenbarnevelt; quoted in "Brieven van Samuel Blommaert aen den Zweedschen Rijkskanselier Axel Oxenstierna, 1635-41," ed. G. W. Kernkamp, BMHG, XXIX (1908), p. 23n.

up forts, from which they march out and into which they withdraw, and try, when opportune, to surprise and burn the Spaniards' cities, houses, and other places, at the most unexpected times. They have also learned to use the weapons which they first took and conquered from the Spaniards as their own.[8]

Chile offered not only allies against Spain, but also commercial possibilities. Not only was the land fertile and healthy and the climate temperate, but it also possessed rich gold mines.[9]

The Zeelanders had been active in Guiana, the thousand-odd mile coast from the Amazon to the Orinoco, since the late nineties of the previous century. Their initial efforts, at Forts Nassau and Orange on the Amazon and on various of the more westerly rivers, probably comprised no more than trade with the natives for tobacco and dyes, but they soon began to plant tobacco for themselves. Colonization attempts in 1613 and 1614 seem to have failed in 1615, but Jan de Moor, a burgomaster of Vlissingen, and his associates sent out more durable colonies to the Amazon and Essequibo in 1616.[10] Thus, by 1623, the Dutch had gained considerable direct experience with this region. De Laet, drawing largely upon Robert Harcourt's *Relation of a Voyage to Gviana . . .* of 1613, was enthusiastic about Guiana's possibilities. Although the seacoast was low, hot, and unhealthy, the inland regions were " temperate, healthful, and fruitful." [11]

> The principal commodity of this land is sugar cane, which is very plentiful in these quarters. The soil is as suitable for this as in any other part of the world; it grows very large in a short time. By planting and building up suitable places to extract the sugar (which would cost much at first) one could gain great wealth, as can be seen by what is done by the Portuguese in Brazil and other places.[12]

8. De Laet, *Nieuwe Wereldt*, p. 365.
9. *Ibid.*, pp. 357–58.
10. For the early ventures of Jan de Moor and other Zeelanders, see two articles by George Edmundson in the *English Historical Review*: " The Dutch in Western Guiana," XVI (1901), pp. 642–50 and 662–63; and " The Dutch on the Amazon and Negro in the seventeenth century," XVIII (1903), pp. 647–51.
11. De Laet, *Nieuwe Wereldt*, p. 470.
12. *Ibid.*, p. 472.

Other products were tobacco "which is now much desired in most all lands" and "from the planting of which a very great profit can be gathered in a short time," dyes, cotton, numberless "well-smelling gums of great worth and efficacy in Medicine and Chirurgery," and minerals.[13] Far back in the interior was reputed to exist the gold-rich kingdom of El Dorado, though this was already regarded by some Netherlanders as a fable invented by Walter Ralegh.[14]

West of Guiana proper the great salt pan of Puncto del Rey had already assumed considerable importance in the Dutch economy, and the inclusion of this salt trade was generally regarded as important insurance for the Company's success. By the end of 1622, however, the Spanish had effectively kicked out this important economic prop from under the Company. In January 1623 a Dutch salt fleet discovered that the Spaniards, during the heated negotiations between the States General and the North Holland cities over the inclusion of the trade in the Charter, had ungraciously fortified the salt pan.[15] Henceforth Puncto del Rey had to be reckoned among the regions under effective Spanish control.

Though the larger Caribbean islands, Honduras, and several other regions were also important sources of wealth to Spain, the Dutch probably regarded West Africa, Brazil, Peru, and Mexico as the four cornerstones of the Iberian colonial empire in the Occident.[16] In one of these, West Africa, the vital source of American manpower, the Dutch had already made a significant incursion. Although the Portuguese remained strongly entrenched at many places along the coast and neighboring islands,[17] Dutch merchants had conducted a profitable trade in West Africa for some thirty years, exchanging various European manufactures for gold dust, ivory, and slaves. In 1612, confronted with a vigorous Portuguese effort to root out Dutch commerce, the States General

13. *Ibid.*, pp. 472–73.
14. N. G., *Reys-boeck van het rijcke Brasilien, Rio de la Plata ende Magallanes*, p. 65.
15. Wass., V, p. 105.
16. One would perhaps look in vain for an explicit statement to this effect among contemporary Dutch writers, but this is the impression one gets from de Laet and Ruiters, who surveyed large sections of the *Octroy* at the advent of the West India Company, and from the various pamphlets written to promote subscription to the West India Company.
17. E. g., Elmina on the Guinea coast, Arguim Island near Cape Blanco, Sto. Antão in the Cape Verde Islands, and São Thomé, as well as many smaller posts.

had established Fort Nassau at Mouree, slightly to the east of the Portuguese stronghold of Elmina on the Guinea coast; and in 1617 the island of Goeree at Cape Verde was fortified as a second Dutch stronghold. The days of the truly princely profits in West Africa had been brought to an end by the competition there between Portuguese, Dutch, French, and English. Ruiters, probably referring to the years immediately preceding the founding of Fort Nassau, wrote:

> This Gold Coast, where our nation trades, is so spoiled, that no one knows what sort of merchandise to bring there that will be in good demand. Yes, it is so spoiled there, that the Negroes with the value of five guilders in gold go to 10 or 12 ships before they will buy . . . .[18]

Nevertheless, the Guinea trade was perhaps the most valuable single asset taken over by the Company: mere continuance of its predecessors' operations would be profitable, and military expansion might establish a virtual monopoly of the African slave trade.

Mexico and Peru, the prime sources of the precious metals that filled the treasure fleets, and agriculturally fruitful to boot, were less precarious pillars of the Iberian empire. Of Lima, de Laet wrote:

> There is at present great trade and excessive wealth in this city. . . . From here ships are often cleared for Panama which are worth eight hundred thousand ducats, and sometimes no less than a million ducats.[19]

Though extremely remote, Peru was not poorly defended. Van Spilbergen's fleet had been confronted by a Spanish army of eight companies of cavalry and four thousand foot troops when it appeared before Callao, the port of Lima, in 1615.[20] The conquest of this distant region would not, therefore, be really practicable

---

18. Ruiters, *Toortse*, p. 72.
19. De Laet, *Nieuwe Wereldt*, p. 326.
20. *Oost ende West-Indische Spieghel waer in beschreven werden de twee laetste navigatien ghedaen inde jaeren 1614. 1615. 1616. 1617. ende 1618.*, p. 71. On the other hand, *Missive daer in kortelijck en grondigh wert verthoont/ hoe veel de Verenighde Nederlanden gelegen is aen de Oost ende West-Indische navigatie* pointed to the possibility that the Indians would come to the assistance of the Dutch and "deliver to us the Mountain Potasy and other places where the gold and silver mines are."

until it could be undertaken from military bases much nearer than the Netherlands.

Over no section of the New World did de Laet wax more eloquent than Mexico, " one of the best provinces of the New World, and the most suitable to live in." [21] Besides rich mines of silver and other minerals, the province possessed vast herds of cattle, abundant grain, cochineal, costly resins and gums, and even some sugar mills. Its conquest, however, would be difficult, because Mexico was extensive, securely colonized, and close to Havana and other strong Spanish military bases.

Brazil, the sugar colony, was much better known to the Dutch than either Mexico or Peru. Dutch ships had traded in Brazil since at least the late 1580's, and when the King of Spain forbade this trade by a severe placard in 1594

> then many good and faithful Portuguese, mostly living in Viana and Porto, offered a hand to the merchants of this country and carried on the trade with them in common and in their names.
>
> The fruitfulness of the above mentioned Portuguese to those of this country being so great . . . as if they had been our fathers, and living in our midst.[22]

During the Twelve Years Truce this clandestine trade had grown so happily that in 1622 Amsterdam possessed a thriving sugar refining industry with twenty-five refineries and Dutch merchants could estimate that a half or two-thirds of the Brazil trade was in Dutch hands.[23] Such familiarity with the Brazilian trade naturally inclined the more aggressive supporters of the West India Company to look Brazilwards for the scene of their first conquests.

The optimists belittled the risks and extolled the advantages of a conquest of Brazil. In their view the Portuguese were neither able nor willing to offer effective resistance, especially as many of them were Jews, sworn enemies of the Spanish inquisition. The only two places of importance, Bahia and Pernambuco, were

21. De Laet, *Nieuwe Wereldt*, p. 144.
22. "Deductie vervaetende den oorspronck ende progres van de vaert ende handel op Brasil . . . ," in *Journael van de reis naar Zuid-Amerika (1598–1601) door Hendrik Ottsen*, ed. J. W. Ijzerman, pp. 99-100.
23. *Ibid.*, p. 100. For the number of sugar refineries, see D. W. Davies, *Primer of Dutch seventeenth century overseas trade*, p. 123.

both not particularly well fortified, and, moreover, since both lay on the coast, they could be unexpectedly attacked and, when captured, easily reinforced. The wealth to be obtained from Brazil's conquest was simply fabulous according to some. One particularly sanguine writer estimated that by confiscation of the property of the King of Spain, the clergy, and merchants resident in Portugal and by imposition of a moderate poll tax, the Company would immediately recoup the expenses of conquest. He projected further that the yearly *profit* from sugar exports to Holland and the import of merchandise into Brazil would amount to 63 tons of gold, i. e. f 6,300,000. Brazil wood would yield a profit of $1\frac{1}{2}$ tons of gold, and tobacco, ginger, sirup, and preserves an additional 3 to 4 tons. Taxation of the inhabitants and the rent from the confiscated lands would bring in an additional 9 to 12 tons of gold. At the very least then, the Company would derive about f 7,700,000 yearly from its conquest. Reckoning the costs of defense at f 2,700,000 per year, one could expect a pure profit of an even f 5,000,000 annually. In other words, this optimistic writer expected the Company to get its entire capital out of Brazil in just a year and a half! [24] Besides affording enormous commercial possibilities, Brazil was also strategically located to serve as a base for privateering expeditions. Not only would it be easy to strike at the carracks returning from the Portuguese East Indies, but, since Brazil lay to the windward of the West Indian islands, privateers based on Brazil could swoop down on the Spanish fleets in the Caribbean at any time.[25]

The pessimists—the slight enthusiasm to invest in the West India Company indicates that they must have been by far the majority of the more affluent inhabitants of the United Provinces—

---

24. Jan Andries Moerbeeck, *Redenen, waeromme de West-Indische Compagnie dient te trachten het landt van Brasilia, den Coninck van Spangien te ontmachtigen, en dat ten eersten*, pp. 6 ff. Moerbeeck also pointed out the expected cooperation of the Jews and the vulnerability of Bahia and Pernambuco (pp. 3–5). Writing in 1623/24, Wassenaer reported that for the defence of Pernambuco "there are not 300 men capable of bearing arms; in both castles lay eighty men, troops that live in a very disorderly way . . ." (Wass., VI, p. 68v). For a good summary of the arguments for the conquest of Brazil, see Boxer, *Dutch in Brazil*, pp. 14–15.

25. Samuel Blommaert, one of the first directors of the West India Company, declared that these advantages were among the prime considerations that induced the West India Company to attack Brazil in a letter to the Swedish Chancellor Axel Oxenstierna, dated September 30, 1637 (in "Brieven van Blommaert aan Oxenstierna," BMHG, XXIX, pp. 136–37).

regarded these expectations as chimerical. Willem Usselincx succinctly expressed the more conservative viewpoint as follows:

> As for Brazil, that is no cat to be touched without gloves
> . . . even assuming that we arrive on land there, wage war
> there, building fort against fort, and force the Portuguese
> to flee inland, then they would lay waste to and burn their
> plantations, houses, and sugarhouses . . . and I offer for consideration how pleasant a war on sea and land would be
> there without profit, and how quickly we would be consumed.[26]

✳

Confronted with these manifold opportunities for trade, colonization, privateering, and conquest, the directors of the West India Company naturally directed their first operations towards securing the already established trades. In November 1623 the Company had fifteen ships at sea, mostly bound for West Africa and the Amazon, one of which, the yacht *Maeckereel*, sailed for New Netherland in July to inaugurate the Company's trade there.[27] But the capital required to sustain these trades was trifling compared to the enormous resources of the Company.[28] Large-scale

---

26. "Corte aenwysinge van de voornaemste verschillen . . ."; in van Rees, *Geschiedenis der staathuishoudkunde*, II, p. 419.

27. The number of ships at sea in November is given by Boxer, *Dutch in Brazil*, pp. 13–14; from Wass., VI, pp. 38, 58, 61. The date of sailing of the *Maeckereel* is given in "Journal du voyage faict par les peres de familles envoyes par Mrs les Directeurs de la Compagnee des Indes occidentales pour visiter la coste de Gujane; . . .", in Mrs. Robert W. de Forest, *A Walloon Family in America; Lockwood de Forest and His Forebears 1500–1848*, II, pp. 190–93. At the Historical Society of Pennsylvania, I discovered an interesting memento of the *Maeckereel's* voyage, a letter or draft of a letter from P(ieter) Courten, a prominent Zeeland merchant, to the Amsterdam Chamber of the West India Company, dated November 26, 1626. This missive was written on behalf of Jan Price, the barber on the *Maeckereel*. It appears that Price had obtained some peltries from the natives as remuneration for bleeding them, but that the Company had confiscated these furs and also his wages (Historical Society of Pennsylvania, West India Company Papers).

28. In 1622, a propagandist for the Company estimated that yearly only about twenty ships, 400 men and f 1,200,000 in merchandise was employed in the Guinea trade (*Levendich discovrs vant ghemeyne lants welvaert*). A seemingly well padded estimate of the effects of the West India Company in September 1626 gave the value of eighteen ships and their cargoes "trading to all quarters where the Company hath any free trade," to be f 1,969,000, little more than a fourth of the Company's capital (DCHNY, I, p. 35). In 1633 the directors of the Amsterdam

agricultural colonies in Guiana or other regions unoccupied by
the Spanish or Portuguese could in time have consumed a very
large investment, but a heavy investment in colonies could not be
made safely in the near future: intelligent agricultural colonization
would have to build on the trials and errors of small beginnings.
Thus the very size of the Company's capital endowment tended
to commit the directors to make a major military effort. They were
further biased in this direction by the realization that the raison
d'être of the Company lay in part in the destruction of the national
enemy. De Laet, who, we must remember, was a director of the
Amsterdam Chamber of the Company, wrote in his history of the
Company's operations that the directors,

> the trade to Guinea and several other places in Africa and
> America having been attended to, . . . began to consider what
> they best might attempt against the enemies of this state. For
> they were well aware that the great desire of the good inhabi-
> tants of these United Netherlands and the great expectations
> that everyone had formed could not be sufficiently satisfied
> by only carrying on the aforementioned trades. . . .

They considered further

> that through one event or another they had to expect the
> same [war with the King of Spain], though they might avoid
> his as best they could.[29]

Finally, the government, as might be expected, was not behind in
prodding the Company to make a major military demonstration.[30]
Even before the Company had commenced its operations, the government urged it to join the expedition under Admiral L'Hermite,
which was being sent to harry Spain on the West Coast of the
New World, or at least to cooperate with a follow-up expedition.[31]

Moved by these pressures and considerations, the directors
deliberated where they could best make a spectacular blow. They
declined to participate in the L'Hermite expedition itself, which

Chamber estimated that by commerce alone not a sixth part of the Company's
ships could be employed ("Remonstrance of the West India Company against a
peace with Spain," in DCHNY, I, p. 67).

29. De Laet, *Historie ofte Iaerlijck Verhael,* (1644), p. 5.

30. "To this having also in particular been urged on by the government of this
country, . . ."; *ibid.*

31. *Ibid.*

after some delay sailed in April 1623, but many of them were in favor of " following the footsteps of that fleet and continuing the work it had begun." At one time this plan to attack the Pacific side of the New World was nearly approved, but eventually considerations of risk and remoteness prevailed to enjoin operations on the Atlantic coasts, where an invasion fleet, prevented from attaining its first objective, could easily find attractive alternatives, and where a beachhead could more easily be reinforced. Bahia, the capital of Brazil, was selected as the site of the Company's first conquest, and an expedition for its reduction consisting of twenty-six sail and carrying 3,300 men was dispatched in December 1623 and January 1624.[32]

Bahia fell on May 10, but the Company's troops were closely invested within the city. Upon receipt of the news of the conquest, both the Company and the King of Spain strained to ready fleets to decide the fate of the city. The Company's relief fleet was held up for several months by contrary winds in the Channel, however, and the Iberian relief armada compelled the surrender of the Company's demoralized and mutinous garrison on April 30, 1625. It was with these momentous events as a background that New Netherland was first colonized.

*

A survey of the West India Company's hemispheric opportunities and activities enables us to look at New Netherland in perspective. The region was obviously of very slight import in relation to the Company's total concerns. For this reason estimates of New Netherland's profitability to the Company cannot be inferred from, say, quotations of the Company's shares or the Company's over-all financial position, as might be possible in the case of a firm with a single enterprise such as the Virginia Company of London. This position of relative insignificance could have either favorable or unfavorable effects on New Netherland's economic development. Prosperity in the Company's principal fields of activity might tend to foster a greater liberality of investment than the prospects of New Netherland warranted. On the other hand, financial disaster elsewhere might enjoin diminution of investment below commercially justifiable levels.

32. The directors' inclination to follow up L'Hermite's expedition and the reasons which eventually persuaded them to attack on the Atlantic coasts are given in *ibid.*, p. 6. Boxer (*Dutch in Brazil*, p. 21) describes the strength of the expedition.

Why the Dutch took the advantage of New Netherland

Our survey also reveals that New Netherland was the only territory within the limits of the Charter clearly outside the sphere of influence of the Spanish crown. The effect of this anomalous position was that fortification and colonial expansion in New Netherland could not be rationalized, as they often were elsewhere, as the undermining of the national enemy. Instead, these activities would have to be justified on the basis of expected profit. In fact, enterprise in New Netherland could have a decidedly negative influence on the national interest, since both England and France, otherwise friendly powers, were interested in the region. However strongly the States General might support the Company in its operations against the Spanish and Portuguese, their High Mightinesses could show scant sympathy for a willful alienation of powerful potential allies.

Yet, despite the relative insignificance of New Netherland and the absence there of major national political objectives, there is no evidence that the directors ever scorned to undertake the direct exploitation of the region. As we have seen, one of their first acts, in the summer of 1623, was to dispatch a yacht thither to take over the trade from the representatives of the *voorcompagnieën*. In the absence of explicit contemporary explanations of the directors' motives in New Netherland, one is inclined to ascribe their immediate interest in the region to the great need for conservative, though small, investment opportunities. Although Brazil, Peru, and the Silver Fleets offered vastly more glittering prospects, their conquest would be very risky, and the most elementary principles of investment diversification demanded the inclusion of modest yet reliable undertakings. This need became particularly acute after the Spanish put an end to the Puncto del Rey salt trade. In relation to the totality of the remaining secure and established opportunities—besides New Netherland, Guinea, Guiana, and minor salt deposits in the Caribbean and elsewhere—the New Netherland fur trade assumed a less insignificant position.[33]

*

33. Some idea of the relative importance of the New Netherland trade in the early years of the Company can be obtained from a comparison of the exports of trading merchandise to New Netherland and to West Africa, where by far the largest part of the Company's trade was then concentrated. Total imports to Guinea, Cape Verde, Sierra Leone, Gambia, and Senegal amounted to ƒ 2,128,532 from 1624–1628, while imports to New Netherland totaled ƒ 110,895, slightly over 5 percent of the West African figure (de Laet, *Historie ofte Iaerlijck Verhael* [1644], Appendix, pp. 26–28).

What opp lied in New Nether

In New Netherland, as in Guinea and Guiana, the directors
had the opportunity of building upon the experience of their predecessors. Although Arnout Vogels had died in 1620 and Lambrecht van Tweenhuyzen, the Pelgroms, and other moving spirits
of the *voorcompagnieën* seem not to have played any prominent
role in the West India Company, Jonas Witsen, an original participant in the New Netherland Company, and Samuel Godijn, a
member of the New Netherland Company in 1620, were among
the first directors of the Amsterdam Chamber.[34] Presumably these
two were willing and able to provide detailed information. De
Laet, also of the Amsterdam Chamber, had access to the journals
of Hudson and Adriaen Block, accounts from which were printed
in his *Nieuwe Wereldt* of 1625. In addition, the Company was
able to take into its service certain former employees of the *voorcompagnieën*, skippers Cornelis Jacobsz May and Adriaen Jorisz,
for example. The information contributed by these sources was
undoubtedly sufficient for carrying on the fur trade, but there is
no evidence that in 1623 the knowledge of the region's agricultural
possibilities much exceeded that gleaned by Hudson.[35] The potential of New Netherland's timber resources was better known, Block
and others having built sloops and yachts there; but, although it
is not impossible that some timber may have been included in
the return cargoes of the *voorcompagnieën*, there is no evidence
that any real experience had been gained regarding production
costs and freight charges.

It is even possible that the directors were seriously misinformed
about the climate of the Delaware Bay region. Wassenaer, writing
in the first half of 1624, before the reports of the first Company
expedition to New Netherland had returned, evidently had access
to abundant and detailed information on New Netherland, yet he
declared that

> In the South Bay [Delaware Bay], some miles nearer
> Florida, is a more temperate country [than the Hudson
> River]. There is no winter there save in January, and that
> but for a few days.[36]

34. For Witsen's participation in the New Netherland Company, see Chapter 1,
pp. 12–13. Godijn's participation is indicated in GAA, Not. Arch. 164, fol 70
(Hart, *Prehistory*, p. 44n).
35. For example, both de Laet's *Nieuwe Wereldt* of 1625 and Wassenaer's
Historisch Verhael, VI, pp. 144–47, give detailed information on the Indians of
New Netherland, but very little about agricultural possibilities.
36. Wass., VI, p. 146v.

Skipper David de Vries tells us that his companions at Swaenen-
dael on the Delaware River during the winter of 1632/33 doubted
that his sloop had been frozen in up river, as "many a steerman
or astronomer cannot understand that such running rivers can
freeze up at thirty-eight and a half to thirty-nine degrees." [37] That
theoretical geographical considerations took the place of empirical
observations may also be indicated by a statement of the Amsterdam directors in 1633:

> Though these parts [New Netherland], according to cli-
> mate, ought to be as warm and suitable for fruit culture as
> the extreme limits of France adjoining Spain, yet the same
> was found to be nearly colder than these, yes, than more
> northerly countries. For this reason, then, the people con-
> veyed thither by us have as yet been able to discover only
> scanty means of subsistence and have been no advantage
> but a disadvantage to this Company.[38]

In the latter half of 1623, armed with ample resources, and
the information and misinformation indicated above, the directors
faced the problem of what to do with New Netherland. Their
eventual solution to this question was no product of a fit of absent-
mindedness. In fact, the directors split very sharply over the
matter. Very dimly, through the mists of some 340 years, we can
see the XIX discussing the problem, pointing at maps, quoting
reports; but their voices are nearly inaudible: only a single scrap
of direct evidence relating to this controversy remains, a 1633
reminiscence of Kiliaen van Rensselaer in a highly partisan memorial defending the patroon system in particular and colonization
in general.[39] Nevertheless, it is incumbent on the historian to try

---

37. De Vries, *Verscheyden voyagiens*, p. 164.

38. "Een memorie over den toestand der West Indische Compagnie in het jaar
1633," ed. M. G. de Boer, BMHG, XXI (1900), p. 355. English translation in
DCHNY, I, p. 65. The directors could not have been deceived except in regard
to the Delaware region, for de Laet's *Nieuwe Wereldt*, which was dedicated in 1624,
correctly assessed the climate of the Hudson River region as nearly agreeing with
that of Holland, "for it is a good deal colder there than it ought to be according
to the latitude" (in NNN, p. 50). Significantly, de Laet says nothing about the
climate of the Delaware.

39. "Memorie overgelevert in de vergaderinge der XIX[en] der Geoctroyeerde
West-Indische Compaignie, op den 25 Novemb. 1633 in Amsterdamme," printed in
English in VRBM, pp. 235–250, and in Dutch in Nicolaas de Roever's "Kiliaen
van Rensselaer, en zijne kolonie Rensselaerswyck," *Oud Holland*, VIII (1890),

to reconstruct the divergent arguments from the significant economic circumstances that the directors can be expected to have known. Admittedly this is a dangerous expedient, for it is fatally easy for us, unconsciously imbued with nearly two centuries of sophisticated economic theorizing, to impute to the directors a degree of economic rationality which they simply did not possess. Yet there is nothing like a controversy to sharpen the wits, and it is not too far-fetched to imagine that lucid and informed standpoints were developed.

One alternative was to continue the system of exclusively fur-trading operations that had been successfully conducted by the various *voorcompagnieën* for over ten years.[40] This system, it will be remembered, involved the establishment of permanent and strategically located trading posts to attract the Indians, from which sloops and yachts could be dispatched to actively seek out the trade in distant regions. Yearly a ship from Holland brought trading goods and provisions and carried home furs. Except for the three years of the charter of the New Netherland Company, the bane of the *voorcompagnieën* was ruinous competition. From the point of view of the New Netherland fur trade as a whole, its effect was to raise costs through the redundancy of shipping

pp. 55–69. Van Rensselaer, either the first or second director chosen by the *hoofdparticipanten* at Amsterdam, indicates he was not yet in office when the first contingent of colonists was sent to New Netherland (about April 1624) but did participate in the deliberations preceding the dispatch of the large shipment of farmers, cattle, and other agricultural necessities early in 1625. This second shipment was, according to van Rensselaer, " diametrically opposed to the views of those who had no other aim than to send their ships from here to trade in [New Netherland]." Undoubtedly, this anti-colonial opposition had also been aroused by the sending of the first colonists in 1624, who were not, as van Rensselaer implies, instructed to make the fur trade their prime occupation, but were agricultural colonists to whom restricted rights of trade were granted (see Chapter 4). Van Rensselaer mentions some of the arguments used against the opponents of the 1625 shipments, but since the memorial was designed as a strong plea for colonization, he gives none employed by them. Since the memorial was written nine years after the actual debate, it is entirely possible that van Rensselaer's recounting of the arguments used for the 1625 expedition may include or reflect arguments developed during the succeeding decade of at times vehement discussion.

40. Of the standpoint of those in favor of this alternative prior to the dispatch of the second colonizing expedition to New Netherland early in 1625, van Rensselaer, writing in 1633, says only that they " had no other aim than to send their ships from here to trade in the aforesaid places [New Netherland]," and that they were unmoved by arguments that the returns from such operations would not bear the costs and that other nations would occupy an uncolonized region (Memorial of 1633, in VRBM, p. 236).

and personnel, and to turn the terms of trade in favor of the Indians. Endowed with its *Octroy*, the West India Company, like the New Netherland Company, could avoid this pitfall and reap maximum profits.

Anyone cherishing this thoroughly reasonable expectation could not fail to regard proposals for the establishment of an agricultural colony in New Netherland with extreme suspicion, for inevitably a colony would disrupt the fur trade. Even if the colonists were absolutely prohibited from trading furs, evasion of the prohibition would be a virtual certainty, and it would be far less easy to discipline colonists than salaried factors. In addition, colonization would confuse and perhaps endanger relations with the Indians. A trading post occupied only a few square rods of ground, and the real service performed by the trader for the savage inhabitants usually outweighed the annoyance he caused; but would land-gobbling peasants be anything but useless and obnoxious in the eyes of the natives? Finally, a policy uniting colonization with absolute or virtual reservation to the Company of the region's only provenly successful economic activity would be self-defeating, as few colonists would be attracted.[41]

According to van Rensselaer, the early proponents of colonization argued that because the trading posts in New Netherland were so widely separated the costs of the trade would exceed the returns.[42] But to this and similar arguments concerning costs and returns, those opposed to colonization could very properly have replied that since certainty about these matters could only be obtained after a period of experimentation with a trade free from the interference of colonists, there was every reason to delay colonization until such experimentation had been made.

The above are grave and reasonable objections, with which few could differ. To justify the undertaking of colonization, substantial compensatory rewards would have had to be demonstrated. What positive aspects of colonization might its supporters have advanced?

41. Simply taxing a free fur trade was probably never seriously considered at this time, although this system may have been applied in 1622/23, the year before the commencement of the Company's own operations. This system would have been the typical recourse of a capital-poor monopoly, such as the Council for New England; but it could have few attractions for a Company embarrassed rather by a surplus than a lack of capital for investment. Supporters of agricultural colonization would also shy away from a policy which would attract a swarm of *boschloopers* but no agriculturalists.

42. Memorial of 1633, in VRBM, p. 236.

What rewards could the colonies gained from colonization

⊻ The economic worth of an agricultural colony would depend
on its ability to (1) provision the Company's fur-trading establishment or (2) develop an export staple besides furs. In the first
case the colony would remain a tiny appendage of the fur trade,
perhaps no more than a half dozen *bouwerijen*. Only the second
case promised an unlimited and independent development.

⊻ The advantage of establishing farms in New Netherland to
provision the fur traders lay in the elimination of the expense and
uncertainty of shipping supplies across the Atlantic. Theoretically,
if the return cargo of furs from New Netherland were considerably bulkier than the America-bound cargo of trading truck (which
does not seem very likely), the provisions might have been transported in the empty New Netherland-bound holds for little more
than the costs of loading, unloading, and insurance. However,
there is little doubt that the expense of transatlantic provisioning
was indeed very heavy. Memorializing a presumably informed
Nineteen in 1633, van Rensselaer wrote that colonization had been
undertaken, among other reasons, " in order thus to relieve the
Company of the heavy expense of transporting all sorts of provisions needed by the people in that land "; and about 1617 Champlain urged the " great expense " of importing provisions from
France as a reason for colonizing Canada.[43] The precise magnitude
of the cost of shipping provisions to New Netherland is uncertain,
but it may well have been in the vicinity of 50 percent of the
original purchase price of the stores.[44] Whether the total saving
resulting from the establishment of agricultural enterprise would

43. Van Rensselaer's statement is in VRBM, pp. 235–36. Champlain's in *Works
of Samuel de Champlain*, ed. Henry P. Biggar, IV, p. 350.
44. In 1636, van Rensselaer and his partners shipped supplies to their colony
of Rensselaerswyck at a probable cost of about 42½ percent of the original purchase
value. The supplies, consisting of at least some foodstuffs, were shipped on a " small
vessel " owned by van Rensselaer, his partners in Rensselaerswyck, and other
associates in October 1636. Van Rensselaer directed his representative in New
Netherland to sell the goods to his own colonists at an increase over the original
wholesale price in Holland of somewhat more than 50 percent, as the original price
did not include " any expense of packing, insurance, damage, etc. (not even your
commission of one stiver on the guilder, . . .)" (VRBM, pp. 325–26). A 50
percent advance probably represented a negligible profit, since the maximum markup
to be charged van Rensselaer's own colonists, 60 percent, is described as below
market prices. Assuming then that 150 percent of the wholesale price just about
covered costs and subtracting the 5 percent commission of the agent, I estimate that
the total shipping charges were thought to be about 42½ percent of the value
of the goods. A larger ship would undoubtedly have reduced the freight rate
somewhat.

be equal to the saving in shipping charges would, of course, depend on whether production costs in New Netherland could be brought down to the level in Europe.[45] In any case, dependence on the fortune and floatability of a single provisioning vessel from the home country would be more risky than dependence on the harvest in New Netherland.

An important consideration in the evaluation of the worth of a provisioning colony was the attitude of the Indians. If it would be possible profitably to exchange agricultural products for peltries, the value of the agricultural enterprise would be considerably enhanced.[46] On the other hand, if the traders could regularly and cheaply obtain an important part of their provisions from the Indians, the justification of a heavy investment in a provisioning colony would be undercut. That such an exchange was indeed feasible was probably known to the directors, since at least one of the *voorcompagnieën* was bartering large amounts of merchandise for provisions shortly before the beginning of the West India Company's operations. The amenability of the savages to this form of exchange is also indicated by the barter of trading truck for maize, fish and other food between the colonists and Indians at the Manhattans in 1626 and in Rensselaerswyck prior to about 1632.[47]

At the eve of New Netherland's colonization, the directors favoring colonization contemplated a large variety of products as potential export staples other than furs. The producibility of some of these products (grain, high quality timber and timber products such as tar and pitch, and grapes for wine) was either certain or very probable; and the directors were hopeful that these commodities would prove exportable.[48] The existence or produci-

---

45. For the unlikelihood of this, see below, pp. 69–70.

46. William Bradford relates that the Pilgrims exchanged grain for peltries in 1625 and 1626 (*Bradford's History*, ed. Davis, pp. 208, 212). The Rensselaerswyck colonists, forbidden to obtain standard trading truck, seem to have conducted a small exchange of this nature about 1636 (VRBM, p. 324).

47. For the exchange of trading truck for provisions by a *voorcompagnie* and at the Manhattans in 1626, see Isaacq de Rasiere to the Directors of the West India Company, September 23, 1626, in Hunt., pp. F24–25, 219–20, and F31, 232. Inscriptions on a map of Rensselaerswyck of about 1632 read: ". . . from the Mohawks one can (principally in the winter) obtain venison enough, that is fat and beautiful; about three, four, or five hands of *sewan* for a deer. The sturgeon is smaller than at the Manathans; one can be bought from the savages for a knife" (VRBM, p. 35).

48. Van Rensselaer asserted in 1633 that the directors, in making their decision

bility of many other products was only wishful conjecture. Besides
the precious metals, the directors were interested in copper, iron,
lead, and sulfur; but, though the natives had copper tobacco pipes
and claimed to know iron, no mines had as yet been discovered.[49]

to colonize New Netherland, considered that the region was "well adapted for
raising all kinds of grain and animals which could be sent here [the Netherlands]
or at least in other limits of the charter" (VRBM, p. 235). I am somewhat
sceptical about the assertion that the directors contemplated exporting cattle very
far from New Netherland, but their interest in grain exports appears reasonable
and is probably attested by the shipment from New Netherland in 1626 of "samples
of summer grain; such as wheat, rye, barley, oats, buckwheat, (and) canary seed"
(DCHNY, I, p. 37). Grain was the Company's principal economic hope for
New Netherland in 1638, when it was determined to renew the region's colonization (*ibid.*, p. 107).

The directors' interest in timber exports is indicated or made probable by a
variety of records. In his *Nieuwe Wereldt* of 1625, de Laet, a director of the West
India Company, emphasized timber for shipbuilding as New Netherland's principal
resource after furs (NNN, pp. 38, 48–50). Willem van Hulst, the provisional
director of New Netherland sent out in 1625, was instructed "to load the ships
with all sorts of wood as far as it is possible so that the ships do not come home
empty" ("Instructie voor Willem van Hulst . . . ," in Hunt., pp. C18, 71); and
according to the anonymous "Journal of New Netherland" of twenty years later,
the Company erected three sawmills "in the beginning" (DCHNY, I, p. 181).
In 1626, the *Wapen van Amsterdam* brought back from New Netherland "considerable oak timber and hickory" (DCHNY, I, p. 38).

In his *Nieuwe Wereldt*, de Laet reported that "wine can be made [in New
Netherland] . . . since vines are already found that require nothing but cultivation"
(NNN, p. 50). Van Hulst was instructed "to pay special attention to the vine-
yards which are there in abundance." If New Netherland grapes were suitable for
wine or raisins, van Hulst was to begin their culture. If unsuitable, he was to
attempt to improve them by transplanting and other means and at least discover
whether brandy, vinegar, or grape juice (*verjuys*) could be extracted from them.
If the New Netherland grapes were totally unsatisfactory, the directors promised
to send over suitable vines from Europe ("Instructie voor Willem van Hulst";
in Hunt., pp. C11, 56). Various other references to viniculture appear in van
Hulst's "Instructie" and his "Further Instructions" ("Naerdere Jnstructie, by de
Bewinthebberen der West-Jndysche compe ter camere van Amsterdam inghestelt,
voor Willem vander Hulst Commis . . . ," in Hunt., but there is no evidence that
any serious effort was ever made to produce wine or other grape products
commercially.

An attempt to produce tanbark was made in New Netherland by 1626 (de Rasiere
to the Directors, Sept. 23, 1626, in Hunt., pp. F33, 23). Probably in answer to
a query of the directors, de Rasiere reported that the burning of tar and pitch was
possible "beyond dispute" in 1626 (*ibid.*, pp. F32, 235).

49. The Nineteen resolved to find two or three mineralogists to search for
"gold, silver, or other metals" in New Netherland on November 25, 1624
(Resolution in Stokes, *Iconography*, IV, p. 60). In addition to gold and silver,
the instructions to the commander of the 1625 expedition mention copper, iron,
lead, and sulphur ("Instructie voor Willem van Hulst"; in Hunt., pp. C21, 76).
The copper pipes and the Indians' knowledge of iron was remarked by Hudson
(de Laet, *Nieuwe Wereldt*; in NNN, p. 49).

Dried or salted fish and pearls were also considered as potential exports, but the existence of nearby fisheries was still unproven, and it was not certain whether the abundant oyster beds bore pearls of good quality. The possibility of salt from salt mountains or artificial pans drew the attention of the directors, though the mountains were as yet undiscovered and no one had yet attempted to make salt in New Netherland by evaporation. Surprisingly, though the Indians produced a green tobacco which Hudson described as " strong and good for use," and though the English had had great success with tobacco little more than a degree south of Delaware Bay, the directors seem to have had but little interest in the weed. Perhaps they regarded their Guiana colony as a much better source of tobacco.[50]

The Republic was heavily dependent on other nations for grain, timber and its products, and wine, all of which could fairly certainly be produced in New Netherland. Southwest France was perhaps the most important source of wine. Rye and wheat were imported largely from the Baltic. Oak, the most desirable material for shipbuilding, was in part floated down the Rhine from Western Germany, but even more was obtained by Dutch ships at Bremen and Hamburg, Lübeck and Stettin, Danzig, Königsberg, and Riga. Fir planks, used to deck ships and for house construction, came from both Norway and the Baltic, and masts were shipped from Norway, Riga, and even Archangel. Pine, which occasionally replaced oak in ship construction, was obtained in Norway and the Baltic.[51] Tar, pitch, ashes and other timber extracts also came from Scandinavia and the Baltic lands. Considering the nation's

50. For the directors' interest in fish, pearls, and salt, see "Instructie voor Willem van Hulst," in Hunt., pp. C21, 76; and " Naerdere Jnstructie . . . . voor Willem vander Hulst," *ibid.*, pp. D22, 125. Secretary de Rasieres gave his opinion on salt making in New Netherland in his 1626 letter to the directors, probably in answer to a query from them (Letter in *ibid.*, pp. F32, 235).

Hudson's appraisal of New Netherland tobacco is in de Laet's *Nieuwe Wereldt*; in NNN, p. 48. Comparing New Netherland and South American tobacco in 1624, Wassenaer wrote " tobacco is planted in abundance [by the Indians in New Netherland], but much better grows in the wild parts of Brasil " (Wass., in NNN, p. 71). The first certain attempt of the Dutch to grow tobacco in New Netherland was that of Governor Minuit about 1630 (VRBM, pp. 219, 233).

51. Johan Schreiner (*Nederland og Norge 1625-1650*, pp. 13–14 and 19–20) gives the Dutch sources of oak, fir, and pine, and mentions the uses to which oak and fir were put. Nicolaes Witsen (*Aeloude en hedendaegsche scheeps-bouw en bestier*, p. 179) mentions the occasional replacement of oak by pine in ship construction.

need for cheap and reliable sources of these commodities, it was natural that the attention of the merchant-directors of the Company would be attracted by New Netherland's promise in regard to these resources. However, those opposed to colonization could have developed a telling a priori argument against the feasibility of exporting to the home country at least two of the commodities in question, timber and grain: except perhaps in times of severe warfare in the Baltic, Baltic exports of these commodities to the Netherlands would have a considerable advantage over New Netherland exports in point of shipping charges (freight + insurance + miscellaneous costs of shipping).

Perhaps in 1623 the directors were unsure exactly how large this advantage would be. Conceivably they could have gotten quotes on insurance rates applicable to a New Netherland voyage; but, since as far as is known no large merchantmen suitable for the grain or timber trade had as yet voyaged to New Netherland, they could have done no more than estimate New Netherland freight rates on the basis of the charges incurred by the small ships of the *voorcompagnieën*. Such estimates, good as they undoubtedly were, cannot be reconstructed directly by the historian, however, since virtually no information on the freight expenses of the *voorcompagnieën* has come to light.[52]

An alternative for the historian is the inference of the directors' 1623 estimates from a comparison of Baltic and New Netherland shipping records of succeeding years. The Gemeente Archief of Amsterdam has so far yielded thirteen charter parties for Netherlands–New Netherlands–Netherlands voyages, of which three date from 1625 and the remainder from 1651–1662.[53] Besides several New Netherland–Caribbean or West African charters, the archives of the provincial government of New Netherland, now at Albany, contain one additional charter of interest, a New Netherlands–Netherlands charter of 1641.[54] Theoretically it would be possible to compare charters for the Baltic and New Netherlands trades

52. The charter party of the *St. Pieter* in 1611 is extant; but this was an atypical, exploratory voyage (see Chapter 1, pp. 5–6).

53. The 1625 charters, two from Not. Arch. Reg. # 226, p. 59v, and one from # 652, p. 11v, are abstracted in Stokes, *Iconography*, VI, pp. 11–12. Dr. Simon Hart of the Gemeente Archief was kind enough to send me abstracts of the later charter parties, viz., Not. Arch. Reg. # 1534, p. 173; # 2194, p. 551; # 2196, p. 470; # 1538, p. 268; # 1539, pp. 20 and 107; # 2793, pp. 414 and 695; and # 2794, pp. 109 and 448.

54. New York State Library, New York Colonial Manuscripts, I, p. 273.

which either (1) specified the freight charges per last of freight
delivered from the Baltic and from the New Netherlands to the
Netherlands, or (2) gave a fixed price for the round trips to these
destinations. None of these fourteen charters specifies the freight
charges per last freight delivered, but one of them, fortunately
one of the very early, 1625 charters, gives a flat rate for the entire
round trip to New Netherland.

This charter agreement was made on May 28, 1625, between
the West India Company and Willem Jansz Boet, skipper and
owner of the 130 last *Ruyter*.[55] Boet, after loading his ship with
provisions, goods, and animals, was to sail with a crew of twelve
directly to New Netherland, where, after unloading and laying
over three weeks, he could be either discharged or loaded with
a return cargo at the option of the charterer. If discharged, Boet
would receive ƒ 2,600. If retained for the return voyage, he would
be paid ƒ 3,100 for the round trip.

The sum of ƒ 3,100 was roughly three times the sum for which
a ship of similar size could be chartered for a round trip voyage
to the nearer Baltic ports, such as Danzig and Königsberg.[56]
Inference of the prevailing freight differential from this single
instance is not, of couse, permissible. However, the 3 : 1 differential is confirmed both by R. G. Albion, who uses it in comparing
transatlantic freight rates with those between England and the
Baltic for an indefinite period from the seventeenth to the nineteenth century,[57] and by my own necessarily inexact estimates based
on reconstructions of the costs of sending ships of identical carrying capacity on the two voyages in question.

These latter estimates are not entirely watertight, for although

55. This charter from GAA, Not. Arch., Reg. # 652, p. 11v is abstracted in
Stokes, *Iconography*, VI, p. 12.

56. Comparison of charter parties to obtain a standard freight price for a given
route is a frustrating undertaking, since any two given charters will almost always
differ in several respects. However, comparison of a number of Dutch Baltic
charters sent to me through the kindness of Dr. Hart suggests that at this time
the freight price for a ship of the *Ruyter*'s size on an Amsterdam-Danzig–Amsterdam voyage was in the neighborhood of ƒ1,000. E. g., a 134-last ship was chartered
June 2, 1622, to sail from Amsterdam to Danzig or Königsberg, unload its cargo
of salt, load an unspecified commodity, and return to Amsterdam, for a total freight
charge of ƒ7½ per last of salt unloaded. If the vessel was fully loaded, the freight
price for this voyage would have amounted to ƒ1,005 (GAA, Not. Arch., Reg. 218,
p. 102v).

57. *Forests and Sea Power: The Timber Problem of the Royal Navy, 1652–1862*,
p. 152.

relative voyage durations and the costs of the additional crew and armament necessary for the more perilous New Netherland voyage can be computed with some assurance, the estimation of both relative insurance costs and the weights which should be assigned to the various cost components tends to become rather arbitrary. However, even when these uncertain factors are permitted to vary by a considerable margin, the result is a cost differential between New Netherland and Danzig or Königsberg voyages which deviates little from 2.5:1.[58] I believe, therefore, considering the probability that a skipper would expect a higher profit margin on a New Netherland voyage, that the 3:1 ratio is a good rough and ready expression of the relative charges incurred in chartering ships of similar capacity to New Netherland and to the nearer Baltic. The ratio would, of course, increase for a port in southern Norway and decrease somewhat for a distant Baltic port such as Reval.

Freight charges were not the only component of shipping charges. A second formidable factor was insurance, which on a cargo of moderate value such as wheat, may have amounted to over one-third of the freight charges on a shipment from New Netherland.[59] As noted above, it is not yet possible to compare the insurance rates applicable to cargoes on well armed and manned ships returning from New Netherland with those obtainable for unarmed ships sailing in convoys from the Baltic. However, considering that in normal times the Baltic was free from privateers and pirates while a ship returning from New Netherland would have to sail through the home waters of the Dunkirk privateers, the principal threat to Dutch shipping in the 1620's and 1630's, I find it hard to believe that the insurance rate differential could have been other than to the disadvantage of the New Netherland trade.

In the composition of total shipping charges, tolls and taxes

58. For a fuller discussion of these estimates, see Appendix I.

59. Price data in N. W. Posthumus' *Inquiry into the History of Prices in Holland*, I, p. 1, indicate that ƒ175 per last of 4,600–4,800 lbs. was a typical price for wheat at this time. Since the ship's last was about 4,000 Holland pounds, a 130-last ship could have carried about $130 \times \dfrac{4,000}{4,700} \times ƒ175 = ƒ19,362$ in wheat. A 6 percent insurance rate on this cargo, for which Appendix I gives some evidence, would therefore yield a total risk cost of about ƒ1,162, 37.5 percent of the charter price of the *Ruyter* in 1625. I use the term "risk cost" instead of "insurance premium," since the insurer did not customarily insure 100 percent of the value of the goods.

were considerably less important than freight and insurance. Imports from New Netherland would have escaped the *convoyen* until at least 1629, since the West India Company's charter exempted it from these taxes for eight years. This exemption would have saved New Netherland wheat two florins per last, or a bit less than one percent of its value.[60] However, uncertainty whether this privilege would be renewed would have prevented the directors from making long-range investments on the basis of its continuance. A more permanent advantage to the New Netherland trade was its freedom from the *lastetold*, which the Danes levied at the Sound. This toll amounted to roughly $1\frac{1}{2}$–2 percent of the value of grain at this time.[61]

If the 6 percent, which some evidence suggests to have been the insurance rate on the return voyages from New Netherland during this period, was about equal to the aggregate of insurance and Sound tolls which the Baltic trade had to bear, and if we assume that outbound voyages to the Baltic and to New Netherland were both made in ballast, total shipping charges incurred by a return cargo of New Netherland wheat in a 130 last vessel would still be roughly twice the total charges borne by the same ship-load from Danzig or Königsberg.[62]

The assumption of an outbound voyage in ballast seems entirely appropriate in the case of New Netherland, since in 1624 the outlook for regular bulk cargos to New Netherland must have been dim indeed. The Baltic trade was in a somewhat better position. Although the eastwards voyage was still often made in ballast, it was becoming increasingly common in the early seventeenth century for Dutch ships to pick up a salt or wine cargo in western France or Portugal before proceeding to the Baltic, thus distributing freight charges over more goods. This development certainly worked to increase New Netherland's disadvantage as to total shipping charges, but to what degree is unknown.

Let us take 2:1 as a very conservative approximation of the ratio of total shipping charges from New Netherland to those from the nearer Baltic ports, keeping in mind that the ratio would have increased for Norway and decreased somewhat for Riga or

60. This is according to the rates of 1625 (van Rees, *Geschiedenis der staathuishoudkunde*, I, p. 228n).

61. Christensen, *Dutch Trade to the Baltic*, pp. 311–312.

62. Six percent of the value of 130 ship's lasts of wheat was about ƒ1,162 (note 59). ƒ3,100 + ƒ1,162 = ƒ4,262 = 1.97 (ƒ1,000 + ƒ1,162).

Reval. What can we say, and what may the directors in 1623 have said, about the prospects for timber or grain exports from New Netherland?

The effect of this millstone of heavy shipping charges on the exports of timber and of grain from New Netherland would be very different. In general, timber, as "the extreme example of great bulk with small value" would be in a hopeless position. A doubling of shipping charges over the Baltic rates, not to speak of the probably higher labor costs in New Netherland, would certainly consume the slight advantage accruing from the presumed initial costlessness of New Netherland timber and go on to price ordinary grades of timber from New Netherland off the Dutch market. The only real hope for regular timber exports lay in choice pieces of timber for the shipbuilding industry such as masts, which might command a high enough price to warrant transatlantic shipment.[63]

Grain, possessing a much higher value-to-volume ratio than most timber, would be in a less hopeless position. In the case of timber, a doubling of the Baltic shipping charges might in itself represent the market price for the wood; but as the cost of shipping wheat, the highest quality grain, from Danzig might be less than 15 percent of the market price in Amsterdam, a doubling of this percentage would not necessarily present New Netherland grain with an insurmountable barrier to its export to Holland.[64] Specifi-

63. Ralph Davis, who describes timber as "the extreme example of great bulk with small value," states that the freight cost of (Scandinavian or Baltic) timber to England commonly equalled its first cost ("Merchant shipping in the economy of the late seventeenth century," *Economic History Review*, IX [1956–57], p. 59n). Albion reports for a vaguely defined period between 1652 and 1862 that the cost of a standing tree in Poland was usually only 5 percent of its final value when delivered in England (Albion, *Forests and Sea Power*, pp. 151–52).

That the upper Hudson did indeed possess good mast timber seems evident from the attempt of a governor of New York to export masts from there to England around 1701 (Albion, *Forests and Sea Power*, p. 247). Whether the directors of the West India Company were aware of the existence of good mast timber in New Netherland in 1623 is another matter. De Laet spoke of good timber for shipbuilding in his *Nieuwe Wereldt*, but not specifically of great timbers for masts.

64. In 1595, the freight charges on wheat shipped from Danzig to Holland were ƒ12 per last (Christensen, *Dutch Trade to the Baltic*, p. 369). Posthumus does not give price data on Danzig wheat for 1595, but he does give the wholesale prices in Amsterdam for Königsberg wheat for several months in 1591, Sep. 1592, and Sep. 1593, the average for these three years being ƒ154.48 per last (*Prices in Holland*, I, p. 1). If Danzig and Königsberg wheat commanded the same price, and if the 1591–1593 average is indicative of the 1595 price, the freight charges on

cally, if, for example, the cost of shipping Baltic wheat were just 15 percent of the selling price in Amsterdam, New Netherland wheat, burdened by double this transport charge, could still be competitive if its cost of production was brought down to about 82 percent of that of the Baltic.[65]

Though shipping charges could have been accurately estimated by the West India Company directors, the question whether production costs could be reduced to this level must have been a matter of pure speculation to them in 1623. To assume that the directors possessed either the time or the economic sophistication to analyze thoroughly so nebulous a subject as potential production costs in the New Netherland wilderness is probably fatuous. However, it must at least have been recognized that labor would present a problem and that its cost would probably offset to some extent the colony's certain advantage over the Baltic in cost of land. Sober consideration would certainly have concluded that European labor would normally demand some sort of material compensation as well as be expensive to transport. Moreover, considerations of security would dictate a high proportion of immigrants from the prosperous, high-wage fatherland. For these reasons, the cost of European labor in New Netherland could only have been expected to run substantially above that of the serf labor of some Baltic lands.

Whether the Indians would provide an effective supplement to white labor was highly questionable, because Indian men eschewed agricultural work, leaving it to the women.[66] Black slaves were, of course, a possibility, but a sceptic could have argued that they

Danzig wheat shipped to Holland would have been only about 7.8 percent of the selling price in Amsterdam. I see no reason why these percentages need have changed very much in the succeeding twenty-eight years. If they did not, c. 8 percent freight plus c. 3 percent for Sound tolls and *convoyen* plus c. 2–3 percent for insurance would have represented the total shipping charges.

65. Small letters refer to New Netherland; capitals to the Baltic. P, p = selling price in Amsterdam; C_t, c_t = total costs of production; T, t = total transport charges.

$C_t + T$ are assumed to = P. $c_t + t$ are assumed to = p. T = .15P. t = 2T.

p = P. c_t = .70P. C_t = .85P. $\dfrac{c_t}{C_t} = \dfrac{.70}{.85} = .8235$.

66. Letter of Isaack de Rasieres to Samuel Blommaert (c. 1628), in NNN, p. 105; *Vertoogh van Nieu-Neder-Land, weghens de ghelegentheydt, vruchtbaerheydt, en soberen staet desselfs* ('s Graven-hage: Michiel Stael, 1650), in NNN, p. 302; "Journal of New Netherland; written in the years 1641, 1642, 1643, 1644, 1645 and 1646," in DCHNY, I, p. 180.

were so necessary to the tropical plantations that it would be far more profitable either to employ available Negroes in Guiana and the expected Brazil conquest or to smuggle them into the Spanish and Portuguese dominions than to ship them to New Netherland.

Considering high shipping charges and the questionability of low production costs, the profitability of exporting New Netherland grain to the Netherlands would have been quite uncertain. However, New Netherland grain would very probably be able to compete with European grain in West Africa or Brazil. According to van Rensselaer, the supporters of colonization were far-seeing enough to consider this possibility, thus in a general way anticipating the eventual solution worked out by the New Englanders to their own acute export crisis after 1640: a triangular trade between New England, the Wine Islands or Africa, and the West Indies.[67] A more limited export alternative also considered by the directors was the establishment of New Netherland as the provisioning base for the Company's fleets in the West Indies, from which New Netherland could be reached in fourteen days.[68]

Our attempt to reconstruct the economic possibilities of New Netherland as they appeared to the Company about 1623 indicates that the directors considered at least four fairly certainly producible exports besides furs: timber, grain, wine, and timber extracts. The home country required all these commodities, but in normal times they could be obtained from countries much nearer to the Netherlands than New Netherland at very substantially lower shipping charges. In the case of a commodity with a very low value to bulk ratio such as timber, the heavier shipping charges would render profitable export to Europe generally impossible. Heavier shipping charges would have a less severe effect on New Netherland grain, though still severe enough to make its export to the Netherlands at least questionable in view of the uncertainty about New Netherland production costs. More hopeful opportunities than Europe for grain exports would be West Africa, Brazil, or the Company's

---

67. In his 1633 memorial van Rensselaer remembered that the directors considered that New Netherland grain or animals could be exported to Holland " or at least within other limits of the charter, as Cape Verde, Guinea, and Brazil " (VRBM, p. 235). Ruiters reported in 1623 that Brazil imported " much flour loaded in barrels " from Portugal, and that Angola exchanged slaves for bread, meal, biscuit, and Brazilian farina (Ruiters, *Toortse*, pp. 9, 12–13). He says nothing about Cape Verde or Guinea as grain importers, however.

68. Van Rensselaer, Memorial of 1633, in VRBM, p. 235.

West India fleets. Wine or timber extracts had considerable value in relation to their bulk and the transport factor would weigh least heavily on them. However, the probable expensiveness in New Netherland of the skilled labor necessary to produce these commodities might not permit a reduction of production costs to even slightly below European levels, and the quality of the eventual products was still uncertain.

The export prospects as summarized above appear rather meager. Whether, in the absence of a West India Company, such prospects would have attracted much free private capital in the economically still expanding United Provinces may be doubted. However, New Netherland's export possibilities may have been more attractive to the West India Company than to the Dutch business community at large. The Company was not free to employ its enormous capital outside the area of its charter, and within that area there were only very limited opportunities for conservative investment without the expense and risk of warfare. The need for investment diversification might therefore countenance investment in a relatively safe commercial venture such as an agricultural colony in New Netherland even if the expected returns were low.

By now it should be abundantly clear that both the opponents and supporters of New Netherland's colonization would have been able to muster telling arguments for their positions. Against the worth of colonists as provisioners for the fur-trading establishment there might have been advanced their undesirability as potential fur smugglers. Against the meagerness of the region's prospects for export staples other than furs, there could have been balanced the undoubted necessity of increasing the number of conservative investments in the Company's entire portfolio. A particularly impressive argument of the directors opposing colonization would have been the desirability of postponing colonization until the profitability or unprofitability of the fur trade under conditions free from the interference of colonists could be determined. However, two other factors encouraged the prompt planting of a colony. One was the current desire of certain families of the Walloon community in Holland to emigrate to the New World.[69] The other was the serious threat, primarily from Eng-

69. See Chapter 4.

land, that another European power might seize a region occupied by only a handful of fur traders.[70]

The English menace was apparent in the Netherlands as early as 1620, when the directors of the New Netherland Company requested the State to assist the future Pilgrims to settle New Netherland,

> having experienced that his Majesty of Great Britain would be disposed to people the aforesaid lands with the English nation, and by force to render fruitless their possession and discovery, and thus deprive this State of its right, and apparently with ease surprise the ships of this country which are there.[71]

In 1622 the English Privy Council, on the strength of an entirely unfounded rumor that the Dutch had already planted a substantial colony in the " Virginias," directed the English ambassador at the Hague to secure the cessation of all such attempts. The ambassador, though he found no evidence of the supposed colony, duly made several remonstrances to the States General, pointing out His Majesty's incontestable right to all the precincts of " Virginia " *de jure primae occupationis*.[72] Rapid action to forestall an English take-over and establish Dutch claims to the region on the basis of prior occupation was thus highly advisable.

On November 3, 1623, during the second gathering of The Nineteen, it was resolved

> that a ship be sent to the Virginias, which the Amsterdam Chamber shall outfit and provide with merchandise necessary to continue the trade, to which end they may also take along five or six families of the colonists to plant a beginning there.[73]

Since the avowed purpose of this very tiny colonization effort was the continuance of the fur trade, it may reasonably be doubted

---

70. In his 1633 memorial, van Rensselaer says that it was pointed out on the eve of colonization " that other nations of adjoining regions, when our ships should be away from there, would immediately seize and occupy these [regions, i. e. New Netherland] and keep us out " (VRBM, p. 236).

71. DCHNY, I, p. 23.

72. *Ibid.*, pp. 27–28; and vol. III, pp. 6–8, 11.

73. Resolution book of The Nineteen, 1623–1624, quoted in Jessurun, *Kiliaen van Rensselaer*, bijlage 1.

whether the resolution implies The Nineteen's acceptance of the desirability of a substantial investment in New Netherland's agricultural development at this time. Perhaps at this time no more was envisaged than a token colonization, sufficient only to establish the Company's territorial claims and to carry out a certain amount of agricultural experimentation. However, a policy of relatively large investment was adopted very soon. Thirty, not just five or six, families were dispatched in the first shipload of colonists in the spring of 1624; and early in 1625, despite the continuing scepticism of some of the directors, the Amsterdam Chamber sent several shiploads of cattle and additional emigrants to the colony.[74]

74. Van Rensselaer notes the continuing opposition on the part of some directors in his 1633 memorial (VRBM, p. 236).

CHAPTER FOUR

THE EXPERIENCE OF THE EARLY YEARS

Having adopted the policy of agricultural colonization in New Netherland, the Company faced a large number of purely technical problems. The first constellation of problems concerned labor. The Company had to select suitable people for emigration, induce them to settle in a heathen wilderness, and motivate them to employ themselves productively. Secondly, it had to provide transportation across the Atlantic for these people, along with animals and tools, and maintain an uninterrupted flow of provisions until the colony could supply its own food. Lastly, the directors had to provide their lieutenants with a comprehensive and realistic blueprint for exploiting the region, a plan which harmonized in every essential respect with the dictates imposed by climatic, pedological, and other geographical factors and by the Indians. Broadly speaking, the Company solved these technical problems rather well, and we can probably reckon the plantation of New Netherland among the better conceived and executed of the colonization schemes which had thus far been directed north of Florida.

Leaving the solutions to problems two and three to be revealed hereafter in the narrative of the colony's first years, let us consider some of the Company's answers to its problems of labor recruitment and motivation. In general, the Company approached these along two paths: by offering generous conditions, it encouraged *coloniërs* (free colonists) to emigrate to New Netherland and set themselves up there on their own account in farming or other permitted occupations; and, secondly, it hired farmers and craftsmen to work in New Netherland for a contracted term of years, setting up and operating Company owned plantations, sawmills, smithies, and the like.

The Virginia Company of London, the Plymouth adventurers, and many other colonizers had considered the early introduction of private enterprise to be incompatible with the necessity of strong

74

central direction in the anxious first years of a colony. In their view, only after a colony was firmly established could the colonizing agency relax its monopoly of the colony's economic life. Yet under the West India Company, *coloniërs* formed the advance guard of 1624, and only in the following year was hired labor sent to the colony. Exactly what prompted this singular procedure is unknown. Conceivably, the notable suitability of the first applicants for emigration placed them in a bargaining position capable of exacting liberal economic concessions from the Company.

All too often the main body of a colonizing expedition had been composed of waterfront punks, who were attracted by promises of loot and adventure or simply impressed. Needless to say, such men seldom made determined pioneers. The " 30 families, mostly Walloons," [1] who sailed off as colonists in 1624, were obviously a different sort, however. The well forged resolution of these Protestant refugees from the Southern Netherlands is indicated both by their willingness to risk wives and children and by their probable initiative towards emigration: some or all of these families were very probably among the " good number of colonists " which the *Poincten van beschrijvinge* for the very first gathering of The Nineteen described as " presenting themselves." [2]

The willingness of whole families to emigrate may have demonstrated determination, but was the family a really suitable unit for the vanguard of colonization, considering the inevitable initial dangers and hardships and the heavy expense of shipping provisions across the Atlantic? To the French and English colonizers of Port Royal, Jamestown, Sagadahoc, and Quebec the answer had been no. But in each of these all-male undertakings, the first

1. So described by Wass., VIII, in NNN, p. 75.
2. Quote from the *poincten van beschrijvinge* in G. J. van Grol, *De grondpolitiek in het West-Indische domein der generaliteit*, II, pp. 30–31; from Resolution book of The Nineteen, 1623–1624. The Nineteen's November 1623 resolution which inaugurated New Netherland's colonization authorized the Amsterdam Chamber to send over " V or VI families of *the* colonists " (italics mine) ; and it is reasonable to assume that " the colonists " of November were the same as or included in the " good number of colonists " of the previous July. Some, perhaps most, of this " good number " were Walloon and French refugees whom Jesse de Forest, a Huguenot émigré dwelling in Leyden, had been recruiting since 1621. De Forest's efforts to lead these refugees to the New World under English or Dutch patronage are admirably described in Volume I of Mrs. Robert W. de Forest's *A Walloon Family in America*. The possibility that some of the fifty-six signers of de Forest's 1621 petition to the King of England for permission to emigrate to Virginia were among the first emigrants to New Netherland is discussed in Vol. I, pp. 34–35.

effusion of enthusiasm quickly gave way to factionalism, idleness, or general demoralization. These symptoms seem to have been most acute in the two English settlements, although Champlain was nearly murdered by a conspiracy of his Quebec colonists. Port Royal's extreme laxity—after the construction of the watermill the " workmen had plenty of leisure and for the most part did nothing "—and organized bon-vivantism was probably instrumental in preventing serious quarrels there,[3] but Marc Lescarbot, who spent a year at Port Royal in 1606/07, pointed to the apathy which tended to grip the members of an all male society. In speaking of the remedies for scurvy, the scourge of the French settlements, he wrote

> One further preservative is necessary to complete a man's content and to fill up his pleasure in his daily task, which is that each man should have the honorable company of his married wife; for if that be lacking, the good cheer is not complete, one's thoughts turn ever to the object of one's love and desire, home sickness arises, the body becomes full of ill humours, and disease makes its entrance.[4]

Perhaps mindful of the experience of these predecessors, a London and Bristol company for the plantation of Newfoundland sent a group of both sexes to initiate its colonizing effort in 1610. The experiment was successful, and its example was followed consciously or unconsciously by various other English colonizers of Newfoundland and New England in the half dozen years preceding the settlement of New Netherland.[5] Thus there existed abundant precedents for the suitability, even desirability, of making an immediate settlement of families by the time the West India Company directors got around to considering the problem in 1623/24. It is reasonable to suppose, therefore, that these gentlemen considered the eager Walloon families as highly promising emigrant material and were thus willing to offer them rather liberal terms, including the right to enjoy immediately the fruits of their private enterprise.

3. For the " Order of Good Cheer " and the idleness of the workmen, see Marc Lescarbot, *History of New France*, ed. W. L. Grant, II, pp. 342–44 and 347.

4. *Ibid.*, pp. 270, 522.

5. E. g., Vaughan's 1618 colony in Newfoundland, Plymouth Plantation in 1620, and Calvert's Newfoundland colony of 1622. (Charles M. Andrews, *The Colonial Period of American History*, I, pp. 268–69, 306, 308). Andrews also describes the 1610 colonization of Newfoundland (*ibid.*, pp. 304–05).

The conditions on which the 1624 *coloniërs* agreed to settle New Netherland were laid down in a *provisionele ordere*, drawn up by three members of the Company's Amsterdam Chamber, Johannes de Laet, the famous student of the West Indies, Samuel Godijn, a former partner of Arnout Vogels in the New Netherland Company, and Dr. Albert Coenraets Burgh, a member of the municipal council of Amsterdam. This document was approved by the XIX on March 28th, 1624, perhaps altered in one important respect a day or two later, and read to the colonists on March 30th.[6]

By the standards of the day, the main economic provisions contained in the *Provisionele ordere* were extremely generous to the *coloniërs*. The " greate Charter " issued by the Virginia Company in 1618 had provided for the granting of land to shareholders of that company or to persons who paid their passage to Virginia; but impecunious persons had been obliged to work for the Virginia Company for seven years on half shares just to repay the costs of their passage, without obtaining at the end of this term any grant of land.[7] The first colonists in New Netherland, on the other hand, would immediately,

> without paying any recognition therefor, receive from the Company the costs of passage, as also the places and lands which are assigned to them to cultivate by the Commander and his Councillors, according to [the size of?] their families and their families' industry.[8]

These lands were to be held in some form of ownership by, not merely loaned to, the colonists; for after the expiration of six years, during which the colonists were obligated to remain in New Netherland, or before that, if moved by order of the Company, the settlers might " barter or sell their houses, cultivated fields, or

6. " Provisionele ordere daer op de respective colonen aengenomen ende affgesonden sijn in dienste vande Westindische Compe naer Nieu Nederlant om haer verblyff te nemen op de rieviere vanden vorst Mauritius, ofte op andere soodanige plaetse als hen luijden doorden Commandeur ende synen raet aengewesen sal worden." The version of March 28th from the Resolution book of The Nineteen, 1623–24, is in Jessurun, *Kiliaen van Rensselaer*, as Appendix 2. A copy of the version read to the *coloniërs* on March 30 is printed in Hunt., pp. A1–A9, 2–19. For the principal difference between the two versions, see p. 79 of this chapter.

7. Wesley Frank Craven, *The Southern Colonies in the Seventeenth Century 1607–1689*, pp. 127–28.

8. " Provisionele ordere," Art. 6.

animals to someone else among the remaining colonists.[9] That the produce of these lands was to remain the property of the *coloniër*, not of the Company or the community, is evident from the instructions given the commander of the relief expedition of 1625:

> If the families of colonists have in stock any grain, hay, flax, hemp, or other good which is serviceable to the Company and which the Company needs, that such be bought from them at a proper price and put on their account. . . .[10]

Private enterprise was thus established in the as yet incorporeal agricultural sector of the New Netherland economy; but a precarious outpost in the wilderness obviously required a coordinated effort. The dilemma was solved by two temporary provisions. One required the *coloniërs* " at first " to till and sow their land according to the dictates of the Company's representatives.[11] This insured a balanced selection of crops in the initial absence of the market mechanism and also the organized experimentation which was to lay the basis of agriculture in New Netherland. A second stipulation preserved the cohesion and defensibility of the settlement and also permitted its location according to the over-all design of the directors: during their six years of required residence in New Netherland, the *coloniërs* were obliged to dwell in the places assigned to them by the Company's officers.[12]

---

9. *Ibid.*, Art. 16.

10. "Instructie voor Willem van Hulst," in Hunt., pp. C12–C13, 59–60.

11. "Provisionele ordere," Art. 17. Wieder, ignoring the little word *vooreerst* (at first), sees in this provision, as in several others, manorial (*landsheerlijk*) precedents and even goes so far as to speak of the serfdom (*hoorigheid*) of the first colonists (Wieder, *Stichting van New York*, pp. 21–23). Van Grol refutes Wieder's contention that the position of the first immigrants was equivalent to that of a serf, pointing out that " in a legal sense, by serfdom was understood a particular social class " and that the "legal position [of the *coloniërs*] was of a purely contractual nature" (van Grol, *Grondpolitiek*, II, 33n). Van Grol asserts, however, that the *provisionele ordere* as a whole and the cultivation requirement in particular were " meant . . . to give [the *coloniër*] a position agreeing with that of the old Netherlands *huisman* or *geërfde*, who, without being a serf, held his property from a lord " (*ibid.*, p. 33). There are undoubtedly many similarities between the obligations laid on the first New Netherlanders and various obligations of the European peasant; but in view of the virtual extinction of the manorial system in the province of Holland by 1624 and the temporary nature of the obligations to cultivate particular crops and dwell at places specified by the Company, it seems more fruitful to explain these obligations as forming part of a business contract between labor and capital and as reactions to specific problems of colonization than as conscious applications of manorial principles.

12. "Provisionele ordere," Arts. 4 and 16.

Besides agriculture, the *coloniërs* were allowed a carefully circumscribed field of pursuits. They were permitted the "internal" trade, including the fur trade with the Indians, "on express condition that they sell their purchased and gathered wares to no one other than those of the Company, and that provisionally, until in this matter experience [shall lead us] to dispose otherwise." [13] The real significance of this provision depended, of course, on the Company's willingness to permit the settler a little profit in turning in his furs. Otherwise the privilege would be valueless. Evidently the Company's instructions of 1624 did allow this little profit, since, according to van Rensselaer's 1633 memorial, the *coloniërs* were expected to gain a part of their livelihood from the fur trade.[14] Useful skills such as carpentry or blacksmithing were undoubtedly allowed the *coloniërs*, but it was strictly forbidden to them to practice or teach others "handicrafts upon which trade is dependent" without permission of the Company.[15] This evident application of the doctrine that colonies should provide outlets for the manufactures of the mother country was specially directed against weaving (*weveryen*) in the version of the *Provisionele ordere* approved by The Nineteen on March 28. The copy of the same document as read to the *coloniërs* two days later inserts the word "dying" (*verwerije*) in place of "weaving" as the specially prohibited handicraft. It is thus possible that the colonists had objected to the comprehensive prohibition of the textile handicraft, which many of them may have practiced in Europe, and obtained a considerable concession. However, the general similarity of the two words as written and the evident sloppiness of the copyist of the March 30 document in other places argues for a purely stenographic explanation. It may also be significant that the "Freedoms" for patroons in Guiana of June 12, 1627, March 8, 1628, and November 22, 1628 and those for New Netherland of June 7, 1629 all forbid the weaving, not just the dying of textiles.[16] A third restriction of the *coloniërs'* choice of occupation was the reservation to the Company of the mining of metals and precious stones. But though mining was forbidden to the *coloniërs*, their discovery of a mine would be rewarded. The finder of a mine

13. *Ibid.*, Art. 8.
14. VRBM, p. 235.
15. "Provisionele ordere," Art. 13.
16. All these "Freedoms" are discussed in Chapter 5.

would receive ten percent of the net profits during the first six years of the mine's operation.[17]

Besides subsidizing colonization by the offer of free passage and free land, the Company extended a partial subsidy in the form of a guarantee to advance the settlers provisions and clothing " at reasonable prices " during the first two years, repayment to be made without interest in an unspecified future. On the other hand, the *coloniërs* were expected to perform certain services to the Company, the most important of which was military service in case of war. They were also required to fortify their settlement and construct the necessary public buildings, a loosely worded obligation, which very soon seems to have been given a satisfactorily narrow interpretation as they were not required to construct Fort Amsterdam on the Manhattans.[18]

If, with the notable exception of the prohibition of handicrafts for profit, the economic provisions were decidedly generous to the *coloniërs*, the political and religious provisions were certainly not. The essential political stipulation bound the *coloniërs* unconditionally " without any objection to fulfill and follow the commands of the Company, already given to them or yet to be given, as also to receive from the aforementioned Company all orders on the matter of their government and justice." [19] Considering the oligarchical constitution of the Fatherland and the unquestioned necessity of a strong central authority in the first stages of the colony, this exclusion of the *coloniërs* from even the most rudimentary participation in government is not particularly surprising. What does surprise, however, is the colonists' acquiescence in a political arrangement which failed to assure them of a single one of the basic rights and protections enjoyed in the home country. The English settlers in Virginia, by contrast, though politically unrepresented until 1619, had at least been granted the " liberties, franchises, and immunities " of Englishmen from the very inception of the Virginia Company. Fortunately this serious constitu-

17. For the conditions concerning mining, see Arts. 10–12 of the " Provisionele ordere."

18. The offer to advance provisions and clothing is found in Article 7 of the " Provisionele ordere." Articles 3 and 4 define the *coloniërs'* obligation to fight for and fortify the colony. For the exemption of the *coloniërs* from compulsory labor on Fort Amsterdam, see " Particuliere instructie voor den ingenieur ende lantmeter Cryn Fredericxz als mede voor den Commis ende Raden om haer daer naer te reguleren; . . ."; in Hunt., pp. E4–E5, 139–40.

19. " Provisionele ordere," Art. 1.

tional lacuna in New Netherland was filled the following year by the Company's provision that legal proceedings in New Netherland were to be in accord with the ordinances and customs of Holland and Zeeland. A second vital safeguard introduced in 1625 protected the colonists from the arbitrariness of the colonial authorities by providing that all serious offenders be returned to Holland for punishment. Finally, Johan Lampo, one of the *coloniërs*, was appointed to the Council of the colony.[20]

The *Provisionele ordere* introduced a religious arrangement for New Netherland, which, though not always effectively enforced, remained the guideline for policy in this area until the demise of the Company's rule. This regulation, modeled on that of the Republic, permitted everyone freedom of conscience, but forbad public religious worship deviating from that of the reformed religion as practiced in the United Provinces.[21] This policy was undoubtedly entirely satisfactory to the first Walloon settlers; but its long-run effect was to discourage the immigration of sizeable Remonstrant, Lutheran, Mennonite, or Catholic groups from the Netherlands, which might conceivably have taken advantage of an offer of genuine religious freedom in New Netherland and eventually formed a barrier against English encroachment.

*

The first colonizing expedition to New Netherland was carried out smoothly. Probably early in April 1624, the pioneers set sail in the 130-last *Nieu Nederlandt*, commanded by Cornelis Jacobsz May, who had made many voyages to New Netherland in the service of various *voorcompagnieën*.[22] Very probably May had been instructed to settle at least a token colony on each of the three great rivers between Cape Cod and the Chesapeake, the

20. The " Naerdere Jnstructie . . . voor Willem vander Hulst " raised Lampo to the Council and provided that legal proceedings be in accord with those in Holland and Zeeland (in Hunt., pp. D5, 90, and D16–D17, 113–14). For the requirement that serious offenders be returned to Holland, see " Instructie voor Willem van Hulst "; in Hunt., pp. C2, 39; and Wass., XII; in NNN, p. 84.

The assurance to the Virginia settlers was given by the charter of 1606 which incorporated the Virginia Companies of London and Plymouth (Andrews, *Colonial Period*, I, pp. 85–86).

21. " Provisionele ordere," Art. 2.

22. Wass., VII, in NNN, p. 75, gives the name of the ship and skipper, but states the vessel sailed in the beginning of March. The preface of the version of the " Provisionele ordere " appearing in the Resolutions of The Nineteen indicates that the colonists were only mustered on March 29 however.

Connecticut, Hudson, and Delaware, in order to establish a valid claim to all of New Netherland *de jure primae occupationis.* Upon arrival in the Hudson, he dispatched two or four families and eight men to the Delaware [23] and two families and six men to the Connecticut River,[24] and he left a small garrison to construct a fort near the mouth of the Hudson on Governors Island.[25] The

23. The deposition of Catalijna Trico Rapaille of 1684–85 mentions four families (*The Documentary History of the State of New York,* ed. E. B. O'Callaghan, III, p. 49); her deposition of 1688 mentions two (*ibid.,* pp. 50–51). Both agree on their being accompanied by eight men. These depositions have been attacked as hopelessly inaccurate by Victor Hugo Paltsits (" The founding of New Amsterdam in 1626," *Proceedings of the American Antiquarian Society,* new series, XXXIV (1925), pp. 48–49) and by George T. Hunt (*The Wars of the Iroquois: A Study of Intertribal Relations,* pp. 28–30). Her relation has two principal discrepancies: (1) the Dutch could not have made a treaty with all the Indian tribes she mentions, and (2) the ship she came over on was not the *Unity* or *Eendracht,* as she related, but the *Nieu Nederlandt.* Hunt is probably right in assuming that Governor Dongan, upon whose request the depositions were made, was responsible for the inclusion of the anachronistic statement about a Dutch treaty with various western Indian tribes; but Royden Woodward Vosburgh (" The Settlement of New Netherland, 1624–1626," *New York Genealogical and Biographical Record,* LV (1924), pp. 11–12) has a very plausible explanation for the second discrepancy: the name of the *Nieu Nederlandt* was probably changed to *Eendracht,* when the great ship *Nieu Nederlandt* was built in the province about 1631. In support of Vosburgh's contention I offer the fact that although an *Eendracht* made several voyages to New Netherland in the early 1630's, a list of ships bought or built by the Amsterdam Chamber through 1636 given by de Laet gives no ship of the name *Eendracht,* though it does give three *Nieu Nederlandts* (de Laet, *Historie ofte Iaerlijck Verhael* [1644], Appendix, pp. 3–5). For this and various other reasons too long to be related here, I agree with Vosburgh that the account given by Mevrouw Rapaille is substantially accurate.

24. Trico Rapaille, Deposition of October 17, 1688, in *Documentary History,* ed. O'Callaghan, III, pp. 50–51. Historians have generally discounted Mev. Rapaille's assertion, since there is no other evidence of a Dutch occupation of the Connecticut before 1633. However, in view of the need to establish a *de jure primae occupationis* claim to the river, the placing of a colony there would have been a very reasonable move to make at first. Might not a tiny colony on the Connecticut have been removed to the Hudson within a few months or a year, just as the colonies on the Delaware and at Fort Orangien were resettled on the Manhattans in 1626?

25. *Ibid.* states that the expedition left eight men " att N: Yorke to take possession. . . ." " Instructie voor Willem van Hulst " of about January 1625 mentions the fort on Governors (Noten) Island (Hunt., pp. C7, 48). Wassenaer (VII, in NNN, p. 76) says " they also placed a fort which they named " Wilhelmus " on Prince's Island, heretofore called Murderer's Island; it is open in front, and has a curtain in the rear and is garrisoned by sixteen men for the defence of the river below." Various conjectures have been made as to the location of " Prince's " or " Murderer's " Island, but since the names do not appear again in the records, its location has never been established. I think it probable that Fort Wilhelmus was really the fort which is known to have been constructed on

main body of colonists was conveyed upriver to a place on the
west bank, slightly above Castle Island, the former site of the
New Netherland Company's Fort Nassau. Here they constructed
bark huts and the small Fort Orange and sowed grain, which
came up well.[26] The Indians in the vicinity "were all as quiet as
lambs & came & traded with all ye freedom imaginable." [27] This
happy circumstance was due to the intelligent Indian policy of the
Company as well as to aboriginal forbearance, as the *Provisionele
ordere* had admonished the *coloniërs* to treat the Indians fairly and
give them no offense on pain of severe punishment.[28] When May
sailed for home, he must have left an ample supply of provisions
with the settlers, for they escaped the agonizing " starving time "
that had once decimated the English colonies to the north and
south.

The great preoccupation of the West India Company during the
fall and winter of 1624/25 was the dispatch of a relief expedition
to the beleaguered defenders of Bahia. Nevertheless, the directors
of the Amsterdam Chamber, which The Nineteen had continued
in September 1624 as manager of New Netherland affairs " as
yet without any prejudice to other chambers," spared neither time
nor money in following up the auspicious beginnings in New
Netherland.[29] Their evident design was to supply all the requirements of a self-supporting agricultural colony in one major effort.

In all, the Company chartered or itself equipped six ships to
sail to New Netherland in 1625. The first, the *Orangen boom* of
about seventy-five lasts, carried additional colonists, most of whom
were to strengthen the tiny outpost on the Delaware, " divers
trees, vines, and all kinds of seeds," and undoubtedly provisions
and other agricultural necessities. Willem van Hulst, the commander of this contingent, was especially charged to explore, conduct agricultural experiments, and maintain good relations with
the Indians. The ship sailed unusually early, probably in late
December or January, perhaps for the purpose of arriving in time

Governors Island, and that Noten (Governors), Prince's, and Murderer's Island
were all one.

26. Trico Rapaille, Deposition of 1688, in the place cited. Wass., VII, in
NNN, pp. 75–76.

27. Trico Rapaille, Deposition of 1688, in the place cited.

28. " Provisionele ordere," Art. 18.

29. The quote is from the Resolution book of The Nineteen, 1623–1624; in
Jessurun, *Kiliaen van Rensselaer*, p. 16, and in Stokes, *Iconography*, IV, pp. 59–60

for spring planting; but it had the misfortune to be delayed by contrary winds in Plymouth, England, where it was arrested as a prospective interloper in His Majesty's North American dominions, and where at least eleven of its passengers and crew died of the plague. Eventually, however, it seems to have gotten away to continue its voyage.[30]

The main shipment of livestock, seeds, and agricultural tools departed in the spring. The Company had contracted with Pieter Evertsz Hulft and Pieter Ranst, both of whom were probably *hoofdparticipanten* of the Amsterdam Chamber at this time, for the transportation to New Netherland of 103 horses and cattle, a large number of hogs and sheep, tools, and Company farmers. The price offered for the safe delivery of this menagerie was evidently munificent. Hulft and Ranst chartered two 140-last ships from a Hoorn shipowner and proceeded to fit them out carefully as cattle boats.[31] Wassenaer described their preparations enthusiastically:

> Each animal has its own stall, with a floor of three feet of sand, arranged as comfortably as any stall here in this city. Each animal has its own servant who takes care of it and knows what he will get if he delivers it there alive. All sorts of forage is there, oats, hay, and straw. . . . The most remarkable thing of all is that nobody in the two ships can find where the drinking water for these animals has been stowed. . . . [Hulft] had a deck built in the ship. Under it he stowed three hundred tons of fresh water, which is pumped out and thus distributed to the animals. On the deck lies the ballast, and on that the horses and bulls stand; . . .[32]

30. "Instructie voor Willem van Hulst" in Hunt. is Commander van Hulst's (or Verhulst's) written instructions. In it is mentioned the *Orangen boom*'s cargo (Hunt., pp. C3, 40, and C11, 56). For the arrest of the vessel, see Wass., VIII, p. 123v, and DCHNY, III, p. 12, which latter source mentions the vessels tonnage. That the ship was eventually permitted to leave England is evident from the fact that the "Naerdere Jnstructie" of April 22, 1625, expected it to have reached New Netherland by the summer of 1625 (in Hunt., pp. D12, 105).

31. Abstracts of the charter parties of these two ships, the *Griffioen* and the *Swarte Paert*, are in Stokes, *Iconography*, VI, pp. 11–12; from GAA, Not. Arch., Reg. #226, p. 59v. The freight price was *f* 125 for each horse or cow delivered alive in New Netherland, indicating that, having made very careful preparations, the partners shifted the risk to the shipowner. Wassenaer's account of this shipment mentions only Hulft, but the charter parties were signed by both him and Ranst.

32. Wass., IX, p. 40.

In company with a 100 last *fluit*, which the partners chartered to carry extra provisions in case the voyage should be prolonged, the cattle ships sailed for the Hudson about the end of April 1625. Narrowly escaping the Dunkirkers, who captured their escort, the Company's yacht *Maeckereel*, they reached New Netherland with the remarkable loss of only two animals.[33] On May 28, the Company chartered in its own name a 130 last ship to carry an additional increment to the colony's farming establishment: "sheep, hogs, wagons, ploughs, and other implements of husbandry." Sadly enough, this latter vessel was captured by a Moorish pirate and never delivered its cargo.[34]

The households sent with the *Orangen boom* very probably went on the same conditions that had been made with the 1624 *coloniërs*;[35] but the directors were evidently sceptical of the ability of private enterprise to establish quickly an agriculturally self-supporting colony, for the emphasis in 1625 was clearly on transporting Company hirelings rather than free colonists. Some of the Company workers were destined for the Delaware, but most of them, some with their families, probably sailed with the cattle ships to the mouth of the Hudson. In this vicinity, midway between the Connecticut and Delaware rivers and blocking access to the Hudson and one end of Long Island Sound, the directors had correctly discerned the defensive key to New Netherland. There, according to their meticulous plans, a surveyor was to lay out a boldly conceived fort and nine Company *bouwerijen*.

33. The ships must have sailed after the "Naerdere Jnstructie . . . voor Willem vander Hulst" was issued on April 22. Wassenaer records that the ships sailed in April. He also mentions the use to which the third vessel (the *fluit*) was put (IX; in NNN, p. 79).

The charter party of the *fluit*, which was named the *Schaep*, is abstracted in Stokes, *Iconography*, VI, p. 12, from GAA, Not. Arch., Reg. # 226, p. 59v. The capture of the *Maeckereel* is mentioned in Wass., IX, p. 37; the great success of the shipment in *ibid.*, X, in NNN, p. 82.

34. The charter party of this vessel, named the *Ruyter*, is abstracted in Stokes, *Iconography*, VI, p. 12; from GAA, Not. Arch., Reg. # 652, p. 11v. The cargo is mentioned in Wass., XII, in NNN, p. 82. Stokes, *Iconography*, IV, p. 60, presents evidence concerning the ship's capture.

35. Wassenaer (VII, p. 123v) mentions that colonists sent with the *Orangen boom* were "families of the Walloons"; thus they were probably from the same group of persons from which the first contingent of colonists was drawn, rendering probable that they secured the same conditions. Van Hulst was instructed to distribute to these families as much land as they could cultivate, which distribution was also provided by the "Provisionele ordere" of 1624. ("Instructie voor Willem van Hulst"; in Hunt., pp. C3, 40).

Most of the horses and cattle and probably most of the other
livestock and tools transported in 1625 were destined for these
farms, although if all the cattle reached New Netherland safely
there were to be a limited number of cows for allotment to the
coloniërs on liberal terms.[36]

In 1625, besides assuming a dominant role in the agricultural
sector of New Netherland's economy, the Company tightened its
control over the fur trade. As related previously, the practical
effect of permitting the *coloniërs* the internal trade of New Netherland depended solely on the price the Company, the ultimate
monopsonist, offered for the colonists' furs. In 1625, this price
became pegged to the going price at the Company's trading posts,
thus eliminating the *coloniër* as a middleman, unless he was bold
enough to venture deep into the interior in quest of furs.[37] Since
in this the *coloniër* would face the competition of Indian middlemen, the new policy, if it could be enforced, must needs result
in the virtual exclusion of the *coloniërs* from the fur trade.

Upon arrival in the Hudson, the livestock was unloaded on
Governor's Island, but after a day or two it was transferred to
Manhattan. The directors had issued very foresighted instructions
regarding the unloading of the animals, including a warning not
to let them graze too much at first. Nevertheless, twenty horses
and cows died on the Manhattans, probably poisoned by unknown
wild plants. This loss must have nearly consumed the extra stock
which was destined for the *coloniërs.* In mid-September the animals went to "meadow grass, as good and as long as could be
desired," and with this comment the colony disappears from view
for about a year. When it reappears in September 1626, the island
of Manhattan had been purchased from the Indians for *f* 60 in
merchandise, Fort Amsterdam had been staked out on its southern
hook, and thirty bark houses and one stone counting house had
been constructed there. Undoubtedly, the clearing of land for the
Company farms had already been commenced.[38]

36. That at least some of the hirelings were sent to the Delaware is indicated
by "Instructie voor Willem van Hulst" (Hunt., pp. C8, 51). The plans for the
fort, the nine farms, and the distribution of the animals are found in the "Particuliere instructie voor den ingenieur . . ." (Hunt., pp. E1–E19, 132–68). Each
of the nine *bouwerijen* were to be provided with four cows and four horses, i. e.
seventy-two horses and cows in all. One hundred and three horses and cows were
shipped over; if this number was about equally divided between horses and cows,
there would be about fifteen cows left for the *coloniërs* if all lived.

37. "Instructie voor Willem van Hulst," in Hunt., pp. C16, 67.

38. The unloading of the animals and their subsequent fate is described in

By this time it had been decided to withdraw the colonists from the Delaware River and Fort Orange (and presumably also from the Connecticut, if that tiny outpost had not already been abandoned) and concentrate them at the Manhattans. Henceforth the Company's presence on the Delaware and the Connecticut was to be maintained solely by its traders, who probably manned the posts there only seasonally during most of the next decade. Since there was no immediate danger that other nations would occupy these rivers, this new policy was probably well advised, despite the setback which abandonment of huts and cleared land entailed. Dispersion into isolated settlements was becoming increasingly perilous as the Indians acquired growing familiarity with the Dutch and their weapons. Concentration meant increased security and also the economic benefits of a better division of labor: henceforth, a small number of skilled craftsmen could serve the needs of the entire colony without long delays. Several additional circumstances encouraged the evacuation of the settlers at Fort Orange. The Mahicans there had been unwilling to part with their maize lands; and, since the West India Company was very scrupulous in recognizing Indian land rights, " so that the wrath of God come not upon our unjust principles," the Indians' refusal effectively barred expansion. An even more compelling reason for evacuation was probably the nuisance which the *coloniërs* were creating at the Company's principal trading post. Only with " great difficulties and threats" and by offering a somewhat excessive price, was a Company agent able to extract a considerable stock of furs from these families in 1626.[39]

Wass., XII, in NNN, p. 83. The directors' instructions regarding their unloading may be found in " Naerdere Jnstructie . . . voor Willem vander Hulst," in Hunt., pp. D5-D6, 90, 93. For the probable size of the extra stock for the *coloniërs*, see note 36, this chapter.

The colony's progress by September 1626 is described by Wass., XII, in NNN, p. 83; and in DCHNY, I, p. 37.

39. The Company's decision to concentrate the colony at the Manhattans and the danger from the Indians' growing familiarity with Dutch ways and weapons are related by Wass., XII, in NNN, pp. 84–85. The unwillingness of the Mahicans to sell their lands is mentioned by Kiliaen van Rensselaer's " Account of the jurisdictions, management and condition of the territories named Rensselaerswijk . . . This 20 July 1634," in VRBM, p. 306. For the Company's policy regarding Indian land rights, see " Naerdere Jnstructie . . . voor Willem vander Hulst," in Hunt., pp. D12–D13, 105–06.

The *coloniërs'* interference with the fur trade is related by de Rasieres in his September 23, 1626 letter to the Directors (Hunt., pp. F22–F23, 215–16).

In the three years following 1625, the Company failed to increase appreciably its investment in the agricultural colony in New Netherland. Neither livestock nor a sizable increment to the colony's human population was sent over; and, presumably after expiration of its agreement to provision the *coloniërs* for two years, the directors even curtailed the shipments of provisions, with the unforeseen result that the Company's officers in New Netherland were obliged to sell trading truck to the settlers so that they could obtain food from the Indians.[40] This parsimonious policy can be adequately explained as the result of a conviction that the tools, animals, and people which had been sent over in 1624 and 1625 were in themselves sufficient to achieve the immediate goals of colonization, agricultural self-sufficiency and experimentation, and that until these goals had been attained there was little sense in proceeding further. But it is also possible that the Company's severe financial depletion in these years discouraged further investment.

This depletion was the result of the failure of the Company's great 1625 expedition for the relief of Bahia, to preserve Dutch control over that city or to achieve anything else of value. This expedition reached Bahia about a month after the capitulation of the Dutch garrison. Finding the Portuguese firmly entrenched there, the Dutch force split up, one squadron sailing for Puerto Rico and the other for Guinea. Both were completely unsuccessful. San Juan de Porto Rico was entered, but long and sanguinary siege operations failed to capture the citadel. Finally, the commander of the expedition, a director of the Company, abandoned the struggle and sailed away to privateer in the Caribbean. After months of cruising brought only trifling results, the dispirited squadron sailed for home in July 1626. Meanwhile the Guinea expedition had fared even worse. It launched an attack on the Portuguese stronghold of Elmina, but native auxiliaries surprised and routed the Company's landing troops and inflicted heavy casualties.[41] This succession of failures must have swallowed a large part of the Company's capital and shaken the directors'

40. The necessity of selling trading truck to the settlers is mentioned by van Rensselaer (Memorial of 1633, in VRBM, p. 236) and by de Rasieres in his letter to the Directors of September 23, 1626 (in Hunt., pp. F31, 232).

41. De Laet, *Historie ofte Iaerlijck Verhael* (1644), pp. 59–63, 65–70, records the Porto Rico and Elmina operations. Boxer, *Dutch in Brazil*, pp. 27–28, summarizes them briefly.

confidence. Fortunately, in 1627 Piet Heyn made two successful attacks on the Portuguese shipping at Bahia, which were remunerative enough to allow the Company "to catch its breath and get to its feet again," in the words of de Laet.[42]

*

1628 was a year of reappraisal of the Company's economic policy in New Netherland. The accounts of the colony were frequently reviewed by The Nineteen, and there was general dissatisfaction with the situation they revealed.[43] What was this unpromising situation, which stimulated the introduction of the patroon system into New Netherland? The original account books of the Company are lost, but three very informative letters written in or about 1628 give a sketchy picture of the colony's progress as of that year.[44]

There is very little doubt that the directors considered their 1624–25 shipments of men, animals, and tools to have been sufficient to establish within a very few years an agricultural community capable of both supporting itself and producing a surplus for the support of the Company's non-agricultural personnel in New Netherland.[45] Whether by 1628 the *coloniërs*, who were probably inadequately supplied with animals and who had been obliged to abandon their original residences in 1626 to come to the Manhattans, had established much more than kitchen gardens there is uncertain; but by about 1628 six of the nine proposed Company farms had been set up, containing sixty morgens of land ready for sowing.[46] Exactly how close this agricultural establishment had come to attaining the goal of provisioning the

42. De Laet, *Historie ofte Iaerlijck Verhael* (1644), p. 105.
43. The review of the colony's accounts prior to March 10, 1628, is noted in a memorial of the patroons of New Netherland to the States General in June 1634, in DCHNY, I, p. 84.
44. Jonas Michaëlius to Joannes Foreest, August 8, 1628; Dutch and English texts in Dingman Versteeg, *Manhattan in 1628*, pp. 37–79. Jonas Michaëlius to Adrianus Smoutius, August 11, 1628, Dutch and English texts in *Ecclesiastical Records of the State of New York*, ed. Edward T. Corwin, I, pp. 49–68; English in NNN, pp. 122–33. Isaack de Rasieres to Samuel Blommaert [c. 1628], English text in NNN, pp. 102–15.
45. Van Rensselaer noted that "since there were now farmers and animals, they [the Company] decided that little or no provisions ought to be sent" (Memorial of 1633, in VRBM, p. 236).
46. Rasieres to Blommaert, in NNN, p. 104. The morgen contains slightly more than two acres.

entire population of New Netherland is unknown, but it is certain
that the goal had not been attained. When Jonas Michaëlius,
the colony's first minister, arrived in New Netherland in the spring
of 1628, he was obliged to live on rations given out by the Company, "hard, old food, such as one was used to eat aboard ship
. . . beans and gray peas, which are hard enough, grits, stockfish,
etc." [47] This indicates that an unknown proportion of the colony's
basic nutritional staples was still being imported from Holland.
Dairy production was also inadequate to fill the needs of the
entire population of New Netherland. Some milk and butter came
on the market, but at very high prices, prohibitive prices for a
minister's pocketbook.[48]

The explanation for this inadequate agricultural production
must be sought in several directions. One difficulty was the shortage of horses and cows after about one-fifth of their original
number had perished shortly after arrival in New Netherland.[49]
A second was the slight industriousness of the Company's hired
labor force. Judgments upon their fellow men of Michaëlius, the
Calvinist dominie, and the exaggeratedly conscientious Secretary
de Rasieres erred perhaps toward the ungenerous, but the picture
of idleness which they present remains substantially convincing.
In 1626 de Rasieres professed to be amazed at the "lazy irresponsibility of many persons, both farmers and others, who want to draw
board and wages, and that for doing almost nothing." [50] Michaëlius
reported the same disinclination to work in 1628, and added that
the daily complaint of the common people was "that they had not
come to work, that to work they might as well have stayed home;
and that it was all the same what or how much one did if it was
in the service of the Company." [51] Perhaps more disturbing to the

47. Michaëlius to Smoutius, in *Ecclesiastical records*, I, pp. 62–63. The colony
was still dependent on European grain as late as 1631 (Arnoldus Buchelius,
"Koloniale aanwinsten 212B," p. 111v, in the Rijksarchief at the Hague, in
Stokes, *Iconography*, IV, p. 944). By 1636 agricultural self-sufficiency had apparently been achieved, since "a large quantity" of locally grown grain was in stock
(Buchelius, pp. 129–129v, *ibid.*, p. 949).
48. Michaëlius to Smoutius, in NNN, p. 130.
49. Michaëlius stresses the need for animals in his letters to both Foreest and
Smoutius (Versteeg, *Manhattan in 1628*, pp. 43–44; and in NNN, p. 130,
respectively).
50. Rasieres to the Directors, Sep. 23, 1626, in Hunt., pp. F18–F19, 207–08.
For the lack of industriousness of the master farmers on the Company's farms
about 1628, see Rasieres to Blommaert, in NNN, p. 104.
51. Michaëlius to Foreest, in Versteeg, *Manhattan in 1628*, pp. 49–50.

directors, because probably less foreseen, was the mediocre quality
of the land at the Manhattans, which, as the defensive key to the
province, needed to be occupied first. About 1628 de Rasieres
described the greater part of the cleared land there as exhausted
by the wild herbage, and feared that the shortage of manure would
cause a part of the cleared land to remain unsown. Of the six
Company *bouwerijen*, he regarded two as good, but the remaining
four as sandier and best suited for rye and buckwheat.[52] The soil
in other places in New Netherland was reported to be better,
however. A particularly promising spot was the Fort Orange
region, "amazingly fruitful and pleasurable" in Michaëlius'
words, where the Mahicans had abandoned their lands after a
severe defeat by the Mohawks.[53]

Limitations of capital, labor, or land seem not to have blocked
further agricultural expansion, however: by May of 1630, probably
without an additional shipment of animals or laborers, the number
of Manhattan *bouwerijen* had grown to eight.[54] This continuing
growth suggests to us that time was the fourth factor in the
inability of New Netherland's agricultural establishment to provision the colony by 1628: even under ideal conditions a certain
period was required to clear fields and build houses, barns, and
fences before rich harvests could be reaped. In 1628 the Manhattan colony had existed at the most for three years, and it was
only two years since all New Netherland's settlers had been
concentrated there.

If agricultural production was still disappointing, timber was
being produced at an uneconomically high rate by 1628. In 1625
the directors had ordered vessels returning from New Netherland
to load wood, even fire wood in the absence of better, in order not
to return home empty.[55] In 1628 much more wood was being cut
than the returning ships could carry.[56] Though the want of
shipping space for timber suggests the directors realized that the

52. Rasieres to Blommaert, in NNN, p. 104. Michaëlius said of the Manhattans
that it "is somewhat less fertile than other places and gives more trouble as a
result of the multitude of roots of bushes and trees" (Michaëlius to Foreest, in
Versteeg, *Manhattan in 1628*, p. 44).

53. Michaëlius to Foreest, in Versteeg, *Manhattan in 1628*, p. 45. Michaëlius
to Smoutius, in NNN, p. 131.

54. Letter of Kiliaen van Rensselaer [to Pieter Minuit?], dated July 2, 1631,
in Edward Van Winkle, *Manhattan, 1624–1639*, pp. 43–46.

55. "Instructie voor Willem van Hulst," in Hunt., pp. C18, 71.

56. Michaëlius to Smoutius, in NNN, p. 131.

value of the commodity was too slight to warrant sending ships expressly for the purpose of bringing it home, the directors were not yet willing to abandon the attempt to exploit New Netherland's magnificent timber resources. About 1628 or 1629 they conceived the idea of establishing a shipbuilding industry in New Netherland, by which means New Netherland timber could be made to provide rather than require shipping space over to Europe. An experiment was carried out with the building of the very large 400-last ship *Nieu Nederlandt* about 1630; but the results (technically successful, financially unsuccessful) were, of course, not known during the discussion over the patroon system in 1628/29.[57]

No progress had been made in producing wood extracts by 1628. Tar and pitch had been considered, but there is no certain evidence that any experiment had yet been made with them. About 1626 an attempt had been made to produce tanbark, but it seems to have run aground on the ignorance and irresponsibility of the craftsman to whom the experiment was entrusted. An attempt to burn potash seems to have failed about 1628.[58]

No evidence points to any serious experimentation with viniculture through 1628; nor had any valuable mines been discovered. De Rasieres feared in 1626 that salt making would not succeed because of the summer rains, but he promised to attempt it at the proper time. If he did indeed make the attempt by 1628, it proved a failure, since the *Vertoogh van Nieu-Neder-Land* of 1650 tells us that salt making was one of the experiments which had " gone to naught or come to little." [59] Though no valuable fishing grounds

57. " A certain ship," undoubtedly the *Nieu Nederlandt*, was almost ready in September 1630 (VRBM, p. 169). De Vries met the ship coming from Texel in July 1632 and described it as " a large ship that was made in New Netherland " (*Verscheyden voyagiens*, p. 149). An English source described it as " 600 tunnes or thereabouts " (DCHNY, III, p. 17). The only *Nieu Nederlandt* which de Laet mentions as approaching this size in his list of ninety-eight ships built or bought by the Amsterdam Chamber through 1636 was of 400 lasts (*Historie ofte Iaerlijck Verhael*, [1644], Appendix, pp. 3–5). The excessive cost of its building is mentioned in *Vertoogh van Nieu-Neder-Land*, in NNN, p. 321.

58. De Rasieres mentions the failure of the attempt to produce tanbark and the possibility of producing tar and pitch in his 1626 letter to the Directors (in Hunt., pp. F32–F33, 235–36). *Vertoogh van Nieu-Neder-Land* of 1650 (in NNN, p. 321) relates that tar burning was one of the Company's experiments " which through bad management and calculation have all gone to naught, or come to little," but gives no indication when this experiment was made. Michaëlius mentions the failure of potash burning in his letter to Smoutius, in NNN, p. 131.

59. De Rasieres to the Directors, 1626, in Hunt., pp. F32, 235. *Vertoogh*, in NNN, p. 321.

in the immediate neighborhood of New Netherland had yet been discovered, the Dutch may in 1628 have already been aware that whales frequented Delaware Bay.[60]

About 1628 New Netherland's most important industry was, of course, neither agriculture nor timber nor any of the other experimental endeavors, but the fur trade. At the end of its first five years in this trade, the Company had adopted essentially the same techniques used by the *voorcompagnieën*, with the one important exception of its planting of a provisioning colony. Fort Orange, after 1626 no longer burdened with *coloniërs*, was the Company's chief trading post, only a cannon shot away from the site of the New Netherland Company's Fort Nassau. After the abandonment of the colonies on the Delaware and Connecticut, these areas were probably serviced by seasonally occupied trading posts and sloops and yachts. Roughly the same trading goods were bartered to the Indians as in the days of the *voorcompagnieën*, although now duffels and *sewan* are more in the foreground. The exchange of duffels for the *sewan* of the coastal Indians and the shipment of the shell-beads to the *sewan*-poor inland had become a well established trading pattern. Since the French had no *sewan* supply, the Dutch were even able to attract Indians from the St. Lawrence region to Fort Orange by this means.[61]

About 1628 the Company's fur monopoly was threatened from several directions, though as yet none of the threats had assumed very serious proportions. English and French sloops seem to have frequented the coasts of New Netherland about 1626, and in the spring of that year, the Dutch lack of duffels had encouraged the Indians in southern New England and in the Delaware region to take their trade to the nearest English posts.[62] By 1628 the Pilgrims had established a post on Buzzards Bay, and de Rasieres thought them on the point of discovering the rich fur trade of the coast of southern New England.[63] The principal internal threat to the monopoly was the aggression of the Mohawks in the crucial Fort Orange area. In a seeming attempt to gain a middleman's position

60. Samuel Godijn, a director of the Company and patroon of Swanendael, was informed of the many whales in the bay by at least December 1630 (de Vries, *Verscheyden voyagiens*, p. 147).

61. The source for this paragraph is principally de Rasieres' letter to the Directors of 1626, in Hunt., pp. F26–F30, 223–24, 227–28, 231, and *passim*.

62. *Ibid.*, in Hunt., pp. F27, F29–F30, 224, 228, 231.

63. De Rasieres to Blommaert, in NNN, p. 110.

about that fort, these Indians were preventing the "French" Indians from reaching the posts, and about 1628 they drove the Mahicans, the original inhabitants, from the region.[64] To what extent the colonists and the Company's employees were successfully smuggling furs out of New Netherland is unknown, but Secretary de Rasieres suspected such practices in 1626.[65] Despite these various encroachments and hindrances the returns from the Company's trade trended generally upwards through 1628. De Laet gives the following figures for New Netherland exports: [66]

1624	4000 beavers	700 otters	ƒ 27,125
1625	5295 beavers	436 otters	ƒ 35,825
1626	7258 beavers	857 otters, etc.	ƒ 45,050
1627	7520 beavers	370 otters	ƒ 56,420
1628	6951 beavers	734 otters, etc.	ƒ 61,075
			ƒ 225,495

De Laet also gives a list of "goods and merchandise purchased and sent from this country [the United Provinces]" to New Netherland, which probably represents the imports of trading truck.[67] The total imports in this column for the same five year period amounted to ƒ 110,895, or a little less than one-half the exports. Whether the sum expended on merchandise plus the various overhead costs of the trade afforded the Company much profit is unknown.

64. The prevention of the "French" Indians is mentioned in de Rasieres to the Directors, 1626, in Hunt., pp. F22, 215.
65. *Ibid.*, in Hunt., pp. F23–F24, 216, 219.
66. *Historie ofte Iaerlijck Verhael* (1644), Appendix, pp. 29–30.
67. *Ibid.*, Appendix, pp. 26–27. For a fuller discussion of what this classification probably includes, see Chapter 6.

Chapter Five

THE PATROON SYSTEM

In the absence of the minutes of The Nineteen after 1624, it is impossible to say exactly when this body first deemed the agricultural colony in New Netherland sufficiently unpromising as to dissuade the Company from making further investment in it. However it is probable that The Nineteen had already made this appraisal by March 10, 1628, when " freedoms " were approved which permitted the agricultural development of New Netherland to private individuals while reserving the fur trade to the Company. Whether at this time The Nineteen was already contemplating divesting itself of a large part of the investment in New Netherland agriculture which it had already made is uncertain. This step was taken in January 1630 when the Manhattan *bouwerijen* were leased and many of the Company's cattle sold.

What prompted the surprisingly early decision of The Nineteen to abandon further Company investment in New Netherland agriculture? Two plausible hypotheses present themselves.[1]

1. It is possible, as van Rensselaer alleged in his 1633 memorial defending New Netherland's colonization, that The Nineteen obtained an overly pessimistic picture of New Netherland's potential through its failure to appreciate fully the magnitude of the initial difficulties attending the establishment of an agricultural colony.[2] This failure may have encouraged the incorrect assumption that the Manhattan colony had nearly attained its maximum production potential by about 1627, hence that the unsavory balance sheet

1. The hypothesis that The Nineteen was deceived as to the true state of New Netherland's agricultural possibilities by the commissioners for New Netherland must be rejected. The commissioners seem to have been the first to offer to undertake the agricultural colonization of New Netherland as patroons, and they could not have reconciled their own announced willingness to colonize the region privately with statements that colonization was unprofitable to the Company.

2. Van Rensselaer suggests this in his memorial of November 1633; in VRBM, p. 236.

for that year was more or less indicative of future results. In so doing, The Nineteen would have estimated the potential yield of present or future investments in New Netherland agriculture to be much lower than it really was.

2. Alternatively, the Company may have acted on perfectly realistic considerations in abandoning further investment in its New Netherland plantation. The Nineteen may have made realistic estimates of its agricultural potential on the basis of the experimentation of the first few years and concluded that in view of the cold climate, the mediocre quality of the tree, root, and rock-ridden soil, and the unsatisfactory productivity of hired labor, there could no longer be any reasonable expectation that a Company managed program of economic development could develop profitable export staples in the foreseeable future.[3]

Although the Company's claim to New Netherland had not gone unchallenged by either the English or the French in North America, both England and France were friendly powers, and the directors hoped that New Netherland could be secured by treaty.[4] Since the existing colony already provided a *de jure primae occupationis* claim to the Hudson and its fur trade, there was therefore little reason to expand it for defensive reasons. Furthermore, the natural development of the existing agricultural colony may have been expected to be able to provision the Company's fur traders within a few years. In short, once the idea of

3. A brief summary of the state of New Netherland contained in a letter from The Nineteen to the States General dated October 23, 1629, says nothing about the problems with land and labor which de Rasieres and Michaëlius mention in their letters, but traces the inability of the colonists to obtain more than a " scanty means of livelihood " to the unexpectedly cold climate (DCHNY, I, p. 39). This explanation is obviously an oversimplification.

4. The directors' hope appears in a letter from a committee of The Nineteen to the States General exhibited October 16, 1627 (DCHNY, I, p. 38). Letters from New Netherland had reported William Bradford's warnings of a possible English attack and requested forty soldiers to protect the colony. The directors commented that they " would rather see [New Netherland] secured by friendly alliance."

The French threat to New Netherland was apparent when the first colonizing expedition under May had to drive a French vessel from the Hudson and later from the Delaware River in 1624 (Wass., in NNN, p. 75). A letter from The Nineteen to the States General dated October 23, 1629, mentions that the French were disputing the Company's possession of New Netherland and that " the Company, on that account, have suffered, of late years, notorious damage by reprisals " (DCHNY, I, p. 39). It is not known to what incidents this refers. De Rasieres mentioned that French sloops had frequented the coasts of New Netherland in his 1626 letter to the Directors (in Hunt., p. 224).

agricultural exports had been abandoned, the Company may have been entirely clear-sighted in deciding to allocate its no longer ample funds to more remunerative undertakings.

Perhaps the New Netherland colony's most immediate rival for the Company's investment funds was the colonies in Guiana. With the exception of tobacco, the potential exports of the two regions, which differed greatly in climate, were entirely different. Yet, if it is true that the directors appreciated the necessity of investment diversification, and hence sought in the plantation of extensive and fruitful, though unoccupied, regions some ballast to the riskiness of privateering and conquest, Guiana and New Netherland must have occupied the same niche in the Company's investment program. We should ask, therefore, whether about 1627/28 the Company was harboring great expectations for the plantation of Guiana and had therefore diverted funds from New Netherland.

In 1628 there were at least five and perhaps six Dutch posts or colonies in Guiana. The uncertain sixth was a colony established by Jan de Moor on the Essequibo in 1616, which may or may not have been withdrawn at the advent of the West India Company.[5] An entirely certain expression of private initiative was a colony on the Berbice in 1627 by Abraham van Pere with the Company's approval.[6] The remaining four establishments were

5. The first resolution book of the Zeeland Chamber, which would undoubtedly permit certainty in regard to the withdrawal or continuance of this colony, has been lost. Virtually the only evidence for its continuance is given in an English account of the late 1660's: John Scott's description of Guiana (in *Colonizing Expeditions to the West Indies and Guiana, 1623–1667*, ed. V. T. Harlow, pp. 132–48). George Edmundson has made skillful use of this document in his article "The Dutch in Western Guiana" (*English Historical Review*, XVI, pp. 640 ff.). W. R. Menkman (*De West-Indische Compagnie*, p. 88) and Davies (*Dutch Seventeenth Century Overseas Trade*, pp. 120–21) have followed Edmundson's account. A newly discovered letter written from officers of the West India Company's own Essequibo colony in 1627 mentions nothing about any other colony on the river, however (copy of a letter from Jan Adriaensz vander Goes and Johannes Beverlandt to the Zeeland Chamber, September 30, 1627, in the James Ford Bell Collection of the University of Minnesota). In view of the great dearth of evidence, it appears impossible to obtain certainty at present.

6. P. M. Netscher, *Geschiedenis van de kolonien Essequibo, Demerary, en Berbice*, pp. 57 ff. Van Grol, *Grondpolitiek*, II, pp. 25 ff. The frequent assertion that the Dutch merchants van Ree and van Pere had a small trading colony on the Berbice in 1624 (Menkman, *West-Indische Compagnie*, p. 87; Davies, *Dutch Seventeenth Century Overseas Trade*, p. 120) is based on Scott's description of Guiana of over forty years later (Scott, in *Colonizing Expeditions to the West Indies and Guiana*, p. 140). While a 1624 Berbice post is not impossible, it is much more probable that Scott was referring to the post van Pere established in 1627.

founded and operated by the West India Company through Chamber Zeeland. Of these Company colonies, one, perhaps somewhere near Cabo do Norte and probably no more than a trading post, was the last remnant of the Company's incipient enterprise on the Amazon, other Dutch posts and colonies having been broken up by a Portuguese offensive from 1623–1625.[7] Westwards, Chamber Zeeland had settled colonists on the Wiapoco and on the Cayenne in 1627, on conditions somewhat similar to those laid down in the *Provisionele ordere* for the New Netherland *coloniërs* in 1624.[8] But the only Guiana colony under the direct management of the Company which had been in operation for any length of time was the Company's establishment on the Essequibo. The fact that this colony was founded less than a year after the planting of New Netherland must have invited comparisons of its progress with that of New Netherland.[9]

Since the first resolution book of Chamber Zeeland, which probably covered the activities of the chamber from its formation to May 1626, has been lost, next to nothing has been known hitherto about the early years of the Company's Essequibo colony. However, a recently discovered copy of a letter written on September 30, 1627, from Jan van der Goes and Johannes Beverlant, two of the Company's officers on the Essequibo, to the Zeeland Chamber sheds considerable light on the colony's early development.[10]

At the time the letter was written, the principal exports of the Company's Essequibo settlement seem to have been dye and *letterhout*, a rare speckled wood. Perhaps employees of the Company gathered some of these commodities, but it was clearly the neighboring Carib Indians who brought in most of these goods.

7. Edmundson, "Dutch on the Amazon and Negro," *English Historical Review*, XVIII, pp. 652–61.

8. Netscher, *Essequibo, Demerary, Berbice*, pp. 53–57.

9. The date of the founding of the Company's Essequibo colony can be inferred from the fact that on August 23, 1627, the Zeeland Chamber resolved to increase the wages of Jan van der Goes, one of the Company's principal officers at Essequibo, after the end of his three year term of service, while van der Goes himself wrote of the approaching end of his term of service on September 30, 1627 (Resolution book of Chamber Zeeland, May 4, 1626–August 30, 1629, quoted in U. S. Commission to Investigate and Report upon the True Divisional line between the Republic of Venezuela and British Guiana, *Report and accompanying papers*, II, p. 45; Vander Goes and Beverlandt to the Zeeland Chamber, September 30, 1627, in the James Ford Bell Collection).

10. The copy, which appears to have been made shortly after the letter was written, is now the property of the James Ford Bell Collection, University of Minnesota.

For purposes of trade, the Dutch were occupying two trading posts constantly and, in season, three or four. It was difficult and expensive to obtain much *letterhout*: the Indians were too lazy, and when they did bring some in, they demanded the best merchandise. A good quantity of dye had been obtained, however, and the Essequibo factors were sure that the directors would be well satisfied with the last shipment. Some English had come to trade for dye on the river, but, according to instructions of the directors, the Dutch were frustrating their trade by systematically offering the Indians better terms.

In addition to trade, the directors had strongly recommended the establishment of plantations. A recent ship had brought over some Negroes, and these had been employed in the gardens and in planting cotton. A large field had been planted with cotton, but worms had eaten off all the leaves and as yet no cotton had been obtained. Despite the fact that many of the Dutch and Negroes were boys, too weak to fell trees and undertake the heavy work of plantation building, the Essequibo captains claimed to be doing all they could to further agricultural development. They stressed especially the potential profits of tobacco, but envisaged also the culture of cotton and dye. In the future, they hoped that men, preferably farmers used to hard labor, be sent over, but suggested for the present that the attempt at plantation be made with the already available labor force in order to spare the Company expense.

The third area of activity was the search for minerals. A " gold-seeker " had arrived recently, and he and van der Goes had just completed a journey deep into the interior. There they had narrowly escaped death at the hands of hostile Indians, but had been unable to discover any mines.

From the foregoing summary of the letter of van der Goes and Beverlant, it is evident that the Company, or at least Chamber Zeeland, was optimistic about the prospects of agricultural development in Guiana. At the same time, the culture of plantation crops at Essequibo, the only Company colony which had been in existence for any length of time, was only just entering the experimental stage. We can be certain, therefore, that it was not marked success with tropical cultures in the Guianas which made the further agricultural development of New Netherland seem unattractive.

*

The Company's decision not to make further investments in New Netherland agriculture did not necessarily imply that private capital would be invited to undertake the colony's development. An alternative was to terminate further agricultural colonization altogether, thereby permitting unhampered concentration on the fur trade; and van Rensselaer's 1633 memorial permits the inference that certain directors, probably the same who had opposed New Netherland's colonization in 1623 and 1624, had just this in mind.[11] In this memorial van Rensselaer also relates that it was the directors entrusted with the management of New Netherland affairs, the *commissarissen voor Nieu Nederlandt*, who suggested the possibility of developing New Netherland through private enterprise: all the blame for the unsatisfactory affairs in New Netherland

> was laid mainly to the account of those who favored the colonization, and especially to the commissioners for that region, who to clear themselves asserted that they were willing to undertake the colonization at their own expense and without cost to the Company, if the Company would only favor the matter a little and render some assistance, and that they would make no objection and would be satisfied if all participants should be thereunto invited, and public freedoms and exemptions framed concerning it.[12]

One is tempted to believe this avowal that the initiative towards the patroon system in New Netherland came from the commissioners, because in 1633 it was clearly in van Rensselaer's interest not to admit it, and because in other places in the memorial he is at pains to show that he, one of the *commissarissen voor Nieu Nederlandt*, was not instrumental in bringing about the acceptance of the " Freedoms." [13] But although the initiative towards the introduction of the patroon system into New Netherland probably came from the commissioners, they were hardly the originators of a scheme of colonization with which the Company was not already well acquainted. Precedents for the New Netherland patroon system already existed in " freedoms " permitting private capital to undertake colonizing ventures in Guiana, and it is virtually cer-

11. VRBM, pp. 236–37, 244.
12. In de Roever, *Oud Holland*, VIII, p. 57; VRBM, pp. 236–37.
13. VRBM, pp. 237–38.

tain that these precedents exerted a significant influence on the Company's decision to adopt a similar policy in New Netherland.

Whether or not Jan de Moor was permitted to continue his Essequibo colony at the advent of the West India Company, the Company was not prepared in 1623 to admit private investment within the limits of the *Octroy* as a general rule. The question whether private merchants ought not to be permitted the exploitation of certain coasts upon payment of a proper recognition to the Company was discussed at the October 1623 gathering of The Nineteen; but the proposal was "unanimously rejected and annulled." [14] Probably at this time the Company's great need for conservative investment opportunities dissuaded The Nineteen from farming out any of its limited opportunities for trade or colonization.

Three and one-half years later, the Bahia disaster and other misfortunes had seriously depleted the Company's available capital. This fact, perhaps, emboldened the merchant Jacob Martsen of Vlissingen to request the Zeeland Chamber in February 1627 that he be permitted to plant a colony of sixty to eighty persons on the West Indian island of Tobago for the purpose of cultivating sugar, cotton, tobacco, and other crops. His request was turned over to a committee, including, among other directors, the veteran Guiana colonizer Jan de Moor, burgomaster of Vlissingen. The next month, another member of the committee, Abraham van Pere, *hoofdparticipanten*-director from Vlissingen, presented his own plan for colonization to the *hoofdparticipanten*, at the same time inviting them to participate in a colonization attempt in accordance with it. On April 22, van Pere reached a tentative agreement with the Zeeland Chamber, whereby van Pere was authorized, on various conditions, to plant a settlement on the river Berbice. [15]

In June 1627 The Nineteen reviewed the requests of van Pere and Martsen, and on the 12th of that month issued a general charter, empowering directors, *hoofdparticipanten*, or lesser participants in the West India Company to plant colonies in Guiana on conditions in most respects more liberal than those originally offered van Pere by Chamber Zeeland. [16] This general charter, sig-

14. Van Grol, *Grondpolitiek*, II, p. 24.

15. Van Grol discusses both Martsen's and van Pere's colonization plans (*ibid.*, pp. 25–26). Netscher (*Essequibo, Demerary, Berbice*) discusses the agreement with van Pere (p. 57) and prints its text (pp. 346–50).

16. The text and an English translation of this charter is printed in U. S. Commission on Boundary between Venezuela and British Guiana, *Report*, II, pp. 47–53.

nificantly revised in 1628, became the original precedent for the 1629 *Vryheden*, the basis for the patroon system in New Netherland. It was also probably the first instance in which the Company admitted a significant amount of private investment within the limits of its charter.

Under the 1627 charter private capital shouldered the burden of the investment in colonization. A " patroon "—the term is first used in the final accord with Martsen and his associates of June 21—was expected to enlist twenty families of at least three members each, provide them with weapons and all necessities, and pay their passage across the Atlantic. He was also expected to provide his colony with a well armed yacht of from 12–20 lasts, which fact in conjunction with the complete absence of any mention of the Company's responsibility to defend the colony, suggests that the patroon was to be responsible for the colony's defense. The Company assisted the patroon by permitting payment for the colonists' passage and outbound cargo to be deferred until it could be made from the first returns from the colony. The freight rates to and from the colony were fixed by the charter for the succeeding seven years, but whether the rates were in general low enough to represent a subsidization of the colonization is uncertain, though they were generally significantly lower than those offered van Pere in April by Chamber Zeeland. Cattle, however, could be sent over for nothing, if provided with food and other necessities, and if there was room on the Company's ships.

The principal advantage accruing to the Company under this charter was a monopoly of the overseas carrying trade of the patroonships: all imports and exports of the colonies were to be carried exclusively on the Company's ships. No provision was made for the Company's collection of tithes, duties, or other imposts, with the single exception of a recognition on exported minerals, which, lumped together with freight charges, amounted to twenty percent.

In return for his investment the patroon received land and the minerals found within it, the privilege of sending and receiving goods to and from his colony despite its situation within the limits of the *Octroy*, the right to carry on an internal trade with the Indians, and restricted governmental authority over his colony. His ownership of land could be extended to all lands cultivated within three years of his having laid claim to them. Probably both to permit each colony to expand and to preserve extensive lands for the Company's own disposition, no patroonship could be planted within seven to eight leagues of another without the special approbation of the Company's officers. The patroon's governmental privileges over his colony comprised the right to issue instructions, conformable to "the political ordinance," and subject to the scrutiny of the directors. The Company warily subjected the colonists to all present or future regulations of the Company regarding their government and administration of justice and also placed the patroonships under the vague supervision of the Company's commander at Cayenne.

Martsen, who by this time had entered partnership with the influential Jan de Moor, contracted with the Company to plant Tobago on June 21, 1627. The basis for this contract was the general charter, approved by The Nineteen a week and a half previously; but Martsen and de Moor were also subjected to several additional stipulations. The most significant of these preserved the Company's right to plant a colony or fortification on Tobago and provided for the devolution of the patroons' land and privileges to the Company if for any reason the colony was abandoned. In case of such devolution, no compensation could be demanded of the Company. The Zeeland Chamber offered van Pere his choice between the general charter and the tentative agreement of April. He accepted the general charter, with a minor change and several insignificant additional stipulations, on July 12th.[17]

In March 1628 The Nineteen approved two general colonization charters, on the 8th of the month new articles for Guiana, and on the 10th the first charter for New Netherland.[18] The New Nether-

17. Van Grol (Grondpolitiek, II, pp. 25–26) discusses the additional stipulations for Martsen and de Moor. Netscher, Essequibo, Demerary, Berbice, prints the additional conditions made for van Pere, pp. 353–54. The "minor change" from the general charter was the substitution of forty men and forty boys for twenty families.

18. Van Rensselaer, Memorial of 1633, in VRBM, p. 237, states that the New Netherland freedoms were actually passed. The memorial to the States General of the patroons in June 1634 relates that on 10 March 1628 The Nineteen merely directed freedoms to be drawn up (DCHNY, I, p. 84). I accept van Rensselaer's version, however, because N. C. Lambrechtsen discovered freedoms and exemptions for New Netherland of this date in the resolutions of The Nineteen before these documents were lost (Korte beschrijving van de ontdekking en der verdere lotgevallen van Nieuw-Nederland, Middelburg: S. v. Benthem, 1818, translated by F. A. van der Kemp in New York Historical Society Collections, series II, v. I (1841), p. 93 and 93n.

land charter has been lost, and of it is known with certainty only that it permitted agricultural colonization in the province while reserving the fur trade exclusively to the Company.[19] However, it is highly probable that both the Guiana and the New Netherland charter of 1628 were conceived in the same spirit, because the final charter for New Netherland of 1629, the *Vryheden*, which must logically have used the 1628 New Netherland charter for its prototype, contains a large number of paragraphs which literally reproduce paragraphs in the 1628 charter for Guiana. It will, therefore, be appropriate to investigate the nature of the second (1628) Guiana charter, for, although it is not in the direct line of precedents to the *Vryheden*, it is at least a sibling, so to speak, of the lost New Netherland charter of 1628.

The March 1628 " freedoms and exemptions "[20] for private colonizers in Guiana represented a considerable revision of the June 1627 charter. In general, the new charter (1) extended the patroons' territorial and commercial privileges, while, apparently, subjecting the patroonships to eventual taxation by the Company, and (2) couched many of the patroons' territorial and governmental privileges in alluring feudal terms. Another significant innovation was a provision enabling individuals or groups of colonists too small to obtain patroonal rights to obtain as much land " in full ownership " as they could conveniently cultivate.

Under the revised arrangement, the entire area within a radius of seven to eight leagues became the property of the patroon, not just that part of it he was able to cultivate. This extended area was not to be simply and prosaically " owned " by the patroon. Instead, the land with its " fruits, superficies, minerals, rivers, and springs " was to be held from the Company as a " perpetual fief of inheritance with middle and lower jurisdiction, taxes, tithes, fisheries and rights of grinding." The commercial concessions included a significant reduction of the freight rates on imports for the following six (not seven) years (20 to 10 percent). The rates on exports were permanently fixed at rates in some cases considerably lower than the temporary rates of the June 1627 charter. If

19. Van Rensselaer, Memorial of 1633, in VRBM, p. 237.
20. " Vryheden ende exemptien voor particuliere die op de Wilde Custe van Brasil ofte de eylanden daeraen ende ontrent liggende, eenige colonien ende vee sullen planten, toegestaen ende vergunt by de geoctroyeerde W I Compaignie," printed in U. S. Commission on Boundary between Venezuela and British Guiana, *Report*, II, pp. 56–64.

the Company declined to send sufficient shipping space to the colony, the patroon might be granted permission to send a ship of his own. The patroon was also permitted to trade along the entire coast from the Amazon to the Orinoco, and he was allowed two-thirds of the proceeds of any prizes his ships captured.

Perhaps in compensation for the cession of these new commercial and territorial privileges, the new charter contained a clause which, though ambiguous, seems to have given the Company the right to levy duties and direct taxes on a patroonship after ten years from 1628. This clause, the essentials of which were incorporated in the *Vryheden* of 1629 and which plagued Rensselaerswyck during the later part of the Dutch regime in New Netherland, provided that during the period specified the Company would not levy any

> *convoy* [an import and export duty in the Netherlands granted the Company by the States General], toll, excise, imposts, or any other contributions, and after the expiration of 10 years, at the highest, such *convoy* as the goods pay here in this country at present.

Two interpretations of the clause are, of course, possible, but it seems probable that the eventual imposition of "tolls, excises, and imposts" as well as *convoyen* was envisaged, and that the Company's financial objectives in permitting private colonization were no longer purely commercial.

Despite the lofty grant of "middle and lower jurisdiction" the Company retained virtually the same political control over the colonies as in the general charter of 1627. Judgments of the patroon's court involving more than 50 florins could be appealed to the Company's officers, and the patroon's instructions to his colonists were still to be conformable to all present and future regulations of the directors. Curiously enough, the vital question of the responsibility for the defense of the patroonships was entirely passed over. In the new charter the patroon was not even obligated to arm his colonists or provide an armed yacht for their defense.

Between the enactment of the Guiana and New Netherland freedoms of March 1628 and the passage of the revised *Vryheden* for New Netherland on June 7, 1629, nearly a year and three months elapsed. Since it has been alleged that the *Vryheden* was scurrilously bagged by an inside ring of the Company's directors, it would be highly desirable to obtain for this period an accurate record of the nature and frequency of the deliberations on the New Netherland patroon system in this period. However, our only two sources, van Rensselaer's 1633 memorial to The Nineteen and a 1634 memorial of four New Netherland patroons to the States General, both proceed from the patroons, members of the supposed inside ring; and moreover, the two memorials were composed for the precise purpose of demonstrating the validity of the procedure by which the *Vryheden* was obtained.[21] Considering the fact that the missives were addressed to the States General and to a hostile and informed Nineteen, it is unlikely that obvious falsehoods would have been introduced. On the other hand, damaging evidence would almost certainly have been omitted and favorable evidence stressed. Specifically, the patroons' accounts can be expected to have emphasized the lengthiness of the deliberations and the approval of the *hoofdparticipanten*, who were generally regarded as the truest representatives of the Company's interests.

The patroons' memorials reveal deliberations on the New Netherland freedoms at The Nineteen late in October 1628 but no other discussions within the Company and no readiness on the part of colonizers to accept the Company's March terms before the arrival of the news of Heyn's capture of the Silver Fleet in mid-November.[22] However, in December 1628 Godijn, Blommaert, and van Rensselaer, all directors of the Amsterdam Chamber, arranged to send two persons to New Netherland to purchase land from the Indians, and on January 13, 1629, three days after Heyn and his treasure fleet reached the Netherlands, these three formally notified the Amsterdam Chamber of their intention, in case their agents should make favorable report, to plant a colony in New Netherland according to the restrictive freedoms of March 1628.[23] Whether the prospective patroons were ingenuously con-

21. Van Rensselaer's Memorial of 1633, in VRBM, pp. 235–50. The memorial to the States General from Paauw, Blommaert, van Rensselaer, and Hamel is in DCHNY, I, pp. 84–88.

22. The October deliberation in VRBM, p. 237. The news of the Silver Fleet's capture arrived in the Netherlands with the yacht *Ouwevaer*, which anchored before Rotterdam on November 15, 1628 (de Laet, *Historie ofte Iaerlijck Verhael* [1644], p. 144).

23. Van Rensselaer, Memorial of 1633, in VRBM, pp. 238–39. The notification to Chamber Amsterdam appears in an extract of the resolutions of the Amsterdam Chamber, in VRBM, p. 154.

templating colonization according to the restrictive freedoms of March, which completely excluded the patroons from New Netherland's fur trade, is at least open to reasonable doubt. They may have suspected that more liberal freedoms would soon be enacted in the jubilant atmosphere following the capture of the Spanish treasure and hence desired to obtain the best sites in New Netherland before others became interested.

The first steps toward amplification of the first New Netherland freedoms appear to have been made in February 1629. According to van Rensselaer the restrictiveness of the freedoms " caused great discontent" among the *hoofdparticipanten*. This dissatisfaction was publicly expressed to either The Nineteen or the Amsterdam Chamber on February 1st, and the request was made that a committee be appointed to amend the present freedoms. Two days later this committee was indeed appointed, and it drafted several amendments. Shortly after February 21, delegates of the *hoofdparticipanten* appeared before The Nineteen " in competent numbers " and requested a liberalization of the New Netherland charter; but they were unable to obtain a decision because of the opposition of the " contrary minded," evidently those persons opposed to any sort of colonization in New Netherland. On February 26, the " commissioners," presumably the committee appointed earlier in the month, presented their report, and The Nineteen resolved to refer the controversial points to the chambers and to discuss the matter at its next meeting.[24]

The importance which the Amsterdam Chamber attached to the amending of the New Netherland freedoms is indicated by that chamber's having made it the second subject for discussion in the *poincten van beschrijvinge* issued on April 18, 1629.[25] On May 29th, at the ensuing gathering of The Nineteen, a committee was appointed to draft a revised charter. " After many long debates," the committee agreed upon a draft and presented it to The Nineteen, which granted it full approval on June 7.[26]

The *Vryheden* of 1629, " freedoms and exemptions for the patroons, masters or private persons who will plant any colonies

24. For the debate on the amplification of the freedoms, see DCHNY, I, p. 84; and van Rensselaer's 1633 Memorial, in VRBM, pp. 237–39.

25. DCHNY, I, p. 84. Van Rensselaer gives the text of this second article of the *poincten* in his memorial (VRBM, p. 238).

26. VRBM, p. 238. DCHNY, I, p. 84.

in, and send cattle to New Netherland," [27] shows great similarities
to the general charter for Guiana of March 1628: Ten of its
thirty-one articles are literally reproduced, and most of the other
articles either conveyed a similar meaning or embodied phrases
from the Guiana charter. Undoubtedly, the likeness between the
Vryheden and the lost March 1628 freedoms for New Netherland
was even greater, because the difference in geographical situation
and economic potential between New Netherland and Guiana
made some differences between a Guiana and New Netherland
colonization charter inevitable. Let us summarize the principal
differences between the Guiana charter of 1628 and the *Vryheden*
of 1629 under two heads: (1) those differences which represented
a fundamental change in the relationship between the Company
and the patroon, and (2) those which resulted simply from differences in the geographical and economic situations of the two
regions.[28]

1. The provision that no second colony might be planted within
seven to eight leagues of a first was retained; but the patroon no
longer possessed all the land within a radius of this distance. A
patroonship might extend four leagues along the coast or one side
of a navigable river, or two leagues along both sides of a river.
No limit was placed on the inland expansion of a patroonship, but
the territory which would necessarily be left vacant between
colonies was expressly reserved to the Company. Within his
colony, the patroon could exercise high as well as middle and low
jurisdiction; however, the right of appeal to the Company from
judgments exceeding ƒ 50 was retained, as was the subjection of
the patroon's governmental instructions to the Company's present
and future regulations. The *Vryheden* was the first charter for
private colonization which admitted the Company's responsibility
to defend the colonies. The Company accepted the obligation to
defend the colonies against internal and external attacks " with
the forces it has there [in New Netherland]" and promised to
put Fort Amsterdam on Manhattan in a proper posture for de-

27. "Uryheden ende Exemptien voor de patroonen/ meesters ofte particulieren/
die op Nieu-Nederlandt eenighe colonien ende vee sullen planten geconsidereert
ten dienst van de Generale West-Indische Compagnie in Nieu-Nederlandt/ ende
het voordeel van de patroonen/ meesters ende particulieren." I have used the Dutch
text and English translation in VRBM, pp. 136–53.
28. Van Grol, *Grondpolitiek*, II, pp. 37–43, presents a thorough discussion of
the similarities and differences of the two charters.

fense. The charter also differed from all of its predecessors in containing a promise that the grant be presented to the States General for approbation and confirmation.

2. For the Guiana patroons' right to trade from the Amazon to the Orinoco were substituted trading privileges from Florida to Newfoundland on payment of a 5 percent recognition to the Company. The New Netherland patroons were also permitted to fish for cod and to sail with their catch directly to Italy or other neutral countries. By far the most important stipulation arising from the peculiarities of New Netherland's situation was Article XV, which regulated the patroons' limited rights to the fur trade. This clause, the ambiguity of which exacerbated the subsequent dispute between the patroons and the Company, permitted the patroons to trade goods produced in New Netherland for all goods except peltries " all around on the coast of New Netherland and places circumjacent thereto." Trade for furs was permitted " where the Company has no agent," provided that all traded furs pay an export duty of one guilder for each beaver or otter.

*

Was the " Vryheden " obtained by fraud?

The question whether, in the picturesque phraseology of S. G. Nissenson, " the system of patroonships in New Netherland had been conceived in a rape of the Company by its commissioners for the province " receives scant elucidation from the fragmentary, superficial, and perhaps even wilfully distorted accounts of the patroons regarding the deliberations preceding the adoption of the Vryheden. Charges to this effect appear to have been raised by opponents of the first New Netherland patroons within the Company by at least the fall of 1631, when the Company began a determined effort to eliminate the patroon system in New Netherland.[29] About a decade later it was reportedly the opinion of Frederick de Vries, a director of Chamber Amsterdam and a commissioner of New Netherland from 1633, that after the plantation of New Netherland had gotten fairly started

then they [Godijn, van Rensselaer, Bloemaert, and Jan de Laet, all commissioners of New Netherland] helped them-

29. See Chapter 6.

selves with sinister merchants' tricks; and the Company, having about that time gotten a good Piet Heyn's booty, never thought about its best trading post of Fort Orange, whether farms were set up there or not: but these fellows . . . succeeded in getting it away from the other directors, their confreres. . . .[30]

Recently these allegations have been echoed by Nissenson's *Patroon's Domain* (1937), which must be regarded as the standard work on Rensselaerswyck and the patroon system.[31]

Nissenson asserts that " so broad were the privileges conferred and so comparatively few the obligations imposed, that this alone would be persuasive of the fact that the policy was initiated by the Amsterdam directors with their own prospective advantage in view." [32] However, our previous consideration of the precedents of the New Netherland patroon system indicates that the privileges and obligations laid down by the *Vryheden* were essentially similar to those contained in previous charters for Guiana, which were deemed perfectly satisfactory. The general liberality of the *Vryheden* is thus no proof of the malfeasance of the directors. However, the transfer of the patroon system to the peculiar economic conditions of New Netherland or specific concessions of the New Netherland charter might conceivably bear witness to the directors' culpability.

In the opinion of the opponents of the New Netherland patroons in the early 1630's, the really prejudicial aspect of the *Vryheden* was the opportunity it gave the patroons to appropriate part of the Company's fur trade.[33] In retrospect we can perceive several ways in which the patroons could have done this. One was smuggling on the patroons' accounts (as opposed to the private illicit trade of their colonists, which would have harmed the Company but not redounded to the benefit of the patroons). Legitimately, the patroons could make use of the limited trading privileges which were indubitably theirs according to even a narrow interpretation of the *Vryheden*. How significantly the patroons could impair the Company's trade if their activities were restricted to those sanctioned by an interpretation favorable to the Company

---

30. De Vries, *Verscheyden voyagiens*, p. 247.
31. S. G. Nissenson, *Patroon's Domain*, especially pp. 21, 27–28, 169.
32. *Ibid.*, p. 27.
33. Van Rensselaer, Memorial of 1633; in VRBM, pp. 239–40, 244.

is debatable, however. Such an interpretation would have barred the patroons from trading within a *considerable distance* of any place where the Company had sent *or might in the future send* a trading agent, hence from all lucrative areas of trade which had been or were yet to be discovered. Since in the remaining areas the patroons could trade only goods produced in New Netherland, they would be unable to make use of any of the standard trading truck except *sewan*. Furthermore the furs they obtained were subject to an export duty of *f* 1 per skin, which in 1629 probably represented about 12 to 13 percent of the final value of a lot of New Netherland furs.[34] In view of these considerations it becomes questionable whether the patroons' fur trading privileges really represented a significant concession at all. However, the ambiguous wording of the *Vryheden*, a typical phenomenon of the period to judge from the colonization charters for Guiana, made it possible to interpret the patroons' trading rights as substantially greater. These defects in wording (1) permitted the interpretation that the restrictions on the patroons' trade applied only to the coast of New Netherland and places *immediately circumjacent*, but not to the inland trade, (2) failed to make explicit that the obligation laid on the patroons' fur traders to keep at a distance from the Company's posts applied not only to posts already in existence but also to all future posts which the Company might choose to establish, and (3) neglected to specify exactly how far the patroons' traders must stay from those of the Company. All these ambiguities were later appealed to by the patroons.[35]

The part of the New Netherland fur trade which was made the indubitable prerogative of the patroons was, as pointed out above, of the most marginal nature. Whether conspiratorial commissioners of New Netherland could reasonably have expected to be able to gain much advantage from the above-mentioned ambiguities or from possibilities for smuggling is questionable. In view of the Company's diffuse organization, the frequent changes of directors, and the constant supervision of the *hoofdparticipanten*

34. The lot of furs obtained by the West India Company from New Netherland in 1628, consisting of 6951 beavers and 734 "otters, etc.," was sold for *f* 61,075, or an average of *f* 7.96 per skin. See Chapter 4.

35. Paauw, Blommaert, van Rensselaer, and Hamel, Memorial to the States General of June 1634, in DCHNY, I, pp. 87–88. Van Rensselaer, "Instructions for Rutger Hendricxssen van Soest" of July 1632, in VRBM, p. 209. Letter of van Rensselaer to Dirck Cornelissz Duyster of July 20, 1632, in VRBM, p. 216.

and the States General, the ability of the commissioners and their cohorts to prevent the Company from opposing activities hurtful to it could only have been of relatively short duration. Furthermore, when once roused to opposition against the patroons, the West India Company would have been a most formidable adversary, because it possessed not only sufficient wealth and influence to fight off legal attacks based on the tenuous grounds of equivocal wording, but also abundant opportunities to retaliate by frustrating or hampering the patroons' activities in the New Netherlands. When viewed in this light, the totality of the patroons' licit and illicit opportunities in the fur trade seems very meager, certainly too meager to raise the suspicion that the *Vryheden* was fraudulently procured.

This suspicion is raised, however, by the probability that a large proportion of the Commissioners for New Netherland took advantage of the *Vryheden*. Since the records of the Amsterdam Chamber in the late 1620's are lost, certainty regarding either the size or the composition of the New Netherland Commission in 1628 and 1629 is impossible. However, Kiliaen van Rensselaer can definitely be identified as a commissioner at the time on the basis of his 1633 memorial to The Nineteen, and the previously quoted memoirs of David de Vries, who was once associated with the Swanendael patroons, described Samuel Godijn, Johannes de Laet, and Samuel Blommaert as commissioners along with van Rensselaer. In addition to these four, several other directors were associated with New Netherland affairs during the 1620's, and their commissionership must at least be regarded as a possibility.

Two tests of this association are (1) signatures on documents concerning New Netherland and (2) names applied to geographical features there in the 1620's. The first criterion yields the following names: [36]

36. Godijn: The "Provisionele ordere" of March 28, 1624, the "Naerdere jnstructie" for van Hulst and the "Particuliere instructie" for the surveyor, both dated April 22, 1625, and the charter party of the *Ruyter*, dated June 17, 1625. It is also significant that Dominie Michaëlius wrote to Godijn complaining of bad treatment on his voyage to New Netherland in 1628 (Michaëlius to Smoutius, in NNN, pp. 123).

Van Rensselaer: "Naerdere jnstructie," "Particuliere instructie," and the charter party of the *Ruyter*.

Coenraets: "Provisionele ordere" and "Naerdere jnstructie."

De Laet: "Provisionele ordere."

Bicker and Spranger: The charter party of the *Ruyter*.

Samuel Godijn (4 documents, 1624 and 1625)
Kiliaen van Rensselaer (3 documents, 1625)
Albert Coenraets (2 documents, 1624 and 1625)
Johannes de Laet (1 document, 1624)
Cornelis Bicker (1 document, 1625)
Gommer Spranger (1 document, 1625)

Applying the second criterion of nomenclature, we find: [37]

Samuel Godijn
Kiliaen van Rensselaer (Probably)
Albert Coenraets
Hendrick Hamel
Samuel Blommaert
Jacob Pietersz Hooghkamer

That as many as nine of the Amsterdam Chambers' twenty directors were on the New Netherland Commission when the *Vryheden* was enacted seems very improbable, though it is possible that all the above listed directors served at some time in the 1620's. At any rate, we do have a list of likely prospects, which can be examined for connection with the patroonships.

Van Rensselaer, Blommaert, Godijn, and Coenraets, all registered patroonships in New Netherland soon after the adoption of the *Vryheden*. In 1630 Johannes de Laet assumed Coenraets'

---

37. Godijns Punt, now Sandy Hook (de Rasieres to Blommaert, c. 1628, in NNN, p. 102).

Rensselaers Hoeck, a cape about ten miles south of Sandy Hook. I have not found this name on maps or documents dated as early as 1629. However, the decidedly cool relations between the patroon and the Company which developed after 1631 would hardly have encouraged the formal bestowal of his name after that date. Nor is there any obvious connection between this cape and the colony of Rensselaerswyck. It seems more reasonable to assume that the name dates from the early period when the principal geographical features at the mouth of the Hudson were named for the commissioners or other prominent directors.

Coenraets Baij, now Sandy Hook Bay (de Rasieres to Blommaert, c. 1628, in NNN, p. 102).

Hamels Hoofden, the narrows between Long Island and Staten Island (*ibid.*, pp. 102–03).

Blommaerts Vallei on the Manhattans (*ibid.*, p. 105). It is also significant that de Rasieres, the Secretary, wrote to Blommaert c. 1628.

Hoogcamers Eylandt, now Governors Island. The Dutch usually called this island "Nooten Eylandt" (Nut Island), but an anonymous Dutch map which was apparently copied c. 1660 from a map of Governor Minuit's time gives this name (Stokes, *Iconography*, II, plate 39).

rights and with Blommaert, Godijn, and van Rensselaer formed a single partnership for the plantation of the several colonies they had registered. Hendrick Hamel became a minor participant in Godijn's colony (though not in the general partnership of the aforementioned four) after about August 1630. As far as is known, Bicker, Spranger, and Hooghkamer never had any interest in the New Netherland patroonships.[38]

The only other person who registered a patroonship in New Netherland in the early period was Michiel Paauw, who was not one of the first directors of the Company but entered the director-ate by November 1627. There is no evidence that he was ever on the New Netherland commission and some indication that he operated independently of the patroons who appear to have been commissioners. Frederick de Vries, a director from 1633, re-portedly believed that Paauw registered his patroonship opposite the Manhattans " when he discovered that they [Godijn, van Rensselaer, Blommaert, and de Laet] took the land of Fort Orange "; and he never pooled his patroonship with the others.[39]

It is very reasonable to ask why, if the colonization of New Netherland was deemed unprofitable for the West India Company, the very men who were best acquainted with the Company's New Netherland affairs leapt to undertake it. Van Rensselaer offers a plausible explanation for this inconsistency when he intimates that the commissioners did not back the Company's decision to abandon the further agricultural development of New Netherland on its own account.[40] If this was the case—and van Rensselaer could not easily have deviated too far from the truth in a memorial to The Nineteen—there would be nothing sinister about their undertaking a project which they had consistently defended as profitable but which the Company as a whole was inclined to give up.

If the commissioners had really been disposed toward appro-priating the Company's fur trade rather than the legitimate plant-

38. For the initial registrations of van Rensselaer, Blommaert, Godijn, and Coenraets, see VRBM, pp. 155–56. The partnership agreement of 1630 is printed in *ibid.*, pp. 71–75. Hamel's participation in Godijn's colony is noted in de Vries, *Verscheyden voyagiens*, p. 147. That Hamel did not join the patroonship pool is evident from the fact that he never possessed a share in Rensselaerswyck.

39. Frederick de Vries' opinion is in de Vries, *Verscheyden voyagiens*, p. 247. That Paauw was a director by November 1627 is evident from DCHNY, I, p. 37.

40. Memorial of 1633, in VRBM, pp. 236-37.

ing of colonies, their activities in New Netherland might be expected to bear witness of this disposition. A study of the patroons' activities through the spring of 1632, by which time their agents would presumably have been warned to proceed with caution in view of the assumption of control over New Netherland affairs by a group hostile to the patroon system, presents somewhat contradictory evidence, however. Godijn, Blommaert, and van Rensselaer sent two persons to New Netherland about January 1629 with instructions to choose a site and purchase land for their patroonships. Although these patroonships were to be established under the March 1628 freedoms, which unambiguously banned the patroons from the fur trade, these agents obtained permission not only to take along trading goods for the purchase of land but also to exchange the goods left over after their land purchases for furs. Evidently the Amsterdam Chamber permitted the agents to take along an inordinately large amount of trading goods, for they managed to bring home, probably after August 1630 and thus much too late to prejudice the chances of amplifying the New Netherland freedoms, some ƒ 5,600 in furs.[41] This haul, slightly over 8 percent of the Company's exports from New Netherland in 1630 and made before any significant colonizing activity had begun, was understandably interpreted by some directors and *hoofdparticipanten* as a sign that

> the patroons were not contemplating colonization at all, but only securing to themselves the fur trade and depriving the Company of the same, which would be the total ruin of the Company as regards [profit from] these regions. . . .[42]

Van Rensselaer regarded this " so little occasion as the return of ƒ 5,600 " as the chief pretext for the anti-patroon sentiment which reached such violent proportions by 1632.[43]

This initial exploit does not reflect well on the intentions of Godijn, Blommaert, and van Rensselaer, who may very possibly have acquired permission to send over the inordinately large supply

41. *Ibid.*, pp. 238–39. I infer the date of the return of the two agents from the fact that the Indians who sold the lands for the Swanendael patroonship appeared at the Manhattans to confirm their sale on July 15, 1630, at which time the agents were probably still in New Netherland (DCHNY, I, p. 43).

42. Van Rensselaer, Memorial of 1633, in de Roever, *Oud Holland*, VIII, p. 59, and VRBM, p. 239.

43. *Ibid.*, in VRBM, p. 240.

of trading goods by devious means; but there is little other evidence that in 1629–1632 the commissioner-patroons made use of the *Vryheden* to encroach on the Company's fur trade. Rensselaerswyck surrounded Fort Orange, and in the early years van Rensselaer absolutely prohibited participation in the fur trade to his colonists. Swanendael, the only other patroonship actually begun by the commissioner-patroons, was far from any Company trading post, and in 1631 the commander there had at least some trading goods which he traded for furs. This immediately raises the suspicion of illegal trading, since the *Vryheden* permitted the patroons to trade only goods produced in New Netherland for furs. However, it is possible that for this voyage, as was certainly the case for the 1632 voyage, special permission was granted by Chamber Amsterdam to take over a very limited supply of trading truck.[44]

Evidence for the good faith of Godijn, van Rensselaer, and their associates is afforded by their genuine and undoubtedly very expensive efforts to promote agricultural colonization at Swanendael and Rensselaerswyck. Cattle and colonists were shipped to both colonies; and, in both, efforts were made to plant grain and tobacco.[45] At Swanendael the greatest hopes seem to have been pinned on neither furs nor agriculture, but on whaling in Delaware Bay.[46] In a June 1632 letter to his partner, de Laet, requesting a new contribution to Rensselaerswyck, van Rensselaer envisaged only various agricultural enterprises as potential sources of profit for his colony.[47]

Do the earlier and later careers of the persons whom we think to have been commissioners and who were also patroons reveal a lack of scruples or general uprightness? The characters of Godijn, Hamel, and, despite the voluminous mass of his letters and memoranda, van Rensselaer, are too obscure to permit any presumption of honesty or dishonesty in regard to their dealings with the West India Company. Coenraets, burgomaster of Amsterdam

44. For Van Rensselaer's prohibition of the fur trade, see VRBM, pp. 161–62, 178–79, 193. De Vries, *Verscheyden voyagiens*, p. 156, mentions the fur trade at Swanendael in 1631. For the special permission granted in 1632, see VRBM, p. 241.

45. For these activities at Swanendael, see de Vries, *Verscheyden voyagiens*, pp. 147–48, and van Rensselaer, Memorial of 1633; in VRBM, pp. 240–41. For agricultural activities at Rensselaerswyck, see VRBM, pp. 162, 176–79, 184, 189–90, 195, 200, 233, and 306 ff.

46. De Vries, *Verscheyden voyagiens*, pp. 147–48.

47. Van Rensselaer to Johan de Laedt, June 27, 1632; in VRBM, p. 200.

and international diplomat, and the scholarly Johannes de Laet, author of two major books in the service of the Company, seem poor candidates for fraud. On the other hand, Blommaert was recalled from the East Indies in 1611 under suspicion of having seriously defrauded the East India Company, and in the 1630's his betrayal of West India Company secrets to the Swedes led directly to the Swedish attempt to carve New Sweden out of the southern part of New Netherland. More detailed information on the lives of Blommaert, Coenraets, and de Laet is given in Appendix II.

If the New Netherland commissioners were really inclined to defraud the Company, how might they have engineered the adoption of the *Vryheden?* Two general approaches are conceivable. (1) If the *Vryheden* had been notoriously prejudicial to the Company, the conspirators could only have obtained its enactment if they had been able to gain the support of enough directors to effectively control the Company and simply overpower the opposition. Or, (2) they might have distorted or suppressed information concerning the real situation in New Netherland, thereby deceiving their colleagues as to the necessary effects of the proposed policy.

Nissenson suggests that the *Vryheden* may have been obtained by the first approach when he stresses the "absolute control" of the West India Company directors vis-à-vis the participants and asserts darkly that "it was out of such a situation and in this spirit that the plan for patroonships was soon evolved." [48] However, in view of the decentralized nature of the West India Company and the variety of checks upon the maladministration of the directors which were considered in Chapter Two, an unalloyed power play would clearly have been virtually impossible. On the other hand, various circumstances would have favored the success of a deceptive approach. Even within Chamber Amsterdam, which was charged with the sole management of the province, New Netherland was of minor importance in relation to the total complex of activities. This circumstance, aggravated after November 1628 by the capture of the Silver Fleet, which provided the capital and example for vast new exploits, may not have encouraged directors other than the New Netherland commissioners to inform themselves in detail regarding New Netherland.

However, according to van Rensselaer, the opponents of the

48. *Patroon's domain,* p. 12.

New Netherland patroon system, who had forced the complete exclusion of the patroons from the fur trade in the New Netherland freedoms of 1628, were still maintaining an active opposition to an extension of the 1628 freedoms as late as February 1629.[49] Presumably these opponents would have made some effort to inform themselves concerning at least the basic economic realities in New Netherland, and if they had done so all the commissioners and their cohorts, including Coenraets and de Laet thus, would have had to present a convincing and perfectly united front in withholding or distorting damaging pieces of information.

Let us summarize our considerations.

1. Within about two years of the enactment of the *Vryheden*, the Company disavowed it and sought to eliminate the existing patroonships. Some members of the Company believed that the *Vryheden* had been obtained by fraud.

2. One of the commissioners for New Netherland, Samuel Blommaert, was a thoroughly unscrupulous character, who is known to have been false to the Company in later years.

3. It is possible that the Company's approval of an arrangement whereby the agents of Godijn, Blommaert, and van Rensselaer could obtain a considerable quantity of furs from New Netherland was obtained by connivance or deception on the part of these directors.

4. After the capture of the Silver Fleet, most directors of the Company probably directed little attention to New Netherland.

On the other hand:

1. The breadth of the privileges conferred by the *Vryheden* *per se* is no proof of its fraudulent procurement, since the *Vryheden* was substantially the same as previous freedoms for Guiana.

2. The patroons' participation in the fur trade was the principal grievance leveled against them. But their licit or illicit opportunities here would have been decidedly limited.

3. The fact that the commissioners for New Netherland leapt to take advantage of an opportunity which the Company was rejecting is not necessarily suspicious, since they seem to have advocated that the Company not give up the colonization of New Netherland.

---

49. Memorial of 1633; in VRBM, pp. 237–38.

4. The early activities of the patroons indicate a genuine interest in agricultural colonization.

5. Two of the commissioners, Coenraets and de Laet, seem unlikely candidates for conspirators against the Company.

6. It would have been impossible to have forced a notoriously prejudicial measure through the Company.

7. The proposals that the *Vryheden* be amplified received considerable scrutiny from at least February to June of 1629.

8. The *Vryheden* was eventually proclaimed lawfully obtained (as will be revealed in Chapter 6).

In the opinion of the writer, the case against the patroons is unproved.

CHAPTER SIX

THE CAMPAIGN AGAINST THE PATROONS

The capture of the Silver Fleet enabled the Company to pay all
its outstanding debts and distribute dividends totalling 75 percent.[1]
This full financial recovery emboldened the directors to make a
new attempt at the heartland of the Spanish-Portuguese empire.
Again they determined on Brazil, but instead of Bahia they chose
the captaincy of Pernambuco, rich in sugar and Brazil wood, as
their main objective.

On February 15, 1630, the West India Company's expedition
attacked the Pernambucan port of Recife and the neighboring town
of Olinda. By March 3, the Dutch had completely subjugated
these two places, but, just as at Bahia in 1624, they soon found
themselves closely invested. Substantial reinforcements arrived
from Holland from December 1630 to April 1631, but in the
spring of 1631 the Dutch found themselves no less beleaguered
than a year earlier. When a strong Iberian relief armada left
Portugal early in May, there was obvious danger of a repetition
of the Bahia debacle of 1625. However, in a naval action off Brazil
in September, this fate was narrowly averted.

The gravity of the Brazil situation about June 1631 could not
have failed to influence the directoral elections of that month to
the prejudice of the directors in office and to the benefit of dissident
and reformist spirits. Although the names of five of the six new
directors of Chamber Amsterdam are uncertain—the sixth was
undoubtedly Marcus de Vogelaer [2]—their reformist inclinations

1. De Laet, *Historie ofte Iaerlijck Verhael* (1644), Appendix, p. 9. Boxer,
Dutch in Brazil, p. 30.
2. Vogelaer was director in April 1634 (VRBM, pp. 282, 287) and after the
directoral elections of June 1636 (Blommaert, "Memorie Boeck"). Since the
normal term of a director was six years, he would have to have been elected in
either 1631 or 1633. But the 1633 directors are known, and they do not include
Vogelaer. It is thus apparent that, unless he acceded to the unexpired term of

are attested by their unquestioned responsibility for the radical changes in New Netherland policy which followed close upon their election.[3] Entirely in harmony with the vigor of their New Netherland policy was the 1632 decision to send two directors of the Company, Mattias van Ceulen and Johan Gijsselingh, to take personal charge of the desperate and so far ineffectual efforts to enlarge the Dutch toehold on Pernambuco; and it is reasonable to suppose that both the campaign against the New Netherland patroons and the energetic offensive led by van Ceulen and Gijsselingh in Brazil originated in the same reformist spirit of the new directors of 1631.[4]

In 1634 the aggrieved patroons traced the campaign against them to October 30, 1631,

> when new articles were forged, thereby the previous freedoms and exemptions were no longer obtainable; the patroons particularly commanded to perform things with exactness which experience taught them were impracticable. Yes, all the Exemptions were drawn into dispute.[5]

From this time until about the end of 1633, the Company prosecuted a systematic anti-patroon policy; thereafter it adopted a more conciliatory attitude, leading eventually to the extinguishing of the Swanendael and Pavonia patroonships by purchase in 1634/35.

The exact nature of the anti-patroon campaign during its virulent period is difficult to determine, because, in the absence of the resolution books of The Nineteen or the Amsterdam Chamber, we must depend largely on a critical assessment of the testimony of the patroons themselves. The broad outlines of the campaign which emerge from this assessment are as follows:

1. The Company disavowed the *Vryheden* as enacted on June 7, 1629, and sought to substitute for it more restrictive freedoms.[6]

another director, Vogelaer became director in 1631. As will be related, he was prominent in the opposition to the patroons.

3. Van Rensselaer to Dirck Cornelissz Duyster, July 20, 1632, in VRBM, p. 215. Van Rensselaer to Bastiaen Jansz Crol, July 20, 1632, in VRBM, p. 217.

4. The sending of van Ceulen and Gijsselingh to Brazil is related in de Laet, *Historie ofte Iaerlijck Verhael* (1644), pp. 295–96, and in Boxer, *Dutch in Brazil,* p. 51. Van Ceulen had a small interest in Swanendael, Godijn's patroonship on the Delaware River.

5. Paauw *et al.*, Memorial to the States General, June 1634, in DCHNY, I, p. 85; Dutch text in E. B. O'Callaghan, *History of New Netherland*, I, p. 130n.

6. *Ibid.*, in DCHNY, I, pp. 85, 86, 88. Van Rensselaer, Memorial of 1633, in VRBM, p. 244.

The ostensible grounds for this action were probably the sup-
posedly illegal means by which the *Vryheden* was obtained.[7]

2. It made strenuous efforts to exclude the patroons from the
fur trade by a variety of means, some implying merely rigorous
enforcement of provisions of the *Vryheden*, some seemingly tend-
ing to abridge the patroons' rights. Among the latter was issuance
on November 18, 1632 of a placard, which, according to statements and insinuations of the patroons, seems to have excluded
their colonists or agents from the fur trade, even in places and
under conditions permitted by the *Vryheden*.[8] A second questionable procedure was the exaction from the patroons' colonists of an
oath constraining them not to trade in furs, *sewan*, or maize.[9]
The Company was on firmer legal ground when it introduced a
factor at Swanendael, thereby terminating the patroons' right to
barter furs there according to Article XV of the *Vryheden*, forbade the patroons the import of trading truck into New Netherland, and confiscated furs which were improperly exported from
thence.[10]

7. On November 24, 1633, the question was proposed in the Amsterdam Chamber "whether the conditions granted to parties planting colonies should be considered as having been lawfully obtained, which is answered in the affirmative . . ."
("Extract uijt Register der Resolutie van: E: Heeren Bewinthebberen van:
westjndische Comp ter camere van Amstl," in New York Colonial Manuscripts,
VIII, p. 36 (badly burned); English translation in DCHNY, XIV, p. 357). This
question carries the strong implication that the Company had hitherto questioned
the legality of the procurement of the *Vryheden*.

8. The placard was a revision of an earlier one which had purported to protect
the patroons against private individuals in the fur trade, and it evidently had the
effect of depriving "the Patroons altogether of the trade" (Paauw et al., Memorial
to the States General, in DCHNY, I, p. 85). It is probably obliquely referred to
in a list of the patroons' "pretensions" adjoined to their 1634 memorial: "The
Company cannot affix, in the Patroons' colonies, without their knowledge, and
against their will, placards excluding everyone from the entire fur trade. . . ."
(*Ibid.*, p. 88).

9. Van Rensselaer complained "it has likewise happened lately that the Director of New Netherland has held his people idle for a long time at the Manhattans
and would not let them travel farther up the river unless they took an unlawful
oath, given him by the Chamber of Amsterdam . . ." (Memorial of 1633; VRBM,
p. 243). This is probably referred to among the patroons' "pretensions" adjoining
their 1634 memorial: "[The Company cannot] constrain the Patroons' inhabitants,
by an oath drawn up for the purpose, not to trade in peltries, wampum or maize"
(DCHNY, I, p. 88).

10. For the introduction of a factor at Swanendael and the prohibition of the
import of trading truck, see van Rensselaer's Memorial of 1633, in VRBM, pp. 247,
and 241, 243. An action similar to the placing of a factor at Swanendael may have
been van Twiller's sending of a Company yacht to accompany David de Vries'
yacht "to the North" in April 1633 (de Vries, *Verscheyden voyagiens*, p. 176).

3. The Company harassed the patroons in various ways. Though the Company did not entirely prevent shipments to their colonies, the patroons claimed that it evaded its responsibility to transport their goods and animals in its ships. Van Rensselaer had to suffer the appointment of a *commis* (factor) at Fort Orange who was avowedly hostile to the patroons, the denial of permission to remove animals which he had purchased from the Manhattan farmers to Rensselaerswyck, and a formal resolution refusing him the occasional hire of idle carpenters and smiths in the service of the Company and the barter of the produce of Rensselaerswyck for needed provisions.[11]

What exactly was the Company's objective in embarking on this repressive policy? In the first place, there was an undoubted necessity of checking the presumption evidenced in the large haul of furs procured by the two agents of Godijn, Blommaert, and van Rensselaer in 1629–30 and perhaps in other operations, for

Van Rensselaer rises to heights of both eloquence and hypocrisy when he describes the Company's confiscation of 205 furs obtained during the second voyage of the Swanendael partners' *Walvis*: " And most intolerable of all is, that after the remonstrants had given these 205 skins upon their arrival into the hands of the Chamber of Amsterdam that it might levy its duty on the same, this chamber threw them among and mingled them with its own skins and also sold them with its own goods, . . . just as if all the goods of the patroons were free booty or confiscated (who is so perfect, that he can bear all this wrong!) . . ." (Memorial of 1633, in VRBM, p. 242). He neglected to add, however, that David de Vries, commander of the *Walvis*, had failed to enter at least some of these skins at Fort Amsterdam as he was required to do, and that, when this was discovered by the Secretary of New Netherland, de Vries refused to hand over the skins and boasted that he would fight off a Company ship which the Secretary threatened to send after him (de Vries, *Verscheyden voyagiens*, pp. 177–78). Whether the *f* 5,600 worth of furs which the agents of Godijn and his associates obtained with merchandise left over after the purchase of Swanendael was justifiably confiscated is entirely unknown. Van Rensselaer, of course, implies that it was not, but in view of his above distortion, his unsupported testimony cannot be accepted (Memorial of 1633; in VRBM, pp. 238–39, 240).

11. Van Rensselaer claimed that the Company had evaded its responsibility to transport goods and animals in his Memorial of 1633, in VRBM, p. 242. Among the " pretensions " of the 1634 Memorial of Paauw *et al.* is the assertion that the Company was not free to refuse to freight the patroons' goods or to charge more than the freight allowed in the *Vryheden*, implying that the Company had done or threatened to do these things (DCHNY, I, p. 87). Yet van Rensselaer sent cattle in the Company's ship *Southerch* in 1632 (VRBM, pp. 242, 274).

The appointment of the hostile *commis*, the refusal to permit animals purchased at the Manhattans to proceed to Rensselaerswyck, and the formal resolution mentioned are all reported in van Rensselaer's 1633 Memorial, in VRBM, pp. 242–43. For the hostility of the *commis* and the difficulty about the Manhattan animals, see also VRBM, pp. 215–16 and 291, 297–98, 310.

otherwise the Company's New Netherland enterprise faced piece-
meal engrossment by the patroons.[12] Might this requirement,
fanned by the emotional need to obtain revenge for what some
regarded, rightly or wrongly, as the fraudulent procurement of the
Vryheden, have prompted punitive measures, designed merely to
discourage the patroons from future effronteries? Slight but convincing evidence indicates that the design of the new directors
transcended this limited objective and contemplated the very extinction or at least severe curtailment of the existing patroonships in
order to clear the way for a fur trade effectively monopolized by
the Company. In his 1633 memorial van Rensselaer asserted " the
main cause of all these differences is nothing but the trade in furs
. . . and the question by whom it shall be conducted " and then
developed a long and persuasive argument against the economic
feasibility of abandoning the colonization and concentrating solely
on the fur trade.[13] The inclusion of this argument as the crux of
van Rensselaer's petition is hard to explain unless the directors
were indeed contemplating such a step.

The long-run result of what was in effect a return to the New
Netherland Company's system of exploiting New Netherland
during the years of its charter could only be loss of the province
to another European power.[14] But, as a business organization, the
West India Company was seeking not colonization for colonization's sake, but profits. If taxation of a privately colonized province would not produce a reasonable profit or if the long-run
political viability of even a moderately populated New Netherland
was questionable, maximization of profits in the short run through
systematic mining of the region's fur resources was the only
reasonable alternative. Eventually the mine would collapse under

12. Van Rensselaer's procurement of cattle for Rensselaerswyck by purchase from
Manhattan farmers whom the Company had ordered to return to the Netherlands,
while strictly legal, still had the effect of denuding the Manhattans to build up
Rensselaerswyck, rather than of strengthening the colony as a whole. In a letter
to his partner Johannes de Laet, van Rensselaer admitted that his cattle dealings
made many " jealous " of him (Letter of June 27, 1632; in VRBM, p. 284).
13. In VRBM, pp. 244–48.
14. That the directors opposing the patroons were aware of this danger is perhaps indicated by a statement imputed to Vogelaer. In a letter to van Twiller of
April 1634, van Rensselaer expressed concern about English encroachments on the
Connecticut River: "but Mr. Vogelaer does not worry much about this, I think,
since he says he would rather be bitten by strange dogs than his own " (VRBM,
p. 284).

French or English pressure, but the vulnerable stock of fixed capital required by a trading enterprise was small, and in the meantime profits might be accumulated, especially if the number of smuggler-colonists was curtailed.

It is perhaps indicative of the basic prudence of a short run approach *per se* that van Rensselaer focused his above mentioned argument not upon the dangers or foregone profits which would attend abandonment of colonization in the long run, but upon the simple inability of the Company to reap a short run profit. The most that could be obtained from New Netherland, he reasoned, was *f* 60,000–70,000 annually, even if the colonists were gone. But, since the fur trade of New Netherland was not geographically concentrated but extremely far-flung,

> it will be found, no matter how economically it may be managed, that the ship which must go with merchandise from the Fatherland and return . . . the garrison and fort at the Manhattans, the garrison and fort at Fort Orange, the yachts and sloops for the trade on the South [Delaware] River and the northern regions, besides the sloops plying between, counting all expenses of building, arming, equipping, keeping up, manning and victualing, will cost so [much] that the aforesaid 60,000 or 70,000 guilders, which are the utmost to be expected thence, will come far short by many thousands.[15]

We must do our best to check this bold assertion. Let us assume that the Company planned to maintain a total resident staff of seventy-five persons in New Netherland, two light yachts and four sloops or shallops, and appropriate armament for Forts Orange and Amsterdam. Let us suppose further that the Company would service the New Netherland trade with a single chartered merchantman each year, and would reduce the risks of famine and lack of trading truck attendant on the fortunes of a single vessel by maintenance of stockpiles of rations and merchandise in excess of normal requirements.[16] What estimates can we make of the costs of this operation?

15. Memorial of 1633, in *Oud Holland*, VIII, p. 65, and in VRBM, p. 245.
16. The staff of Fort Orange at this time was about twenty-five men (VRBM, p. 200). I am assuming, therefore, that the Company would base a staff of double this size at the Manhattans, which would be the only permanent post other than Fort Orange. The use of a single " ordinary freighter of large hold " was practicable, as it was strongly urged by van Rensselaer (Memorial of 1633, in VRBM, p. 236).

Per annum

Wages for 75 men at an average of ƒ 170 per man
per year [17] .... ƒ 12,750

Provisions for 75 men at an average of ƒ 100 per man
per year [18] 7,500

10% annual depreciation of two light yachts, two
sloops, and two shallops, valued in all at ƒ 6000
new [19] 600

Naval stores for the above per year [20] 1,000

Munitions

25% annual depreciation of hand
weapons for 75 men, valued in all at
ƒ 900 new [21] .... ƒ 225

10% annual depreciation of cannon for

---

17. A 1645 project to place Curaçao under the administration of the Director of New Netherland estimated that a 116 man garrison at Curaçao, containing a wide variety of soldiers, sailors, and artisans would cost in wages ƒ 1,327 per month, that is ƒ 15,924 per year. In addition the plan allocated ƒ 2,985:10 in " merchandise necessary to be distributed to the garrisons in part payment of their monthly wages," evidently yearly. ƒ 15,924 + ƒ 2,985:10 = ƒ 18,909:10, which comes to an average of ƒ 163 per man per year (DCHNY, I, pp. 166, 169–70). De Laet estimated the wages paid the Company's personnel from 1625–1636 very roughly at ƒ 180 per man per year (Historie ofte Iaerlijck Verhael (1644), Appendix, p. 8).

18. The 1645 Curaçao project estimated the cost of food for 116 men for one year at ƒ 10,123:6, or slightly over ƒ 87 per man per annum (DCHNY, I, pp. 167–68). In 1632 van Rensselaer estimated the cost of providing the Company's twenty-five man Fort Orange garrison " with everything " at ƒ 2,500 per year (VRBM, p. 200).

19. D'Omvallende Nooteboom, a yacht of 16 lasts about one and one-half years old, well built of dry New Netherland timber, with masts and spars, but without sails and rigging, was valued at ƒ 2000 in 1626. At the same time an 8-last yacht of unrecorded age with all appurtenances except anchors, cables, and armaments, was valued at ƒ 1000. Smaller craft of unknown condition mentioned in the same valuation were a sloop of 3 lasts at ƒ 300, a Zaandam barge at ƒ 150, and a Biscayan shallop at ƒ 80 (GAA, Not. Arch., Portf. 256, Reg. 61, fol. 331, in Stokes, Iconography, VI, p. 13; GAA, Not. Arch. 592, p. 307v, in Hart, Prehistory, p. 38n). In 1645 one-half of a tight and seaworthy " shallop " sold for ƒ 225 in New Netherland ("New York Colonial Manuscripts," IV, p. 239). In 1651 one-half of the yacht Zeepaert with its appurtenances sold for ƒ 300 in merchandise (ibid., III, p. 82).

20. The 1645 Curaçao project estimated the (yearly ?) naval stores for the 5-gun and 30-man ship Paraquit, a sloop, and jolly boat at ƒ 1,896:17. This sum included over ƒ 600 in various sorts of boards which were unobtainable in Curaçao, but probably free for the cutting in New Netherland.

21. The city of Amsterdam estimated the cost of hand weapons and their appurtenances for 150 men to be sent to New Netherland in 1656 at ƒ 1,843 (DCHNY, I, p. 645).

Forts Amsterdam and Orange, consisting of 10 cast iron pieces and 20 light
cannon; valued in all at ƒ 4000 [22] . . . . .   ƒ   400
1200 lbs. new powder yearly at ƒ 35 per
cwt [23] . . . .   ƒ   420
600 lbs. musket balls, 50 cannon balls,
600 lbs. pig lead, 4 reams cartridge
paper [24] . . . .   ƒ   225
                                                                ƒ 1,270   1,270
Charter of a well armed 150-last merchantman at
ƒ 1100 per month,[25] for seven months.   7,700
10% annual spoilage of a stockpile of 6 months
rations, valued at ƒ 3750 [26]   375
5% spoilage of a stockpile of ƒ 10,000 in trading
merchandise   500
Miscellaneous storage and accounting expenses in the
Netherlands   500
                                                                           ƒ 32,195

These estimates are, of course, very inexact: in some cases the
price data has of necessity been taken from twenty-five and thirty
years after 1631–33. Since the figures tend to be padded rather
than deflated, it is probably fair to conclude, however, that the
overhead costs of the fur trade would not exceed by very much
one-half of the gross receipts of ƒ 60,000–70,000 estimated by van
Rensselaer.

22. In 1647 ten *ijsere gotelingen* (cast iron pieces) on the old ship *Swol* were
valued at ƒ 2000 (New York Colonial Manuscripts, II, p. 169). This price is in
general agreement with a statement of David de Vries that heavy cannon usually
cost ƒ 9 or ƒ 10 per hundred pounds in 1618, especially when one considers that
the price of artillery probably rose after the end of the Truce in 1621 (de Vries,
Verscheyden voyagiens, p. 4). *Gotelingen* might weigh anywhere from 800 to
1500 pounds (" Placaten . . . behelsende ordre opte Wapeninge en Manninge van
Schepen . . ."; *Groot Placaet-Boeck*, I, cols. 876-92).

23. The 1645 Curaçao project estimated 1200 pounds of new powder at ƒ 405,
or ƒ 33:15 per cwt (DCHNY, I, p. 168).

24. These quantities, at this price, were judged necessary for the fort at Curaçao
and a five-gun yacht in the 1645 Curaçao project (DCHNY, I, pp. 168–69).

25. This estimate is based on eight charter parties for Amsterdam–New Netherland–Amsterdam voyages from 1651–1662 (but not including voyages during the
first Anglo-Dutch war) (GAA, Not. Arch., 1534, p. 173; 1538, p. 268; 1539,
pp. 20 and 107; 2793, pp. 414 and 695; 2794, pp. 109 and 448).

26. See note 18.

Given these overhead costs, the profitability of the entire enterprise would depend on the terms of trade with the Indians. The only indication of these terms is given by Johannes de Laet in the appendix to his history of the West India Company's operations through 1636. A list of " returns from New Netherland " gives the annual number of " beavers, otters, etc." received by the Company from 1624–35, together with the proceeds of their sale in Europe. The sum of the proceeds for this period was f 725,117. Conceivably a little timber may have been included under the " etc.," but even so the total must closely approximate the value of furs obtained. The rubric " purchase of goods and merchandise which have been purchased in and sent from this country " lists a total of f 331,284 sent to New Netherland in the same period. Evidently this classification does not include the Company's shipments of agricultural capital or provisions, for in 1625, the year of the Company's principal colonization effort, the shipments under this column were unusually light, only f 8,772.[27] The most reasonable explanation is that these imports comprise the goods for which the furs were bartered. If this was the case, the Company received about 2.18/1 on its merchandise over 1624–1635. Applying this ratio to a return of f 65,000 in furs, we get an expenditure on trading merchandise of very nearly f 30,000. When this sum is added to the overhead costs of the trading establishment and when insurance on the merchandise to and furs from New Netherland is computed, our computations do indeed tend to confirm van Rensselaer's claim that the Company could not obtain a profit from its fur monopoly:

Merchandise	f 30,000
Insurance on above to New Netherland and	
f 65,000 from New Netherland at 6% each way	5,700
Overhead	32,195
	f 67,895
Returns	f 65,000
Deficit	f 2,895

Van Rensselaer anticipated that his opponents would reply to his predictions of losses

27. *Historie ofte Iaerlijck Verhael* (1644), Appendix, pp. 26–27 (" purchases ") ; 29–30 (" returns ").

that much more than 60,000 or 70,000 guilders could be gotten there annually, especially if the colonists who so defraud them were gone and if attention were devoted entirely to the benefit of the trade.[28]

Whether a significant increase in the trade as a result of elimination of the colonists was a realistic expectation is debatable: van Rensselaer side-steps the general question by pointing out that the Swanendael enterprise had actually benefited the Company trade by opening up a new region of trade for the Company. But it is reasonably certain that the negligence of the Company's New Netherland employees had hitherto reduced the trade far below its potential. In 1630, for example, a year when the Company obtained 6041 beavers and 1085 otters, grossing together f 68,012, Sijmen Dircxz Pos, a councillor in New Netherland, wrote to van Rensselaer

> The Director-General and Jan Romonde (the Secretary) are very much embittered against one another. Here all is left to drift as it will; they let trade slip away and do not exert themselves to increase it either by sloops or otherwise, but are very diligent in bringing exorbitant suits and charges against one another and in neglecting the interests and business of the directors.[29]

Since, assuming our estimates of overhead costs and terms of trade are correct, the break-even point was a return of about f 71,000, there must have been a good possibility that a new and energetic staff could pull the operation out of the red.

*

One facet of the implementation of the new directors' policy, the repressive measures against the patroons at home and in New Netherland, has already been outlined. A second major aspect was the replacement of objectionable personnel in New Netherland. According to van Rensselaer, opposition within the Company prevented the new directors from full application of their general principle of calling home all the old New Netherland

28. Memorial of 1633, in *Oud Holland*, VIII, p. 66, and VRBM, p. 246.
29. De Laet, *Historie ofte Iaerlijck Verhael* (1644), Appendix, pp. 29–30, gives the number of furs in 1630. Pos's letter of September 16, 1630 is in *Oud Holland*, VIII, p. 70, and in VRBM, pp. 169–70.

personnel, a few excepted, and sending out an altogether new staff.[30] Nevertheless, the reformers were able to recall Director-General Bastiaen Crol, and demote the Fort Orange *commis* to *ondercommis*, along with several lesser changes.[31] The replacements for these officials, the ex-clerk of the West India Company house in Amsterdam, Wouter van Twiller, who replaced Crol, and Hans Hunthum, who had traded in New Netherland in the days of the *voorcompagnieën* and who now combined intransigence against the patroons with the promise to obtain 13,000 skins yearly, sailed away on the *Southerch* about the end of July 1632.[32] Presumably their instructions prescribed energetic and economical measures in the fur trade. A final ascertainable expression of the directors' new policy was economy in shipping. After the *Southerch* in 1632, no vessel was dispatched to New Netherland until the *Eendracht*, which sailed about May 1634.[33]

The *Southerch* arrived in New Netherland after a long and eventful voyage in February or early March of 1633. The new staff was therefore at least partially responsible for the fur returns of 1633 and entirely so for those of 1634. De Laet records a very lucrative 1633 return: 8800 beavers and 1383 "otters/etc.,"

30. Van Rensselaer to Bastiaen Jansz Crol, July 20, 1632, in VRBM, pp. 217–18.
Director-General Minuit, the Secretary, Dominie Michaëlius, and several lesser Company employees were probably summoned home by the *Eendracht*, which sailed from Holland shortly after July 7, 1631. (For the sailing date of the *Eendracht*, see VRBM, p. 189; for the date of the removal of Minuit *et al.*, see note 34.) But though the *Eendracht* sailed at least a month after the fateful directoral changes of 1631, there is no evidence that the new directors were responsible for the replacement of the Minuit government and some evidence to the contrary: Crol, Minuit's replacement, thanked *van Rensselaer* for promoting him to the directorship of New Netherland (VRBM, p. 217). Arnoldus Buchelius, a cousin of the manager of the patroonship of Pavonia, mentions the return of Minuit *et al.*, in 1632 as a result of their "not being able to get along together," but says nothing about the group within the Company which determined on their recall (Stokes, *Iconography*, IV, p. 944, from a manuscript in the Rijksarchief).

31. VRBM, p. 217. Albert Dieterinck, who was summoned home at this time, seems to have been stationed at Fort Orange (VRBM, pp. 216–17). Perhaps he was the old *ondercommis* who was replaced by the demoted former *commis*. Also summoned home at this time was the wheelwright at the Manhattans (VRBM, p. 232).

32. Van Twiller was a nephew of van Rensselaer, but this fact seems to have had no bearing on his appointment. De Vries, no admirer of van Twiller, describes him as an ex-clerk (de Vries, *Verscheyden voyagiens*, p. 174). For Hunthum, see VRBM, pp. 215–16, 243, 273.

33. De Laet records no imports into New Netherland for 1633 (*Historie ofte Iaerlijck Verhael* [1644], Appendix, pp. 26–27). For indications of the sailing date of the *Eendracht*, see VRBM, pp. 300, 315.

yielding together the magnificent sum of f 91,375. However, since the second shipment of 1631–32 furs was unusually light, it is probable that the 1633 figures include furs obtained in the latter part of 1632. The 1634 and 1635 figures are lumped together. The average for these years was 7,445½ beavers and 707½ otters, taken together an improvement over the c. 6,500 beavers and 835 otters averaged from 1628–1632, but no very startling increase.[34]

If the immediate results of the new policy were not spectacular, this was not necessarily the fault of the policy. Indeed, it is a wonder that the trade increased at all in view of the extremely unfortunate circumstances in 1633 and 1634. Hunthum, it developed, had a black reputation with the Mohawks from his *voorcompagnieën* days, and van Twiller proved drunken and incompetent to handle the besetting difficulties of these years. In April 1633 an English expedition brushed past an irresolute van Twiller at the Manhattans and traded for several weeks in the immediate vicinity of Fort Orange before being expelled by the Dutch. The disturbance created by the presence of these intruders, combined with the Mohawks' animosity towards Hunthum, undoubtedly had a depressing effect on the Fort Orange trade, and one or both of these irritants may have led to the burning of a Company yacht by the savages. In September 1633 a more enduring, though less proximal threat developed. A party from New Plymouth defied the newly constructed Fort Good Hope on the Connecticut and proceeded to build their own post farther upriver. An armed troop was dispatched from the Manhattans, but the Plymouth men held their ground, and the Dutch force withdrew without offering any violence.[35]

---

34. O'Callaghan misinterprets de Vries in placing the arrival of the *Southerch* in April (*History of New Netherland*, I, pp. 141 and 141n; De Vries, *Verscheyden voyagiens*, pp. 173–74). Bastiaen Crol placed the arrival of the English traders under Eelckens (18 April) at a month after the arrival of Hans Hunthum, which would place the *Southerch*'s arrival in mid-March (VRBM, p. 303. Date of Eelckens' arrival from de Vries, p. 174). Arguing for a still earlier date are inventories of Minuit's and Bijlvelt's farms dated January 1 and 14, 1632. Since such inventories would logically have been made preparatory to the owners' departure for Holland, it is reasonable to suppose that Minuit had already been removed from office by this time. If this was the case, van Twiller's arrival would have been not after February 1633, since Crol, Minuit's successor and van Twiller's predecessor, served in office thirteen months (VRBM, p. 302).

For the fur returns from 1631–1635, see de Laet, *Historie ofte Iaerlijck Verhael* (1644), Appendix, pp. 29–30.

35. For the incompetence of van Twiller, see van Rensselaer to van Twiller,

In April 1634 the objectionable Hunthum was killed, but towards the end of that year the Fort Orange trade "was doing very badly." [36] In December an expedition was sent deep into the interior to ascertain the cause. Its findings revealed that a truce had been made between the Iroquois and the "French" Indians and that the result, contrary to the expectation of van Rensselaer, who had believed that peace would lead to an import of Canadian furs to Fort Orange, was a flow of Iroquoisan furs toward the French.[37]

*

Hendrick Hamel, a participant in Swanendael, was among the retiring directors in June 1633, but this loss to the patroonal interest was more than compensated by the reappointment to the directorate of the influential Albert Coenraets, recently returned from his embassy to the Czar. Coenraets, as one of the original commissioners of New Netherland and registrant of a patroonship on the Delaware in 1629, shared responsibility for the enactment of the *Vryheden*. His re-elevation to the directorate and subsequent reappointment as commissioner of New Netherland produced, therefore, a counterweight on the New Netherland com-

April 23, 1634, in VRBM, pp. 266–88; and de Vries, *Verscheyden voyagiens*, pp. 173 ff. For Hunthum's reputation with the Mohawks, see "Examination of Bastiaen Jansz Crol . . . ," June 30, 1634, in VRBM, pp. 302–04; and van Rensselaer's Memorial of 1633, in VRBM, p. 243. The English trading expedition to the Fort Orange area in 1633 is documented by (1) "Examination of Bastiaen Jansz Crol . . . ," in VRBM, pp. 302–04; (2) de Vries, *Verscheyden voyagiens*, pp. 174 ff.; and (3) DCHNY, I, pp. 71–81, 93–95.

Van Rensselaer asserted that the yacht was burned and some Rensselaerswyck cattle killed by way of revenge against Hunthum in his 1633 memorial (VRBM, p. 243), but, since in April 1634 he privately admitted his uncertainty as to whether Hunthum was the cause of the killing of the cattle (VRBM, p. 286), this was probably just propaganda. Crol connects Hunthum only circumstantially with the burning of the yacht (VRBM, pp. 303–304). In October 1634 the West India Company laid the blame for "injurious seeds of division sown between the Indians and our people" and "other serious mischiefs . . . such as the killing of men and cattle" on the English intruders (DCHNY, I, pp. 93–95).

O'Callaghan, *History of New Netherland*, I, p. 155, describes the confrontation with the Plymouth men on the Connecticut.

36. "Narrative of a journey into the Mohawk and Oneida Country, 1634–35," in NNN, p. 139. For the death of Hunthum, see Deposition of Corn. Martsz van Buren, from GAA, Not. Arch. 843, printed in "Some Early Dutch Manuscripts," ed. A. J. F. van Laer, *New York State Historical Association Quarterly Journal*, III (1922), p. 230.

37. "Narrative of a journey . . . ," *passim.*, in NNN, pp. 139–57. Van Rensselaer expressed his expectation in his 1633 Memorial, in VRBM, p. 248.

mission to Marcus de Vogelaer, the soul of the opposition to the patroons, and heralded at the very least a rejection of the standpoint that the *Vryheden* was fraudulently procured.[38]

By November 1633 the Company had adopted an attitude of cautious conciliation. November 19, The Nineteen invited the patroons to present their grievances. On the 24th, after receipt of the statement of the Swanendael partners, but a day before van Rensselaer penned his oft-quoted and historiographically highly important memorial, the Amsterdam Chamber passed a resolution of great moment: the *Vryheden* was henceforth to be regarded as lawfully obtained, and the New Netherland commissioners were charged to re-examine the question of the patroonships on that basis. This acknowledgment by the Amsterdam Chamber was confirmed by The Nineteen on December 19, when a committee of six from all the chambers, including Coenraets from Amsterdam, was appointed to negotiate a settlement with the patroons. At the same time the Company adopted the equitable, but potentially dangerous, principle that irresolvable differences be submitted to the States General or the Court of Justice.[39]

Avowal that the *Vryheden* was legally acquired implied acceptance of its conditions as contractually binding. At this juncture, therefore, the Company must have been prepared to observe at least a narrow interpretation of the charter. It soon developed, however, that the Company's desire for conciliation did not extend to acquiescence in a markedly generous interpretation. The patroons pressed hard for the right to trade merchandise for furs in New Netherland, hoping perhaps that their more or less justified claims for compensation for their injuries might enhance the tenuous contractual grounds for the privilege; but this the Company, cleaving to the obvious interpretation of the XVth article

38. Hamel's retirement and Coenraet's reelection are noted in VRBM, p. 270. For Vogelaer's influence on the New Netherland commission, see van Rensselaer to van Twiller, April 23, 1634, in VRBM, pp. 266–88, especially pp. 282 and 287.

39. The Company's invitation to the patroons to present their grievances is mentioned in van Rensselaer's Memorial of 1633, in VRBM, pp. 248–49. For the resolution of November 24, see "Extract uijt Register der Resolutie van: E. Heeren Bewinthebberen van: westjndische Comp ter camere in Amstl," in New York Colonial Manuscripts, VIII, p. 41 (partially burned), translation in DCHNY, XIV, p. 357. For the resolution of December 19, see "Extract uijt het register der Resolutien van: E. Heeren gecommiteerde ter vergaederinge van XIX der Westjndische Compe althans tot amsterdam. Lunae den 19en December 1633," in New York Colonial Manuscripts, VIII, pp. 40–41 (badly burned). Translation in DCHNY, XIV, p. 356.

of the *Vryheden*, refused to grant. This and perhaps other questions of interpretation or compensation blocked an amicable agreement; and on March 27, 1634 The Nineteen, perhaps confident of the justice of its case, perhaps compelled by legal maneuvers of the patroons, perhaps moved by a high-minded but not necessarily politic desire for an equitable solution, referred the differences with the patroons to the binding arbitration and judgment of the States General.[40]

On May 13, 1634, the States General appointed a committee to hear and decide the dispute, but a month elapsed before arbitration actually began on June 14. The proceedings of the hearings are very imperfectly known, but it is clear that the patroons sought a decision on their own aggressive interpretation of the *Vryheden* to prepare the ground for specific claims against the Company, while the Company strove to avoid such a decision and tried to limit eventual claims against it. Ten days after the opening of the hearings, the States General postponed deciding the controversy for twelve days, during which the parties were to try to settle their differences on their own, and there is no evidence that the government resumed official intervention in the dispute. On July 21, 1634 van Rensselaer wrote to his partner in Rensselaerswyck, Johannes de Laet, that the Company seemed to be inclined to extinguish the patroonships by purchase and that the patroons had consented on condition of receiving a reasonable price. This inclination was converted to decision on August 22, when directors were commissioned by The Nineteen to negotiate the purchase of the patroonships.[41]

40. An example of the Company's readiness to observe a narrow interpretation of the *Vryheden* was its willingness to permit the patroons to trade the produce of their patroonships for furs where the Company had no *commis*, that is to enjoy their rights under Article XV of the *Vryheden* which were hitherto denied them (van Rensselaer to van Twiller, April 23, 1634; in VRBM, pp. 266–67).

The patroons' hope that they would be permitted to trade merchandise for furs is mentioned in VRBM, pp. 266, 282, 284. The tenuousness of the grounds for such a concession is revealed in the " pretensions " annexed to the memorial of Paauw *et al.*, to the States General. The patroons deduced the right to send merchandise to New Netherland, though not necessarily to trade it for furs, from their obligation to satisfy the Indians for the soil of the patroonships (Art. XXVI of the *Vryheden*) and their unquestioned right to trade on the North American coasts north and south of New Netherland (Art. XIII) (DCHNY, I, pp. 86–87). Writing in April 1634 to van Twiller, van Rensselaer stated that the sending of merchandise to New Netherland was the only point in dispute (VRBM, p. 266). For the referral of the differences with the patroons to the judgment of the States General, see DCHNY, pp. 69, 90.

41. The States General's summons to the parties to appear on the 14th of June

An agreement with the Swanendael partners was concluded on November 27, 1634. At this time the principal assets of the Swanendael enterprise were (1) claims arising from the Company's campaign against the patroons, (2) rights of jurisdiction and trade under the *Vryheden*, and (3) title to land. The first seems to have been excepted from the transaction by a clause excluding a lawsuit between the Swanendael partners and the West India Company pending before the Court of Amsterdam; but the second and third were taken over by the Company. The two tracts of land in question were on Delaware Bay, one a strip one-half league in depth stretching from Cape Hinlopen eight leagues towards the mouth of the river, the other containing sixteen square leagues on the peninsula of Cape May. On the first tract the partners had begun an agricultural colony in 1631, but it was totally exterminated by the Indians in 1631/32, and the 1632/33 voyage, probably the last equipped by the partners, seems to have been largely directed at whaling and not to have led to the resuscitation of significant agricultural activity. It is improbable, therefore, that the Company acquired as real effects more than a few remotely located buildings and perhaps a shallop, train kettle, or other implement for whaling, besides its land purchase. The purchase price was *f* 15,600 to be paid in three installments from 1635–1637. Computing six percent interest, this represented *f* 13,962 cash down.[42]

is in DCHNY, I, p. 71. For an indication that the hearings were under way by June 15, see DCHNY, I, p. 82.

Three documents proceeding from the hearings have survived: (1) a memorial of Paauw *et al.*, with its annexed "Pretension and Claim" (DCHNY, I, pp. 83–88); (2) a short and evasive answer of the West India Company to the preceding (DCHNY, I, p. 89); and (3) the reply of the patroons to the foregoing answer (DCHNY, I, pp. 89–90). The States General postponed rendering judgment in the dispute to permit the parties to work out their own settlement by its resolution of June 24, 1634 (in DCHNY, I, p. 91).

Van Rensselaer's communication to de Laet is in VRBM, pp. 312–13. The August 22, 1634, decision is mentioned in the conveyance of Swanendael (in O'Callaghan, *History of New Netherland*, I, p. 479).

42. Conveyance of Swanendael, dated Feb. 7, 1635, in O'Callaghan, *History of New Netherland*, I, pp. 479–80. The land deeds mentioned in this conveyance appear in full in DCHNY, I, p. 43, and XII, pp. 17–18.

Two pieces of evidence indicate the abandonment of agriculture at Swanendael. In 1636 Hendrick de Forest, who was engaged by the Swanendael patroons to serve at Swanendael in December 1631, declared that "owing to the sad tidings coming from New Netherland the [patroons] changed their minds and did not think it advisable to settle any people at Swanendael for the time being" (Declara-

The resolutions of the Amsterdam Chamber reveal that that chamber accepted Michiel Paauw's terms for the purchase of his " Pavonia " on January 1, 1635,[43] but not much is known about the content of the agreement. Pavonia at this time included Staten Island and on the mainland Hoboken and the adjoining tract of Ahasimus; and, according to de Vries, it was very favorably located for the interception of the fur trade, since it was from within its limits that the Indians normally crossed over to the Manhattans with their furs.[44] The exact state of its agricultural development is unknown, but it probably possessed two well equipped *bouwerijen*.[45] Transfer of this enterprise entailed the Company's assumption of Paauw's obligations under current contracts with his colonists; and, since Paauw had granted his colonists the right to trade privately for furs, the Company was obliged to continue this privilege to the termination of their contracts, at least to the extent that Paauw's grant had accorded with the *Vryheden*. Aside from this annoying obligation, very little is known about the specific conditions of the contract. If analogous to the Swanendael conveyance, it excluded the patroon's claims for damages. The purchase price was 26,000 florins, but the terms of payment are unknown.[46] If the debt was paid off by the same system of install-

tion of Hendrick de Forest; from GAA; in de Forest, *A Walloon Family*, II, p. 352). David de Vries, commander of the 1632/33 voyage to Swanendael, says nothing about resuscitated agricultural enterprise there in his account of the voyage (de Vries, *Verscheyden voyagiens*, pp. 148–83).

43. Van Grol, *Grondpolitiek*, II, p. 54.

44. The patents to Paauw for these tracts are in DCHNY, XIII, pp. 1–3. De Vries' comment in *Verscheyden voyagiens*, p. 247.

45. The Company owned three *bouwerijen* at Pavonia in 1638–39: (1) that leased to the widow of Cornelis van Vorst, Paauw's director at Pavonia, in March 1639 (New York Colonial Manuscripts, I, p. 92); (2) that leased in July 1638 to Jan Evertsz Bout, who came to New Netherland in Paauw's service in 1634, (*ibid.*, p. 53, in DCHNY, XIII, p. 3); and (3) an only partially completed farm leased to van Vorst's son in March 1639 (p. 76, *ibid.*, p. 4). The Manatus maps of 1639 show no other *bouwerijen* in this area beside these three, though they do show five *plantages*, which in the terminology of the period meant not complete farms but fields for the cultivation of a single crop. (The maps are in Stokes, *Iconography*, II, plates 41 and 42.) Since the Company seems not to have made any effort to improve New Netherland agriculture from 1635 to 1638, it is probable that the two fully operative *bouwerijen* of 1638–39 were set up by Paauw.

46. For the Company's obligation to permit Paauw's colonists to continue trading for furs, see VRBM, pp. 314, 316; and van Grol, *Grondpolitiek*, II, p. 54. The purchase price for Pavonia is given in Cornelis van Tienhoven's " Brief statement or answer to some of the points contained in the written deduction laid by Adriaen van der Donck *cum sociis* before the High and Mighty Lords States General," in DCHNY, I, p. 432.

ments as the Swanendael purchase, the cash down price, computing six percent interest, would have been ƒ 23,270.

In July 1634, van Rensselaer offered to sell Rensselaerswyck for ƒ 36,000 and presented an account of the state of the colony which indicated that two *bouwerijen* had been set up and that cattle, colonists, and supplies were on hand to equip three more.[47] Nothing is known about succeeding negotiations, but the offer was either retracted or not accepted, and Rensselaerswyck was not taken over by the Company.

The willingness to reach a settlement with the patroons, evident since late 1633, was not accompanied by an alteration in the general policy of preoccupation with the probably transitory profits of the fur trade; for van Rensselaer wrote in May 1635

> It seems to me the Company is taking a strange course in New Netherland affairs and that ere long they will be obliged to lease the fur trade to others who will manage it better; or else the whole will go wrong. They want to economize by having few people and they cannot keep the land in that way.[48]

Was the decision to purchase the patroonships made primarily in reference to this continuing policy? In other words, did the directors expect the assets they obtained by the purchases, *i. e.*, (1) a more perfect fur monopoly and (2) the provisioning capability of the Pavonia *bouwerijen*, to be capable of amortizing most or all of the rather formidable debts? No direct evidence of the directors' objectives is available. The sum of the purchase prices is not so large as to render chimerical the amortization of the debt out of the yield from the acquired assets within, say, a decade. Nor is it so small as to make amortization a virtual certainty. In this state of unknowing, we can only adopt the tentative and unsatisfactorily vague conclusion that the desire to reduce competition with the Company's fur trade and to add to the Company's provisioning establishment was a significant motive for the purchases. Then we must look about for other situations which may

---

47. Van Rensselaer's price for Rensselaerswyck is given in his letter to his partner de Laet of July 21, 1634, in VRBM, p. 312. The account of the state of the colony appears in *ibid.*, pp. 306–12.

48. Van Rensselaer to van Twiller, May 24, 1635, in *Oud Holland*, VIII, p. 291, and in VRBM, p. 316.

have inflated the figures. Various inflationary situations are conceivable, but only two are suggested by the available evidence.

1. Before the States General's hearing on the dispute between the patroons and the Company had even begun, van Rensselaer was optimistic of its result:

> I hope that the patroons by [the time] the next [ship] sails will have the free trade in furs, even [in exchange] for merchandise, unless some restrictions are added. Their High Mightinesses have appointed to settle this question Messrs. Arnhem, Weede, and Donck, who well understand the rights of the colonies and the population and that the first adventurers ought to be favored in order to tempt others to follow.[49]

Though the last named gentleman seems not in fact to have served on the committee of arbitration, van Rensselaer's optimism suggests that the Company may have found itself confronted with a decidedly hostile committee.[50] An " out of court " settlement, even if rather expensive, may, therefore, have been preferable to a damaging decision.

2. When Marcus de Vogelaer resigned from the New Netherland commission about the beginning of May 1634, the backbone of the inveterate opposition to the patroons was removed from direct management of New Netherland affairs.[51] Albert Coenraets, who probably succeeded to the leadership of New Netherland affairs and who headed the commission which negotiated the purchase of the patroonships, had himself once registered a New Netherland patroonship, and most of the patroons were or had been his colleagues on the directorate. Moreover, Paauw was said to have " much influence " with him. These circumstances certainly point to the possibility that the Company's offer was over-generous. On the other hand, Coenraets was at least partly responsible for a very astute counter to a maneuver by the patroons during the

---

49. Van Rensselaer to van Twiller, April 23, 1634, in *Oud Holland*, VIII, p. 281 and VRBM, p. 282.

50. The members of the States General's committee are mentioned in DCHNY, I, pp. 69, 82, 83.

51. Van Rensselaer wrote to van Twiller on April 23, 1634, " so long as Vogelaer is on the commission, there can be no dealings with the Company (VRBM, p. 287). Van Rensselaer's letter to Jacob Planck of May 2, 1634 mentions Vogelaer's resignation (in VRBM, pp. 300–301).

States General's arbitration of the dispute.[52] This indicates that he could take a firm stand against his former colleagues. Unless new evidence is unearthed, even reasonable certainty in regard to the Company's generosity or lack thereof in purchasing the patroonships seems unattainable.

52. Coenraets' name heads the list of signatures of the Company's representatives on the deed of conveyance of Swanendael, indicating that he headed the committee for negotiation (Conveyance, in O'Callaghan, *History of New Netherland*, I, p. 481). That Paauw had influence with Coenraets is noted by van Rensselaer in his letter to van Twiller of April 23, 1634, in VRBM, p. 268. The astute counter-maneuver was the "Answer of the West India Company to, and against the Pretension and Claim of Michael Paauw, Kiliaen van Rensselaer, and Samuel Blommaert, Patroons in New Netherland, . . ." signed by Albert Kounraut Burgh and Jacques van Horn, in DCHNY, I, p. 89.

CHAPTER SEVEN

THE PATH TO FREE TRADE

Director-General Wouter van Twiller, the designated imple-
menter of the Company's policy of preoccupation with short run
fur profits, proved neither informative in his correspondence with
the home office nor assiduous in expediting the departure of
Holland-bound ships.[1] As a result, more or less inadequate information handicapped the directors' ability to react promptly to
the related problems of foreign encroachment and a sluggish fur
trade in New Netherland.

When the *Eendracht*, which had sailed for the New Netherlands
in the beginning of May 1634, made its tardy return from there
about November 1635, she probably brought the directors the first
news of the colony since a year and a half back, when letters
written in New Netherland about September 1633 had reached
Holland via New England.[2] The tidings the *Eendracht* must have

---

1. For the directors' annoyance with van Twiller's uncommunicativeness in
1634, 1635, and 1636, see VRBM, pp. 271, 272, 316, 320–21. For mention of
accusations that he delayed the departure of ships, see VRBM, pp. 271 and 333.
2. For the date of the *Eendracht*'s departure from Holland in 1634, see VRBM,
p. 315. The approximate date of its return to Holland in 1635 can be inferred
from the minutes of the Amsterdam Chamber ("Resolutien No. 6, Amsteldam,
van Pmo January, 1635, tot ultimo December, 1636," in "Minutes of the Amsterdam Chamber of the Dutch West India Company, 1635-1636," ed. A. J. F. van
Laer, *New York Genealogical and Biographical Record*, XLIX (1918), pp. 222–23).
Maerten Gerritsz brought a letter from van Twiller to van Rensselaer via New
England, which was dated September 14, 1633, and received by van Rensselaer
about April 21, 1634 (VRBM, p. 266). Undoubtedly van Twiller also wrote to
the directors by Gerritsz at the same time. May 24, 1635, van Rensselaer wrote
to van Twiller that the directors were very much alarmed, having received no
letters from him by way of Virginia or New England (VRBM, p. 316). It is
therefore improbable that at the end of May 1635, the directors had received news
since that sent by Gerritsz. It is conceivable that letters arrived via New England
or Virginia between May and November 1635 (there was no direct sailing from
New Netherland to Holland in this period), but there is no mention of receipt
of letters from New Netherland in this period in the above quoted resolutions
of the Amsterdam Chamber.

brought were exceedingly grave. Since the last communication from New Netherland, the English had acquired a firm foothold on the Connecticut River, one of the three great rivers of New Netherland, and the Iroquois had made a truce with the French Indians, which tended to divert furs towards the St. Lawrence and away from Fort Orange. About the time of the *Eendracht*'s departure from New Netherland, word arrived at Fort Amsterdam that an English party had been arrested at the Company's unoccupied Fort Nassau on the Delaware River, a development which boded ill for the prospects of preserving the trade of that river without a permanent garrison. *f* 134,925 in beavers and otters came back with the *Eendracht*; but, since this represented the returns for two years, 1634 and 1635, the sum did not betoken a significant improvement over the returns of the previous decade.[3]

These grave developments tended to refute the two essential premises on which the present New Netherland policy was based, namely (1) that an economically run fur monopoly could yield a profit and (2) that New Netherland would not be engulfed by another European power in the immediate future. Little is known about the deliberations on New Netherland which the *Eendracht*'s news provoked, but it is certain that by the next summer and before the receipt of further intelligence from New Netherland, the directors were seriously considering the radical step of abandoning the fur monopoly as well as the recall of van Twiller.[4] In September 1636 no decision on either of these pressing questions had yet been made, but the delay need not indicate the directors' neglect of New Netherland affairs. Hitherto incon-

3. For the English foothold on the Connecticut and the diversion of the trade from Fort Orange, see p. 131. The news of the arrest of an English party on the Delaware arrived in New Amsterdam on September 1 (de Vries, *Verscheyden voyagiens*, p. 219). Since a letter sent by the *Eendracht* was dated as late as August 31 (VRBM, p. 319), it is very possible, though not certain, that the ship sailed late enough to have carried news of the event.

De Laet gives the returns for 1634–35 in *Historie ofte Iaerlijck Verhael* (1644), Appendix, pp. 29–30.

4. On September 25, 1636, van Rensselaer wrote van Twiller that " the Company has much discussed certain points which he proposed to them concerning the throwing open of the fur trade, but thus far no decision has been made " (VRBM, p. 320). A revision of New Netherland policy was probably discussed at the June 1636 gathering of The Nineteen, since the seventh *poinct van beschrijvinge* requested the delegates to " come prepared to resume and, if necessary, amend the order for the Director of New Netherland " and for seven other posts and colonies (DCHNY, I, p. 100).

sistency had been the bane of New Netherland policy, and the directors may have been very properly desirous of avoiding another unsettling change before the present administration and policy were thoroughly tested. Since the *Seven Ster* could be expected from New Netherland in the summer of 1636, it was entirely appropriate to wait at least for the news she would bring.

The *Seven Ster*, which reached Holland between September 27 and 29, 1636, brought two letters to the directors, one from van Twiller, and the other from van Twiller and the Council.[5] A lucky accident has preserved both missives, and it is possible, by magnifying the disappointment which the historian experiences upon reading van Twiller's extremely brief and vague letter, to comprehend the frustration and annoyance which the directors felt on receiving this first communication from their director-general in some ten months. The gist of the two letters (that from the director-general and council was fuller, but still hardly circumstantial) was that New Netherland was perilously close to engulfment by the English. These intruders had " complete possession " of the Connecticut River, from which followed not only the loss of the trade on that river but also a threat to the Fort Orange trade, since the English could now " approach Fort Orange from the rear." Fort Nassau on the Delaware was in the process of fortification, but it was feared that the English would not long be held back from there either. Even in the immediate vicinity of Fort Amsterdam, which was falling " entirely into ruin," the Company's trade was not inviolate, for English barkentines were coming in " by night and at unseasonable hours and in inaccessible places " and conducting a clandestine trade with the Dutch of the area. In short, " if your Honors wish to preserve the country, you must people it with free men [i. e. persons not in the employ of the Company]." About 8,000 skins returned with the *Seven Ster*, which again represented no improvement over the returns from before the inauguration of the present policy.[6]

The receipt of this news provoked the Company to an immedi-

---

5. The *Seven Ster* sailed past Texel on September 26 ("Resolutien No. 6, Amsteldam, . . . ," fol. 183v; in "Minutes of the Amsterdam Chamber . . . ," *New York Genealogical and Biographical Record*, XLIX, pp. 226–27). Van Rensselaer received letters from it by Sep. 29 (VRBM, p. 320). The letters, edited and translated by A. J. F. van Laer, are printed in *New York State Historical Association Quarterly Journal*, I (1919), pp. 44–50.

6. VRBM, p. 334. Buchelius, pp. 129–129v, in Stokes, *Iconography*, IV, p. 949.

ate reaction. The directors were very annoyed over van Twiller's uncommunicativeness and complained that they had little advice how things were getting along in New Netherland.[7] On October 28, about a month after the return of the *Seven Ster*, Albert Coenraets, probably the "gentleman" described by van Rensselaer about this time as the person upon whom New Netherland affairs were largely devolving, submitted to the Amsterdam Chamber that a new director-general must be found for New Netherland and a ship sent there. Both proposals were ratified by the chamber, and a week later it was resolved to send the *Haringh* to New Netherland via Curaçao.[8] About the end of November, van Rensselaer, at this time no more than a *hoofdparticipant* in the Company and thus not necessarily accurately informed regarding the Company's policies, believed that the Company would not debate the opening of the New Netherland trade or dispatch the *Haringh* before the following spring.[9] However, since the tenth *poinct van beschrijvinge* for the December gathering of The Nineteen requested the delegates to come prepared "to resume and amend, if necessary, the order on the management of New Netherland" and six other posts and colonies, it is possible that the question was discussed earlier.[10]

A winter, spring, and summer came and went before the *Haringh*, with the new director-general Willem Kieft, sailed away about the end of September 1637. Not only did this long delay put off a much needed change in the administration of New Netherland, but it also deferred a solution to the increasingly precarious state of the colony: although the directors had drafted a new policy promoting the colonization of New Netherland by

7. Van Rensselaer to van Twiller, September 25–29, 1636, in VRBM, pp. 320–21.

8. The ratification of Coenraets' proposals and the resolution to send the *Haringh* appear in "Resolutien No. 6, Amsteldam," fols. 199 and 204, in "Minutes of the Amsterdam Chamber . . . ," *New York Genealogical and Biographical Record*, XLIX, p. 228. Van Rensselaer, writing to van Twiller in September 1636, mentioned "the gentleman who remains fairly favorable to your Honor . . . [who] can easily protect your affairs if he understands them, as the whole work devolves largely on him" (VRBM, p. 321). Coenraets had defended van Twiller in 1634 after the first reports of the latter's misconduct had turned many against him (VRBM, p. 267), and his initiative in proposing the need for a new director indicates his responsibility for New Netherland affairs. It seems likely, therefore, that he was the "gentleman" mentioned by van Rensselaer.

9. VRBM, p. 343.

10. DCHNY, I, p. 102.

the time the *Haringh* sailed, they were understandably hesitant to issue it before they received reports from the new director-general and had a chance to interrogate the returning van Twiller. Specific snags, such as difficulty in finding a suitable candidate for director-general, may explain part of the singular and damaging delay; and it is even possible, though not likely, that pecuniary embarrassment compelled the directors to postpone matters until a sufficient amount of the one-third increase of the Company's capital, a financial expedient resorted to in 1636, had been paid in.[11] But a more tempting explanation is the virulent and acrimonious intercameral dispute over the Brazil trade, which must have had a paralyzing effect on the Company's efficiency.

It is possible that the Brazil dispute had a more direct effect on New Netherland policy than the mere hindrance of its execution. Many of the general questions raised by the controversy over Brazil were so similar to those raised by New Netherland as to suggest that the arguments evoked during the heated debates over Brazil influenced the thinking on the much subordinate problem of New Netherland. It will therefore not be inappropriate to review the dispute over " free " trade to Brazil.[12]

Before the Dutch invasion of Brazil, a free, though taxed, trade existed between that country and Portugal; and, desiring to conciliate its new subjects shortly after the capture of Recife and Olinda, the Company consented to an only slightly less liberal arrangement. According to it, pacified Brazilians as well as inhabitants of the United Provinces were permitted the two way trade

11. The *Haringh* sailed after September 21 (VRBM, p. 351). The delay in its sailing seems not to have been occasioned by a problem in repairing or equipping the ship, since the *Haringh*'s skipper was fretting to be off long before its actual departure (VRBM, p. 400). That the Company had been hampered by lack of funds is evident from van Rensselaer's September 1637 letter to van Twiller, in which he wrote: " it seems now the Company intends to take up the affairs of New Netherland with all diligence, since by the increase of the Company's capital by one-third they have now obtained money which they really lacked before " (VRBM, p. 352). It is probable, however, that by " taking up the affairs of New Netherland " van Rensselaer meant much more than the sending of a single ship there.

In the same letter, which was sent by the *Haringh*, van Rensselaer reported that the directors had " planned some freedoms " but were delaying their issuance until the receipt of further news from New Netherland.

12. A detailed account of the early part of the dispute is given in J. P. Arend's *Algemeene Geschiedenis des Vaderlands*, vol. III, part 5, pp. 46 ff. Another good account is in Boxer, *Dutch in Brazil*, pp. 75–82. I have based my relation on these works and the contemporary pamphlet literature on the subject.

between Brazil and the Netherlands on condition of payment of a "recognition" to the Company which was no higher than the tolls collected previously by the Portuguese and of transport of all goods, at specified rates, on the Company's ships.[13] Little advantage was taken of this concession in the first three years after the conquest of Recife, as Dutch Brazil consisted of no more than a handful of coastal forts. But after the Company was able to extend its control over Pernambuco and Paraiba in 1634 and 1635, enterprising Dutch merchants were encouraged to take advantage of a second concession of January 9, 1934, which was basically similar to the first except that the recognition was fixed at 6 percent *ad valorum* for exports from Holland and 20 percent for exports from Brazil and the freight rates on Brazilian exports were reduced by half.[14] The profits which some of these merchants made were enormous; and, since the recognitions received by the Company in no wise covered the roughly *f* 3,000,000—nearly forty percent of the Company's capital—which represented the Company's annual military expenditure in Brazil at this time, it was natural to look to reestablishment of the Company's monopoly of the Brazil trade as the only solution for the desperate situation.[15]

Amsterdam, the principal beneficiary of the open trade, resisted its revocation, and in this the city was followed by its chamber of the Company. A sharp controversy then developed between the Amsterdam Chamber and the "outer chambers" led by Zeeland, which saw reestablishment of the monopoly as the Company's only

13. [West Indische Compagnie. Generale Vergaderinge der XIX], *Articvlen, met approbatie vande Ho: Mog: Heeren Staten Generael over het open ende vry stellen van den handel ende negotie op de stadt Olinda de Parnambuco, ende custen van Brasil.*
14. "Reglement, op 't open stellen vanden handel op Pernambuco en Brasil. In date den 9 Ianuarij 1634," *Groot Placaet-Boeck*, I, cols. 603–06.
15. Johan Maurits, the Governor of Brazil, wrote in a missive to the States General defending free trade that some merchants had increased their capital four or five times (Johan Maurits van Nassau-Siegen, "Memorie . . . ," in *Kronijk van het Historisch Genootschap*, vol. XI (1855), p. 64). The anti-free-trade pamphlet *Brilgesicht voor de verblinde eyghen baetsuchtige handelaers op Brasil* (1638) asserts that after the conquest of Pariba the Company could have made six to one if it had bought up sugar at the low prices of that time (p. 5).
In 1637 the States General requested the balance of the Company's receipts and expenditures for 1635 and 1636. This revealed that the Company's military expenditures in Brazil were running at *f* 3,030,000 per year and that the Company had received no more than *f* 500,000 to *f* 600,000 during the two year period (Arend, *Algemeene geschiedenis*, vol. III, part 5, p. 48. *Ooghen-Salve tot verlichtinghe, van alle participanten, so vande Oost, ende West-Indische Compagnien*, p. 15).

salvation. When the States General granted its approval to the abolition of " free " trade in December 1636, the dispute was in no way allayed, but in fact exacerbated, since the Amsterdammers pressed hard for annulment of the States General's decision and sought by various devices to postpone the execution of the edict.

The horns of the Company's dilemma were these: monopoly might better enable the Company to meet its vast military budget, but it would also alienate the Portuguese and discourage immigration from Holland, thereby increasing the necessity for a large military establishment and slowing the reconstruction of the war-torn land. The entire problem was enormously complicated by the fact that in 1637 the Company was only just beginning to stabilize the situation in Pernambuco and the other conquered captaincies and therefore had no experience of " normal " conditions on which to base estimates of its returns from either monopoly or " free " trade.

In one important respect the New Netherland problem was simpler. There the directors at least knew what could and could not be obtained from a monopoly, and, since there was no reason to expect from the cession of the fur trade to private persons a very substantial change in the level of fur exports, it was even possible to estimate rather closely the returns from imposts on what must for a long time be the region's principal export staple. But the general question of how much and how fast immigration from Holland would increase agricultural production (sugar in Brazil, perhaps grain in New Netherland) was an imponderable in both cases; and the problem of inducing such immigration, a military necessity in Brazil and New Netherland, was basically similar for both provinces.

The arguments over the means to stimulate immigration to Brazil remind us that, though in New Netherland monopoly seems not to have been profitable and the land faced increasing peril from the English, a solution existed in theory which, if successful, might save the land and make the monopoly pay a profit: if enough immigrants could be attracted to the colony by land grants or other non-commercial concessions, the Company might be able to shift the burden of defending the land from the fur trade to a prosperous agriculture. In the Brazil controversy, the monopolists argued that the immigration necessary to rebuild the war-torn sugar industry and defend the country could be induced by non-commercial concessions, especially if the Company would furnish necessities to the immigrant at civil prices. The abolition of free trade, they said, might discourage speculators and fly-by-night merchants, but these were not the sort of people needed to rebuild the land.[16] The Amsterdamers, however, denied that any significant immigration could be evoked under a monopoly. Nowhere in Europe, they countered, was there a state where the government had absolute control of all necessities. All free people abhor monopoly " knowing well that monopoly is the most odious thing in the world and the most harmful action of all states." [17] It would be hard enough to bear a monopoly of one or a few necessities. A monopoly of everything necessary for sustenance would be intolerable.

If the Amsterdamers' arguments were apropos to Brazil, they were even more so to New Netherland; for the latter province offered no certainty of a valuable agricultural export staple such as sugar which would tend to overcome the immigrants' scruples about monopoly. Another factor which rendered impractical the theoretical solution of fostering immigration to New Netherland while maintaining the fur monopoly was the virtual certainty of ruinous smuggling if the region became well populated. Indeed the defraudations plaguing the Company in the relatively unpopulated New Netherland of 1637 were already exceedingly damaging. In its last despairing edict against private trade in New Netherland, which was probably issued by The Nineteen in the winter of 1637/38, the Company asserted that it had " not only been sufficiently experienced previously, but had now recently become evident before all the world," that persons in New Netherland " have drawn to themselves and away from the Company . . . as many and more peltries and furs, and of better condition and assortment, than have been traded there for the account of the Company." [18] Maintenance of the monopoly while encouraging the immigration of agriculturalists by non-commercial concessions was, then, for several reasons an impractical solution. The only remaining alternatives, if anything was to be salvaged from the

---

16. *Examen over het Vertoogh tegen het ongefundeerde en schadelijcke sluyten der vryen handel in Brasil* (1637), pp. 7–8. *Bril-gesicht*, p. 5. Deduction of the Zeelanders in 1637, summarized in *Ooghen-Salve*, p. 15.

17. " Corte redenen by die van Amsterdam overgegeven om t bewysen de nodicheyt van den vrien handel overgelevert 30 January 1637," in van Rees, *Geschiedenis der staathuishoudkunde*, II, pp. 456–60.

18. New York Colonial Manuscripts, IV, p. 7.

costly investment in New Netherland, were (1) abandonment of the monopoly and encouragement of immigration, or (2) cession of the province to the States General for a reasonable compensation.

In April 1638 the hesitation of the Company in New Netherland affairs was ended by a command from the States General. On April 26, their High Mightinesses, informed of the actual decline of New Netherland's population and the consequent danger of engulfment by foreign powers,

> resolved and concluded, that before the present delegates from the respective chambers to the . . . . present Assembly of the XIX adjourn, their High Mightinesses' deputies to the XIX shall assist in making and enacting such effectual order regarding the population of New Netherland, and thereto invite all good inhabitants of these Netherlands . . . so that this State may not be deprived of the aforesaid New Netherland.[19]

Subsequently The Nineteen empowered Chamber Amsterdam to draft a plan " to promote and improve the trade and population of New Netherland "; but, despite the dispatch required by the States General, the plan was not presented for their High Mightinesses' approbation until August 30.[20] Perhaps the directors were

19. DCHNY, I, p. 106.

20. " Articles and Conditions drawn up and published by the Chamber of Amsterdam, with the approbation of their High Mightinesses, the States General of the United Netherlands, in conformity to the authority of the XIX; on which the respective Lands and Places in and around New Netherland shall, from now henceforward, be traded to, frequented and settled, according to such form of government and police as may at present, or shall hereafter, be established there by the Company or its agents " (in DCHNY, I, pp. 110–114). Brodhead and O'Callaghan believed that this proposal consisted of only the first thirteen articles of the plan, and that the latter part, superscribed " West India Company " was the plan actually put into effect after approbation of the States General (John Romeyn Brodhead, *History of the State of New York*, I, pp. 286–87; O'Callaghan, *History of New Netherland*, I, pp. 192–203). In opposition to this view may be adduced the following arguments. (1) Neither the first nor the second section is complete without the other, the first dealing largely with government and justice and the second with trade and land policy. (2) Several important provisions of the second section, according to Brodhead's and O'Callaghan's supposition the plan actually adopted, contradict the plan which was seemingly put into effect. For example, it appears that the New Netherland trade was opened not only to persons who took up and cultivated lands in New Netherland but to all inhabitants of the United Provinces. Also the second section prescribes tithes on lands after four

awaiting the first reports from their new director-general in New Netherland, or perhaps they were hindered by the intercameral strife over Brazil, which, according to director Blommaert was "making such disturbances that there is no courage to do anything." [21]

Despite the Company's implicit surrender of its monopoly of the fur trade, the draft was not liberal. The entire New Netherland trade was to be opened to "inhabitants of this state or its friends, who may be disposed to take up and cultivate any lands there," but all goods had to be conveyed in the Company's ships at unspecified and hence probably not unduly low freight rates. Cattle, and perhaps other implements of husbandry, seem to have escaped payment of a recognition, though not, as in the 1629 *Vryheden*, payment of freight; but "merchandise" was to be subject to a stiff recognition over and above freight charges: ten percent for imports to New Netherland and fifteen percent for exports. By contrast, the recognitions levied on the infinitely more lucrative Brazil trade, which on April 29, 1638 had been reopened to inhabitants of Brazil, participants in the Company according to the size of their investment, and persons to whom participants had transferred their trading rights, was little more: ten percent on imports and twenty percent on exports plus a small surtax on exported sugar.[22] Immigrants to New Netherland were to be obliged to pay their own passage, but on arrival they would at least receive land on condition that it be properly cultivated. However, tithes were to be levied on new plantations after only four years, a retrogression from the policy then in effect in New Netherland which exempted lands from tithing for ten years.[23] Despite tithes and heavy imposts on imports and exports, the Company sought to shift a significant portion of the costs of defense and

years of cultivation, whereas the system actually placed in effect exempted new lands from the tithe for ten years. (See the following pages.)

That The Nineteen had authorized Chamber Amsterdam to produce an ordinance is evident from the beginning of the second section of the "Articles and Conditions."

21. Samuel Blommaert to Axel Oxenstierna, September 4, 1638, in "Brieven van Blommaert," BMHG, XXIX, p. 153.

22. "Reglement, by de West-Indische Compagnie ter Vergaderinge vande Negentiene, met approbatie vande Ho: Mo: Heeren Staten Generael, over het open stellen van den handel op Brasil, 29 April 1638," in *Groot Placaet-Boeck*, I, cols. 609–12.

23. Patents were granted on condition of payment of tithes after ten years according to resolution of the Director of New Netherland, June 24, 1638 (New York Colonial Manuscripts, IV, p. 11).

other public necessities onto the inhabitants. Assessments levied on the colonists were to pay for the construction of forts and public buildings and for the maintenance of clergymen and school-masters. Though the Company retained the responsibility for garrisoning the forts, "everyone, be he trader or inhabitant" was obliged to fight in the colony's defense and even to provide his own musket and side arms. In short, the directors envisaged an arrangement designed to populate the colony at minimal cost to the Company, yet, once bitten twice shy, they shrunk from turning over the undertaking to private capitalists as in 1629.

Their High Mightinesses were not pleased at the effort of Chamber Amsterdam. On September 2, 1638, after the plan had been studied in committee, the States General resolved that

> the aforesaid articles, instituted by the aforesaid Chamber of Amsterdam, for the service and furthering of the colonies in New Netherland, are not acceptable, as they are, ...

By the same resolution the draft was returned to the Company, along with a "New Project" which had evidently been privately submitted to the States General and which may have proposed a revival of the patroon system on very liberal terms. Their High Mightinesses also directed representatives of the Company to appear at the Hague to review the question with a committee of the States General and declared their intention to frame a "reso-lution" on the colonization of New Netherland on the basis of these joint deliberations.[24] Presumably by "resolution" was meant a general plan for colonization, such as the States General had demanded in April 1638 and received in unsatisfactory form at the end of August, rather than a simple expression of their High Mightinesses' pleasure.

The States General did not subsequently make a resolution of any sort in the matter, and in 1639 and 1640 the Company was still

---

24. Resolution of the States General, Sep. 2, 1638; in DCHNY, I, p. 115. The "New Project" may be the undated draft of "Freedoms, Privileges, and Exemp-tions" appearing in DCHNY, I, pp. 96–100, which conceived very advantageous privileges for patroons. However, it is also possible that these "Freedoms" were the "certain project regarding the planting of colonies in New Netherland" which the States General received from someone (not the West India Company) on April 17, 1638 (DCHNY, I, p. 105) and that the "certain project" of April and the "New Project" of September were distinct.

busy drafting a general plan for New Netherland's colonization.[25] In view of these circumstances, the major revision of the Company's New Netherland policy which occurred in late 1638 or early 1639 must be regarded as a purely provisional solution. Evidently the directors had been able to convince the States General not only of their good faith in searching for a solution but also of the necessity of avoiding a binding, permanent settlement until a certain amount of experimentation had been made.

Despite its provisional nature, the arrangement of 1638/39, by abolishing the hitherto so jealously guarded fur monopoly, marks the end of an era in the Company's New Netherland policy. Adopted by May 1639, perhaps as early as September 1638,[26] the new policy permitted all inhabitants of the United Provinces, not just persons undertaking plantations in New Netherland as provided by the rejected draft of Chamber Amsterdam to send merchandise to New Netherland, trade with the Indians or other inhabitants within the colony, and dispatch their returns back to Holland, on condition (1) that transatlantic shipments be made on ships of the Company and (2) that a recognition be paid to the Company.[27] As far as is known, no goods were excepted from this arrangement except muskets and powder, which, by an ordi-

25. The Nineteen drafted a general plan about October 1639 (VRBM, p. 464). This was probably substantially the same as that submitted to, but apparently not approved by the States General in July 1640 (DCHNY, I, pp. 119–23).

26. That the new policy was adopted by May 1639 is evident from VRBM, p. 432. A March 31, 1639, ordinance of the Director and Council of New Netherland against trading guns and ammunition to the Indians and providing for the registration of private boats sailing to or from Fort Orange, Fort Good Hope, and the Delaware raises the suspicion that the trade was already opened by the date of its promulgation. If this suspicion is true, the news of the opening of the trade must have been brought to the New Netherlands by the *Liefde*, which left Texel on September 25, 1638, and arrived before Fort Amsterdam on December 27 (de Vries, *Verscheyden voyagiens*, pp. 229–31), since no vessel from Holland is known to have reached North America between the arrival of the *Liefde* and the promulgation of the ordinance of March 31.

27. That the privilege of trading to and in New Netherland was not conditional upon cultivation of land or even domicile there is best revealed in the *Poincten van beschrijvinge* for the meeting of The Nineteen on February 21, 1643 (DCHNY, I, pp. 135–36). See also the "Report and advice on the condition of New Netherland" drawn up by the General Board of Accounts of the West India Company about December 1644 (DCHNY, I, p. 154). For the obligation to employ only the ships of the Company see the "Instruction of the Deputies to the Assembly of the XIX . . . for the Director and Council of New Netherland . . . ," of July 7, 1645, in DCHNY, I, p. 162. For the obligation to pay recognition, see van Rensselaer's letter of May 1639 to Willem Kieft, in VRBM, p. 433.

nance promulgated in New Netherland on March 31, 1639, could not be traded to the Indians on pain of death.[28] The size of the recognition is not entirely certain, but, if unchanged through April 1642, it amounted to ten percent on imports to New Netherland, the same amount prescribed by the Amsterdam Chamber's unacceptable draft plan.[29]

Several important noncommercial concessions were either instituted at the same time as the opening of the trade or very shortly thereafter. By May 1640, the immigrant to New Netherland was not obliged to pay his passage, but only his board during the voyage. By contrast the Amsterdam Chamber's draft had exacted both passage and board from the immigrant. A similar relaxation of that draft was a return to the practice of exempting new lands from tithes for ten, not just four years. This ten year exemption was certainly in effect by June 1641. Although, from 1639 on, the Company had warily inserted a new provision in its land deeds subjecting the land owner to "all such taxes and recognitions already devised or yet to be devised by the Company," the Company did not subject the inhabitants to the assessments for defense and public services mentioned in the Amsterdam draft. Until a disasterous Indian war forced enactment of a beer excise in 1644, the recognition on imports and exports and the still generally uncollected tithe were the only taxes in New Netherland.[30]

As we mentioned previously, the opening of the New Netherland trade was not the only alternative left to the Company in 1638. It would also have been possible to abandon the province, perhaps by cession to the States General; and, if there was no reasonable expectation that the new policy would yield a profit or at least permit the Company to break even in New Netherland, this was the only financially rational solution. Abandonment was considered in the depths of the Indian war of 1643–44; but in April 1638, when their High Mightinesses suggested that New Netherland be placed under the States General, the directors had

---

28. New York Colonial Manuscripts, IV, p. 36.

29. Ordinance imposing duties on wares imported to New Netherland which escaped payment of the recognition in Holland, dated April 3, 1642 (*ibid.*, p. 120).

30. For the grant of free passage to immigrants, see VRBM, pp. 481–82; for the ten year exemption from tithes, see DCHNY, XIII, p. 8. The clause reserving rights of taxation to the Company first appears in a patent of November 15, 1639, the first patent issued in that year (New York Colonial Manuscripts, GG, p. 32).

Vertoogh van Nieu-Neder-Land, in NNN, p. 327, mentions the tax situation at the time of the Indian war.

" no intention so to do; unless they receive profit by it." [31] This rejection of a graceful means to divest themselves of the province can only mean that the directors were reasonably hopeful that the region would become a source of profit. What were the encouraging prospects for New Netherland in 1638?

In the same interrogation of the States General's deputy to The Nineteen which reveals the directors were not inclined to abandon New Netherland, it is stated that though the Company had hitherto experienced losses in New Netherland " it could afford profit, principally from grain." [32] This renewed interest in New Netherland agriculture after seven years of neglect need not of itself betoken markedly improved prospects for New Netherland grain exports around 1638: the new interest in grain could merely reflect the expected abolition of the fur monopoly, with which colonization had previously been deemed incompatible. Yet, in fact, a new circumstance had developed which improved the prospects of an agricultural export staple very significantly. By 1638 half of the captaincies of Brazil were under effective control of the Company, and Elmina, the principal Portuguese stronghold on the Guinea coast had just fallen to a Company expedition. A great Dutch empire on the equatorial Atlantic seemed, therefore, on the verge of realization, and though it was perhaps unrealistic to expect New Netherland grain, timber, or fish to compete in Europe with the Baltic lands or the North Sea, it was by no means unlikely that New Netherland exports could compete successfully in Brazil or West Africa. A somewhat similar trade to the West Indies and Africa was conducted with great success by the New Englanders from the 1640's. Were the directors unjustifiably confident when they decided to hold on to New Netherland?

31. That the abandonment of New Netherland was considered in 1643–44 is evident from General Board of Accounts, " Report and advice on the condition of New Netherland," in DCHNY, I, p. 153. The attitude of the directors in April 1638 is expressed in a report on the condition of New Netherland presented to the States General on or before April 30, 1638, in DCHNY, I, p. 107.

32. *Ibid.*

CHAPTER EIGHT

SOME CONCLUDING OBSERVATIONS

Director-General Willem Kieft was sufficiently impressed by the
sorry state of New Netherland at the time of his arrival to cause
depositions to be taken concerning it. One such deposition, made
by two carpenters and one master workman of the Company,
relates

> that on the 28th of March in the year 1638, being the date on
> which Mr. Willem Kieft safely arrived here by the ship
> *Haringh* . . . Mr. Kieft found Fort Amsterdam totally and
> wholly in a ruinous condition, so that people could go in and
> out of said Fort on all sides except alone at the stone point,
> all the cannon off the gun carriages, five farms vacant and
> fallen into decay; there was not a living animal on hand
> belonging to the Company on said farms, or any other places,
> but all from the smallest even to the largest were in the
> possession of other people.
> Moreover, every vessel was unserviceable, the yacht *Prins
> Willem* alone being fit for use and one new one on the stocks.
> The whole of the house in the fort is yet in need of con-
> siderable repair, as well as the five stone houses, the wooden
> church, the lodge and the smith's.
> One grist and saw mill in operation, another which is out
> of repair; the third burned. The place where the public store
> stood can with difficulty be discovered.[1]

This and other statements were interpreted by O'Callaghan and
Brodhead, the great pioneer historians of New Netherland, according to the point of view of the colonists, which, as expressed in
the extremely uncharitable *Vertoogh van Nieu-Neder-Land* (1650)
was simply this: all the evils plaguing New Netherland stemmed

1. New York Colonial Manuscripts, I, p. 96.

154

from the " bad government " of the Company.[2] O'Callaghan and
Brodhead therefore paused at the initiation of the free trade policy
in 1638/39 to deplore the " bad government " (Brodhead) and
" culpable neglect " (O'Callaghan) of the directors, which had
brought the province to such sorry straits.[3] In general, their views
have been followed by subsequent writers on New Netherland.

Our study suggests, however, that the depreciated state of New
Netherland about 1638 was not the result of neglect, but of a
studied attempt to extract a maximum profit from the fur trade
in the short run. This policy, since it would inevitably lead to loss
of the province to another European power, was obviously incompatible with large investments in agriculture or with any other
fixed capital. The only serious suspicion of neglect in the period
we are considering is aroused by the long delayed departure of the
Haringh in 1637; but this delay can probably better be explained
by the paralyzing effect of the Brazil dispute, ultimately a result
of the decentralized organization of the Company, than by the
culpable maladministration of the directors.

The great fault of the Company's early New Netherland policy
seems to have been not neglect but vacillation. Either exclusive
concern with the fur trade or a wholehearted and continuing effort
at agricultural colonization would have been preferable to the
tragic abandonment and even discouragement, during most of the
1630's, of a colonization which had already begun. Had the Company obtained thorough knowledge of the profitability or unprofitability of the fur trade in New Netherland *before* planting a
colony there, it would never have been deceived into making this
mistake.

Though in retrospect it is easy to perceive faults in the Company's New Netherland policy, it is no less easy to appreciate how
intelligent and responsible men could have been led, step by step,
to the same decisions. The threat that other foreign powers would
seize an unoccupied New Netherland provided a strong argument
for the Company's making an immediate demonstration of its
determination to colonize the region. Once the colony was established, it could not lightly be abandoned; and it was reasonable to

2. *Vertoogh*, in NNN, esp. pp. 320–21. Brodhead follows the *Vertoogh* almost
literally (History of the State of New York, I, p. 286).

3. Brodhead, I, pp. 285–86. O'Callaghan, *History of New Netherland*, I, pp.
177–78.

invite the private capital of the patroons to continue what the Company had discovered to be an unprofitably expensive operation. Finally, if doubts existed as to the long run defensibility of the province or the future of export staples other than furs, concentration on the fur trade in the short run, combined with discouragement of the private colonization which undermined the fur monopoly, must have seemed a sensible policy.

ESTIMATES, FROM COSTS, OF NEW NETHERLAND FREIGHT RATES IN RELATION TO BALTIC FREIGHT RATES

The equation I have used to express New Netherland freight costs as a multiple of freight costs to a nearer Baltic port such as Danzig or Königsberg was suggested in large part by Gary M. Walton's article " Sources of Productivity Change in American Colonial Shipping, 1675–1775," which appeared in the *Economic History Review*, Second Series, vol. XX (1967). In this equation, barred letters are New Netherland costs expressed as multiples of Baltic costs, while letters not so barred are the Baltic costs themselves.

$$\bar{c} = [\bar{d}(\bar{t}_1 + \bar{t}_2 + \bar{t}_3)(d/c)] + [\bar{w}(\bar{t}_2 + \bar{t}_3)(w/c)] + [\bar{r}\bar{t}_2(r/c)] + [\bar{i}(i/c)] - [p/c]$$

c = total costs
d = per diem depreciation and interest on hull, spars, and armament
w = per diem wage and provisioning expense
r = per diem repair costs
i = insurance premium on the round trip
p = other protection costs
t_1 = time spent equipping, loading, and unloading in home port
t_2 = time at sea
t_3 = time in foreign port

All but the last term of this equation is fairly self-explanatory. The " other protection costs " represented by this last term were charges levied on unarmed Baltic traders for the privilege of sailing in consortship with armed merchantmen, which in effect convoyed them. Such charges would not have been paid by New Netherland bound vessels, which would have had to be well armed and manned.

A listing of all the scraps of evidence which I used in making quantitative estimates of the unknowns in the above equation would be a tedious undertaking. Suffice to say that, besides charter parties, I have made full use of the very informative memoranda which Dutch merchants submitted in opposition to a proposed general insurance company from 1629 to 1635 ("Koopmansadviezen . . . ," ed. P. J. Blok, BMHG, XXI) and the placards of the States General concerning maritime affairs, which defined such things as proper armament and crew size for various trades and the protection costs for unarmed vessels sailing in consortship. Secondary works which have been particularly helpful have been Ralph Davis' *Rise of the English Shipping Industry*, Violet Barbour's articles on "Dutch and English Merchant Shipping" and "Marine Risks and Insurance," and A. E. Christensen's *Dutch Trade in the Baltic*. Where these standard sources offered no help, I have often had recourse to odd gleanings, such as a comment in David de Vries' *Voyagiens* on the price of ship's artillery in 1618.

Insurance rates on the New Netherland trade were 12 percent for a round trip in 1636. Six years later, when the threat from the Dunkirk privateers, the principal threat to Dutch shipping in the 1620's and 1630's, had abated considerably, the rate on the outbound voyage was 5 percent.[1] At present these rates cannot be compared with the rates applicable to unarmed Baltic traders because no thorough study of Baltic insurance premiums has yet been made. Unfortunately we cannot safely assume that the rates for the Baltic trade which were proposed for the projected but never organized "General Insurance Company" in 1628 and again in the early 1630's accurately reflected actually prevailing rates.

Time spent at sea and in port can be estimated with considerable certainty, and it seems appropriate to give a fuller explanation of the sources and reasoning behind these estimates. Wassenaer's estimate of the usual New Netherland voyage was seven to eight weeks outbound and one month returning, in other words about twelve weeks under sail for the round trip; but, as has been pointed out, a voyage of this duration would have been particularly fortunate.[2] If to Wassenaer's estimate of twelve weeks under sail we add five weeks for equipping, loading, and finally unloading in the Netherlands and four weeks for unloading, refitting, and reloading in New Netherland, we get an approximation of the least possible amount of a ship's time a New Netherland voyage would consume: twenty-two weeks, or about five months. In practice, it would be unreasonable to expect a voyage and its preparations to be completed in this space, but five and one-half or six months was probably a reasonable expectation. Writing in 1640, Samuel Blommaert, a director of the West India Company, claimed that if no intermediate stops were made the round trip (not

1. The *Rensselaerswyck*, which was well manned and carried at least some armament, paid 6 percent going to and 6 percent returning from New Netherland in 1636, a year when the threat from the Dunkirk privateers was considerable (VRBM, pp. 339, 368). The premium on goods sailing to New Netherland in June 1642 on the *Houttuyn*, well manned but of unknown armament, was 5 percent (*Ibid.*, p. 645).

2. See Chapter 1, p. 16.

including the initial equipment and final unloading) could be made " in four to five months, and then still have three or four or six weeks to unload and load [in the New Netherlands]." As an example Blommaert mentioned a West India Company ship which about 1639 carried cattle from the Netherlands to the New Netherlands, sailed to France, where it loaded salt, and returned to the Netherlands within five months, despite its having to wait for the wind in France. Under the highly auspicious conditions which favored this ship it would be possible for a vessel to make two New Netherland voyages in a single year.[3]

In demonstrating the unusually favorable situation of the Netherlands for commerce, a 1644 pamphlet asserts that from the Netherlands, Norway could be sailed to in six or seven days, Danzig or Königsberg in two weeks, and Riga or Reval in three weeks.[4] Probably these represent more or less ideal sailing times, roughly comparable to the figures for New Netherland times given by Wassenaer. To obtain total voyage times for these ports we must add to these sailing times the standard three week lay-over in a Baltic port, which charter parties in the 1620's specified, and also several weeks for loading, unloading, and repairs in the home port. Taking the ideal sailing times, I estimate

(in days)	Norway	Danzig/ Königsberg	Riga/ Reval	New Netherland
t_1	28	28	28	35
t_2	14	28	42	90
t_3	21	21	21	28
$t_2 + t_3$	35	49	63	118
$t_1 + t_2 + t_3$	63	77	91	153

The estimates for total voyage times ($t_1 + t_2 + t_3$) are confirmed by other sources. In 1634 Dutch merchants computed the effect of the insurance rates of the proposed " General Insurance Company " on the basis of six Norway voyages and four Baltic voyages per year. These figures are quite consistent with the above estimates if one assumes that by " Baltic

3. Letter of Samuel Blommaert to the Swedish Chancellor Axel Oxenstierna, January 28, 1640, in "Brieven van Blommaert aan Oxenstierna," BMHG, XXIX, p. 182.
In 1636 the director and council of New Netherland advised the Amsterdam Chamber that a speed up of the turn around time in New Netherland would permit a ship to make two voyages a year ("Letters of Wouter van Twiller and the Director General and Council of New Netherland to the Amsterdam Chamber of the Dutch West India Company, August 14, 1636," ed. A. J. F. van Laer, *New York State Historical Association Quarterly Journal*, I (1919), p. 49). However, a careful reconstruction of the pattern of Dutch shipping to New Netherland until about 1640 has failed to unearth any evidence of a double voyage.
4. *Aenwysinge: datmen van de Oost en West-Indische Compagnien/een compagnie dient te maken.* p. [1] of the " consideratien."

voyages " were meant voyages to the nearer Baltic ports. In his *Rise of the English Shipping Industry*, Ralph Davis does not mention the possible number of voyages per year from England to Danzig or Königsberg, but he does mention the " nearly unvarying pattern " of voyages from England to Norway and to Riga in the eighteenth century. Norway traders usually made five voyages per year from Hull to the Oslofjord. Since winter might close the Gulf of Riga from November through April, Riga traders could make but two voyages yearly, but they often in addition made a winter voyage to the Bay of Biscay for wine. Thus Davis' figures on Baltic voyages as well as those of the Dutch merchants fit in rather neatly with my own estimates.[5]

With this introduction, the reader is now invited to consider my estimates for the unknowns in the original equation, which, it will be remembered, compared the costs of a merchantman of 130 lasts or so, on a voyage to New Netherland with its cost on a voyage to a near Baltic port:

$\bar{d}$ (depreciation and interest)	$= 1.2$
$\bar{w}$ (wages and provisions)	$= 1.5$
$\bar{r}$ (repairs)	$= 1.0$
$\bar{i}$ (insurance)	$= 1.5$
$\bar{t_2}$ (time at sea)	$= 3.22$
$\bar{t_2} + \bar{t_3}$ (time at sea and in foreign port)	$= 2.41$
$\bar{t_1} + \bar{t_2} + \bar{t_3}$ (total sea and port time)	$= 1.99$
d/c	$= .15$
w/c	$= .40$
r/c	$= .15$
i/c	$= .20$
p/c	$= .10$

$$1.2(1.99)(.15) + 1.5(2.41)(.40) + 1.0(3.22)(.15) + \\ + 1.5(.20) - .10 = c.2.49$$

5. For the computations of the Dutch merchants in 1634, see " Koopmans-adviezen," BMHG, XXI, pp. 47, 151–53. Davis' estimates are in his *Rise of the English Shipping Industry*, pp. 195 and 219.

APPENDIX II

BIOGRAPHICAL NOTES ON THREE PATROONS: BLOMMAERT, COENRAETS, AND DE LAET

Samuel Blommaert

Lodewijck Blommaert, Samuel's father, was an Antwerp merchant who served his city in several responsible capacities during its brief period of freedom from Spain.[1] After the capitulation of Antwerp in 1585, Lodewijck took refuge in England, and he died in London in 1591, leaving eight-year-old Samuel, his only surviving child by his first wife, his second wife, and their three year old daughter.

Samuel's stepmother kept him in England for a time, then sent him to school, first to Staden in Flanders and later to the Hague. Thereafter he clerked for merchants in Hamburg, Amsterdam, and Vienna. In 1603, "entirely abandoned by friends," the twenty-year-old found a position as *assistent* (factor) for the Dutch East India Company, and in December of that year he sailed for the Indies on the fleet of Admiral Steven van der Hagen. In the Indies young Blommaert survived sickness and several close calls with the natives and worked himself up to *oppercommis* (chief commercial agent) in West Borneo by 1608. In 1610 he suddenly requested permission to return to Holland, and after a voyage of nine months, arrived there in June 1611.[2]

G. W. Kernkamp has assembled rather convincing circumstantial evidence that Blommaert had been guilty of seriously defrauding the East India Company. It seems that Blommaert left Borneo in August 1610 with "a beautiful lot of diamonds" but arrived in Bantam with "only 154½ carats, as there were few diamonds to be obtained as a result of the internal

---

1. Where not otherwise specified, the information on Blommaert comes from the "Memorie Boeck" of Lodewijck and Samuel Blommaert, now in the GAA. G. W. Kernkamp has also worked much information from the "Memorie Boeck" into his excellent biographical introduction to Samuel Blommaert's letters to Oxenstierna, which were printed in BMHG, XXIX, pp. 3–196.

2. Blommaert's sudden request in 1610, the date of his fourth voyage to Borneo, when he became *oppercommis*, and many other particulars of his life in the Indies which are not recorded in the "Memorie Boeck" are related *ibid.*, pp. 5–13.

wars." [3] Also, by September 1610 the directors of the East India Company in Holland had received disturbing reports about Blommaert and directed their Governor-General in the Indies

> to inquire sharply about the comportment of Samuel Blommaert in Succadana, and if everything is not found to be as it should, to send him, after account has been made, to the Netherlands with the first ships; as we understand that the trade at Succadana is of great importance and that the Company can be greatly defrauded there by unfaithful factors. [4]

There is no evidence, however, that after his return to Holland in 1611, the directors of the East India Company ever called upon Blommaert to justify his conduct. [5]

In 1612 Blommaert married a daughter of Gerrit Reijnst, one of the most prominent merchants of Amsterdam. The following year Father-in-law Reijnst sailed to the East Indies as the new governor-general of the East India Company, and in January 1616 the directors of that Company were seriously concerned lest Blommaert and a brother-in-law of Reijnst, in the hope of Reijnst's connivance, were equipping a ship to voyage to the East Indies via a new passage south of the Strait of Magellan. [6] About the same time Isaac le Maire, the inveterate schemer against the East India Company, sent his son on a similar voyage. Le Maire's instructions to his son do not speak well for either Reijnst's or Blommaert's reputation: upon arrival in the Indies Jacques le Maire was to curry favor with Reijnst by offering to carry back to Holland any goods which Reijnst had obtained dishonestly,

> and especially, if he had any jewels, that you would be glad to send the same back for no charge and deliver them to his son-in-law Blommaert or to that person whom he shall specify. [7]

In October 1622 Blommaert was appointed director of the West India Company, and he continued in this position until about June 1629, when he became one of the first one-third of the board to retire. With Godijn and van Rensselaer he sent out two men to choose a site for a colony in New Netherland about January 1629. In November he declared himself patroon of the Connecticut River and in April 1630 of St. Martin or the Barbados in the West Indies. Both these projected colonies were included in the combination agreement of October 1630 between Blommaert, Godijn,

---

3. *Ibid.*, p. 14; from L. C. D. van Dijk, *Neerland's vroegste betrekkingen met Borneo, den Solo-archipel, Cambodja, Siam en Cochin-China*, p. 142.
4. "Brieven van Blommaert," pp. 14–15; from van Dijk.
5. "Brieven van Blommaert," p. 15.
6. *Ibid.*, pp. 16–17.
7. *Ibid.*

de Laet, and van Rensselaer. Neither of these colonization projects was ever undertaken, but by virtue of this agreement Blommaert retained a share of Rensselaerswyck until his death in 1654.[8]

In the early seventeenth century Sweden was a land of opportunity for Dutch capitalists. Probably by 1626 Blommaert had an interest in a Swedish brass works, and about 1631–1633 he was assisting a Swedish agent in the Netherlands with the sale of copper and in various exchange operations.[9] About July 1634 he offered to become a commercial adviser for the Swedish government. If given such a post, he promised to

> clearly show his faithfulness towards companies [the East India Company in which Blommaert was *hoofdparticipant*, but especially the West India Company where he had long been a director] and everything that he had ever undertaken, all the more as he is piqued at the same [the companies].[10]

Undoubtedly Blommaert's pique stemmed from the West India Company's campaign against his patroonal rights, to defend which he and the other patroons were at this very time presenting their case before the States General.

The Swedish Chancellor Oxenstierna met Blommaert in the spring of 1635 and from this time until about 1642 Blommaert was a regular correspondent of the Swedish government.[11] Having obtained thirty-two votes of the *hoofdparticipanten* in 1636—only one other of the fifteen persons nominated for director received more votes in this election—he was appointed to a second term as director of the West India Company by the burgomasters.[12] Although his " pique " must have been somewhat assuaged by this honor, he accepted the desired position as agent in the Swedish service the following November and about February 1637 sent Pieter Minuit, a former director-general of New Netherland, off to Sweden to prepare the Swedish expedition which carved New Sweden out of the southern part of New Netherland. Later he even contributed money for the expedition and helped to collect its cargo and crew. Besides New Netherland, Blommaert indicated many other regions for Swedish profit within the West India Company's *Octroy*.[13]

8. For Blommaert's activities as a patroon, see VRBM, pp. 154, 157, 166, 171–74. His retention of a share in Rensselaerswyck is noted by Nissenson, *Patroon's Domain*, p. 328n.
9. " Brieven van Blommaert, pp. 24–26.
10. Michel le Blon to the future Swedish Resident Peter Spiering, July 18, 1634, in " Brieven van Blommaert," pp. 29–32.
11. " Brieven van Blommaert," pp. 32–33.
12. Jessurun, *Kiliaen van Rensselaer*, bijlage lle. Blommaert, " Memorie Boeck."
13. His acceptance of the Swedish post is mentioned in " Brieven van Blommaert," p. 34. For his activities on behalf of New Sweden, see *ibid.*, pp. 47–49, 106–10, 115–17.

Blommaert left Swedish service about 1641–42, shortly before his term as director expired. Exactly how much of his double dealing ever came to light is unknown, but in 1645 he was honored with a third term as director; perhaps his real capability and grasp of Company affairs were judged to outweigh suspicions or certainties of questionable conduct.[14] He died in 1654, long in years and heavy in conscience, having not quite fulfilled his father's pious wish that his infant son "may follow the footsteps of the prophet Samuel." [15]

Albert Coenraets Burgh

Albert Coenraets, or Albert Coenraets Burgh, as he was also called, was baptized in Amsterdam in 1593, son of a merchant who seems not to have held any important municipal posts. In 1614 he matriculated at Leyden, and several years later began practice as a physician in Amsterdam. In 1618 he married the daughter of a hide merchant, whose greatest honorific attainment was probably a term as deacon of the hide-merchants' guild. Yet, despite his seeming lack of influential connections, when Prince Maurits purged the city council of Amsterdam of adherents of Oldenbarnevelt in 1618, Coenraets, at the tender age of twenty-five, became one of the thirty-six councilors, and he held this post until his death. In 1622 he was appointed director of the West India Company.[16]

His appointment by Maurits to the city council must indicate his having evinced at the time an unwavering Contraremonstrant sentiment. Yet before Maurits' death in 1625, Coenraets encouraged the poet Vondel to compose *Palamedes*, a tragedy on the death of Oldenbarnevelt, thinly disguised by the use of Greek names.[17] In another important case Coen-

14. Kernkamp discusses Blommaert's departure from Swedish service and his precarious relationship with the West India Company in *ibid.*, pp. 34–35, 56–57; and 59–64. In his letter to Oxenstierna of January 28, 1640, Blommaert gives a summary of all the accomplishments of the West India Company and then writes: " all the aforewritten plans and attempts were mostly undertaken through my leadership and on my suggestion; and I myself prepared the instructions and inquiries, as I make it my job to have punctual knowledge of everything that is happening in the whole area of the *Octroy*, as I am continually getting information from everyone who comes from those quarters, which is not practiced by others . . . ."; *ibid.*, p. 171. In the " Memorie Boeck," however, Blommaert mentions as his activities while a director only his connection with the expedition of Hendrick Brouwer to Chili and with the General Board of Accounts in 1646.

15. Elias, *Vroedschap*, I, p. 373, gives the date of his death. His father's wish is in the " Memorie Boeck."

16. Elias, *Vroedschap*, I, pp. 327–30, gives information on Coenraets' family connections, his matriculation at Leyden, and his entry in the city council. The beginning of his practice is noted in A. J. van der Aa, *Biographisch woordenboek der Nederlanden*, II, p. 1585. Wass., IV, p. 20, lists him among the first directors of the West India Company.

17. Jan Wagenaar, *Vaderlandsche historie*, XI, p. 487.

raets acted in an equally paradoxical manner. In November 1628 he was a foremost proponent of the great scheme to secure Dutch shipping from the depredations of the Dunkirkers and other sea rovers through a chartered insurance company on the scale of the East and West India Companies. The scheme ran into stiff opposition and was not adopted at this time, but when revived in 1634, Coenraets was flatly opposed to the concept.[18] It is, of course, possible to interpret these puzzling changes of opinion as the machinations of an intriguer; but another explanation is that they represented the changing convictions of a conscientious statesman who possessed the rare courage to admit he was wrong.

Elias described him as a " prominent merchant and dyer," but about the time he became a patroon in New Netherland he possessed only very modest means: in 1631 his worth was only f 40,000.[19] Yet he registered two patroonships, on October 22, 1629, for the West Indian island of St. Vincent and on November 1 of the same year, with associates, for the left bank of the Delaware River, opposite Godijn's Swanendael. Although he seems originally to have considered joining with Blommaert, Godijn, and van Rensselaer in the single partnership for the plantation of the patroonships, his appointment as ambassador to the Czar in 1630 and perhaps some differences with the other patroons over the amalgamation agreement caused him to abandon his patroonships.[20] In 1633 Coenraets began a second term as director of the West India Company, and soon he was involved in the renewed controversy over the patroon system. Although he and one other signed in June 1634 a reply of the West India Company to a memorial of the patroons to the States General, van Rensselaer reveals Coenraets as furthering a moderate policy in regard to the patroons.[21]

18. Coenraets' role in the debate about the proposed general insurance company is described in P. J. Blok, "Het plan tot oprichting eener Compagnie van Assurantie," *Bijdragen voor Vaderlandsche Geschiedenis en Oudheidkunde*, 4th series, I (1900), pp. 6–7, 12–13, 37–38.

19. Elias' description in *Vroedschap*, I, p. 327. Blok (*Bijdragen voor Vaderlandsche Geschiedenis en Oudheidkunde*, 4th series, I, p. 13n) gives his financial worth.

20. For Coenraets' initial registrations, see VRBM, p. 156. He was included in a draft combination of colonies of February 1, 1630 (VRBM, p. 164) and also the final combination agreement, which was drafted at an unknown date and signed October 1, 1630, de Laet signing for Coenraets' share "whereas Mr. Albertus Conradj had before ceded him [de Laet] his half and his wife now in his Honor's absence neglects matters entirely" (VRBM, pp. 171–74). Coenraets' dissatisfaction with the combination agreement seems to be indicated in a letter from van Rensselaer to Johannes de Laet, February 4, 1641, in VRBM, p. 532.

21. Coenraets' reelection as director at "the last meeting of the directors" is mentioned in van Rensselaer's letter to van Twiller of April 23, 1634 (VRBM, p. 270). As the biannual retirement of one-third of the directors occurred in June, it appears that Coenraets was reelected in June 1633. For his activities in the patroon controversy in 1633–34, see Chapter 6. That he followed a moderate policy in this controversy is evident from van Rensselaer's letter to van Twiller, April 23, 1634, in VRBM, p. 282.

In 1636 he contemplated purchasing a share in Rensselaerswyck, and van Rensselaer wrote to his partner de Laet that he had let Coenraets read all the letters and instructions concerning the colony " in order that he [Coenraets] may be at ease and do the same [invest in Rensselaerswyck] in good conscience." [22] In 1645 Dr. Coenraets was serving a third term as director of the West India Company.[23]

In a letter to his nephew, Wouter van Twiller, van Rensselaer describes Coenraets as acting " with his wonted discretion." [24] Others evidently appreciated the same quality, for he made three difficult ambassadorial missions for the United Provinces, two to the Czar in 1630-32 and 1647 and one, in 1639, to Denmark. He also served as burgomaster of Amsterdam in 1638 and 1641 and held many other respectable positions. His death occurred in 1647 during his second embassy to Russia.[25]

Dr. Coenraets' career reveals him as a talented and high-minded statesman, one of the finest representatives of the regent class of the United Provinces. Though his personality is not so clearly revealed as Blommaert's, it is difficult to conceive of him as a party to a plot to swindle the West India Company.

Johannes de Laet

We met Johannes de Laet in Chapter Three as the author of the *Nieuwe Wereldt*, a description of the West Indies which went through two Dutch, a Latin, and a French printing between 1625 and 1640. Born in Antwerp in 1582, de Laet settled at an unknown date in Leyden. In 1618–19 he was a member of the famous National Synod of Dordrecht. When Leyden contributed *f* 200,000 to the capital of the Amsterdam Chamber of the West India Company, the city was entitled to name two supernumerary directors in that chamber, and de Laet was one of the directors named. Shortly thereafter he completed his *Nieuwe Wereldt*, written both to attract investors to the West India Company and inform its directorate.[26]

De Laet's scholarly achievements included, besides *Nieuwe Wereldt*, seven volumes of the Elzevier's forty-eight volume pocket library of political and geographic descriptions of the nations of the world, the able

22. Letter of van Rensselaer to de Laet, October 6, 1636, in VRBM, p. 270.
23. Samuel Blommaert, " Memorie Boeck."
24. Van Rensselaer to van Twiller, April 23, 1634, in VRBM, p. 270.
25. Elias (*Vroedschap*, I, p. 327) mentions Coenraets' missions to the Czar, his service as burgomaster, and the date of his death. For a fuller account of his first mission to Russia, see van der Aa, *Biographisch woordenboek*, II, pp. 1585–86.
26. De Laet's birth is given in Académie royale des sciences, des lettres et des beaux-arts de Belgique, *Biographie nationale*, V, p. 273. His participation in the Synod of Dordrecht is mentioned by van der Aa, *Biographisch woordenboek*, XI, p. 27. Blommaert's " Memorie Boeck " lists him as a director from Leyden.
The reasons why he wrote *Nieuwe Wereldt* are given in his dedication to that work, dated November 15, 1624.

classification and publication of the notes of the distinguished naturalist Marcgraff, who had died after accompanying Johan Maurits to Brazil, a treatise on gems, and several very mediocre translations of classical writers. He engaged in a scholarly dispute with Grotius concerning the origin of the American Indians and corresponded with the appallingly learned Joseph Scaliger and with Claudius Salmasius, Scaliger's successor at the University of Leyden. Undoubtedly, de Laet was intelligent and productive, but it has been said of him that despite his excellent compilations he failed to make any really original contributions to knowledge.[27]

De Laet's first term as director of the West India Company on behalf of Leyden extended at least through July 1631.[28] In 1630 he assumed Dr. Coenraets' rights to a patroonship on the Delaware River and entered the patroonship pool of Blommaert, Godijn, and van Rensselaer. Although he seems never to have attempted to develop the Delaware patroonship, he remained until his death in 1649 a participant in Rensselaerswyck; and in this capacity he engaged in two sharp disputes, with van Rensselaer and with van Rensselaer's heirs, over their interpretation of their patroonal rights.[29] After his first term as director of the West India Company, he served again in at least 1635–38 and 1645, indicating that he retained the confidence of his principals at Leyden. During his latter years as director, his literary talents were engaged in the service of the West India Company a second time. His *Historie ofte iaerlijck verhael van de verrichtinghen der Geoctroyeerde West-Indische Compagnie* (1644) served to publicize the achievements of the Company in the war against Spain as the Company's first charter approached its end. Though little is known of the scholar's character, an attempt to defraud the Company would appear inconsistent with his apparent dedication to the Company's cause.

27. *Biographie nationale*, V, p. 276, lists de Laet's scholarly works and states the opinion that he failed to make any really original contributions. His connection with Scaliger and Salmasius is mentioned in van der Aa, *Biographisch woordenboek*, XI, p. 26.

28. Letter of Pieter Janss Blauhaen to the Burgomasters, *Schepens*, and Council of Deventer, July 18, 1631, in Gemeente Archief van Deventer, Netherlands.

29. De Laet's entrance into the patroonship pool is recorded in VRBM, p. 174. For his disputes with van Rensselaer, see Nissenson, *Patroon's Domain*, pp. 320–24.

Van der Aa, *Biographisch woordenboek*, XI, p. 26, gives his date of death. His heirs inherited a share in Rensselaerswyck (Nissenson, p. 324).

BIBLIOGRAPHY: BOOKS AND MANUSCRIPTS CITED

NOTE: *Two very useful bibliographical essays on the sources for the history of New Netherland are:*

Asher, G. M. *A Bibliographical and Historical Essay on the Dutch Books and Pamphlets Relating to New-Netherland and to the Dutch West-India Company and to Its Possessions in Brazil/ Angola etc./ as also on the Maps, Charts, etc. of New-Netherland, with Facsimiles of the Map of New-Netherland by N. I. Visscher and of the Three Existing Views of New-Amsterdam.* 2d edition. Amsterdam: N. Israel, 1960. First published in Amsterdam by Frederik Muller, 1854–1867.

Paltsits, Victor Hugo. "The New York tercentenary: an exhibition of the history of New Netherland," *Bulletin of the New York Public Library,* XXX (1926), pp. 655–84, 759–92.

*

Aa, A. J. van der. *Biographisch woordenboek der Nederlanden, bevattende levens-beschrijvingen van zoodanige personen, die zich op eenigerlei wijze in ons vaderland hebben vermaard gemaakt.* Continued by K. J. R. van Harderwijk and Dr. G. D. J. Schotel. 21 vols. New edition. Haarlem: J. J. van Brede-rode, [n. d.].

Académie royale des sciences, des lettres et des beaux-arts de Belgique. *Biographie nationale.* 25 vols. Bruxelles: H. Thiry; Bruphant-Christophe & c^e, 1866–1932.

[Accarias de Sérionne, Jacques]. *Hollands rijkdom, behelzende den oorsprong van den koophandel, en van de magt van dezen staat; de toeneemende vermeerdering van deszelfs koophandel en scheepvaart; de oorzaken, welke tot derzelver aanwas medegewerkt hebben; die, welke tegenwoordig tot derzelver verval strekken; mitsgaders de middelen, welke dezelven wederom zouden kunnen opbeuren, en tot hunnen voorigen bloei brengen.* Revised by Elias Luzac. 4 vols. Leyden: Luzac and van Damme, 1780–1783.

Acquoy, J. *Deventer's participatie in de West-Indische Compagnie.* Deventer: N. V. Electr. Drukkerij "Trio", 1922.

"Advies tot aanbeveling van de verovering van Brazilië door de West-Indische Compagnie [1622]," *Kroniek van het Historisch Genootschap,* XXVII (1871), p. 228–56.

Aenwysinge: Datmen van de Oost en West-Indische Compagnien/ een compagnie dient te maken. Mitsgaders twintich consideratien op de trafyque, zeevaert, en commercie deser landen. The Hague: Ian Veeli, 1644.

Albion, Robert Greenhalgh. *Forests and Seapower: The Timber Problem of the Royal Navy, 1652–1862.* Cambridge: Harvard University Press, 1926.

Andrews, Charles M. *The Colonial Period of American History.* 4 vols. New Haven: Yale University Press, 1934–1938.

Arend, J. P. *Algemeene geschiedenis des vaderlands, van de vroegste tijden tot op heden.* Continued by O. van Rees and W. G. Brill. 15 vols. Amsterdam: J. F. Schleijer; C. L. Schleijer & Zoon, 1840–1883.

Baker, William A. *Colonial Vessels: Some Seventeenth-Century Sailing Craft.* Barre, Mass.: Barre Publishing Company, 1962.

Barbour, Violet. "Dutch and English Merchant Shipping." *Economic History Review* II (1929–1930), 261–90.

————. "Marine Risks and Insurance in the Seventeenth Century," *Journal of Economic and Business History* I (1929), pp. 561–96.

Berg van Dussen Muilkerk, W. E. J. "Bijdragen tot de geschiedenis onzer kolonisatie in Noord-Amerika." *De Gids,* (1848), part II, pp. 522–54; and (1849), part I, pp. 702–20.

Bijlsma, R. "Rotterdams Amerika-vaart in de eerste helft der zeventiende eeuw," *Bijdragen voor vaderlandsche geschiedenis en oudheidkunde,* 5th series, III (1916), pp. 97–142.

Blok, P. J. "Het plan tot oprichting eener Compagnie van Assurantie," *Bijdragen voor vaderlandsche geschiedenis en oudheidkunde,* 4th series, I (1900), pp. 1–41.

Blommaert, Samuel. "Brieven van Samuel Blommaert aan den Zweedschen Rijks-kanselier Axel Oxenstierna, 1635–41," edited by G. W. Kernkamp, *Bijdragen en mededeelingen van het Historisch Genootschap,* XXIX (1908), pp. 3–196.

Boxer, C. R. *The Dutch in Brazil, 1624–1654.* Oxford: Clarendon Press, 1957.

Bradford, William. *Bradford's History of Plymouth Plantation, 1606–1646.* Edited by William T. Davis. Original Narratives of Early American History. New York: C. Scribner's Sons, 1908.

Brakel, S. van. *De Hollandsche handelscompagnieën der zeventiende eeuw: hun ontstaan—hunne inrichting.* The Hague: Martinus Nijhoff, 1908.

Brilgesicht voor de verblinde eyghen baetsuchtige handelaers op Brasil. By forme van advijs door een lief-hebber van't vaderlandt geschreven aen synen vriendt. [n. p.], 1638.

Brodhead, John Romeyn. *History of the State of New York.* 2 vols. New York: Harper & Brothers, 1853–1871.

Champlain, Samuel de. *The Works of Samuel de Champlain.* Edited by H. P. Biggar. 6 vols. Publications of the Champlain Society. Toronto: The Champlain Society, 1922–1936.

Christensen, A. E. *Dutch Trade in the Baltic about 1600.* Studies in the Sound Toll Register and Dutch Shipping Records. The Hague: Martinus Nijhoff, 1941.

Chronicles of the First Planters of the Colony of Massachusetts Bay, from 1623 to 1636. Edited by Alexander Young. Boston: Charles C. Little and James Brown, 1846.

Chronicles of the Pilgrim Fathers of the Colony of Plymouth from 1602 to 1625. Now first collected from original records and contemporaneous printed documents and illustrated with notes. Edited by Alexander Young. 2d ed. Boston: C. C. Little and J. Brown, 1844.

Colonizing Expeditions to the West Indies and Guiana, 1623–1667. Edited by V. T. Harlow. Works issued by the Hakluyt Society, 2d series, LVI. London: Hakluyt Society, 1925.

Craven, Wesley Frank. *The Southern Colonies in the Seventeenth Century 1607–1689.* A History of the South, vol. 1, eds. Wendell Holmes Stephenson and E. Merton Coulter. Vols. 1—. [Baton Rouge]: Louisiana State University Press, 1947—— .

Dale, [Johan Hendrik] van. *Groot woordenboek der Nederlandse taal.* 8th edition revised. The Hague: Martinus Nijhoff, 1961.

Davies, D. W. *Primer of Dutch Seventeenth Century Overseas Trade.* The Hague: Martinus Nijhoff, 1961.

Davis, Ralph. "Merchant Shipping in the Economy of the Late Seventeenth Century," *Economic History Review*, 2d series, IX (1956–1957), pp. 59–73.
————. *The Rise of the English Shipping Industry in the Seventeenth and Eighteenth Centuries*. London: Macmillan and Co., 1962.
Derde discovrs by forma van missive, daer in kortelijck ende grondich vertoont wort/ de nootwendicheyt des Oost ende West-Indische navigatie/ oock met goede fondamentale redenen bewesen/ dat door gheen ander middel/ eenen vasten versekerden vrede en is te verwachten of te verhopen. Worden daerom alle ghetrouwe patriotten des vaderlandts/ ten voorsten de regierders/ ende volgens alle vermoghende inwoonders vermaent/ om tot dese/ nu nieuwe gheoctroyeerde West-Indiaensche Compaignie mildelijck te contribueren/ ten eynde deselve beter succes tot krenckinghe van de Castiliaensche trafijcke ghewinne. [n. p.], 1622.
Documentary History of the State of New York. Edited by E. B. O'Callaghan. 4 vols. Albany: Weed, Parsons & Co.; Charles van Benthuysen, 1849–1851.
Documents Relating to New Netherland, 1624–1626, in the Henry E. Huntington Library. Translated and edited by A. J. F. van Laer. San Marino, California, 1924.
Documents Relative to the Colonial History of the State of New York. Vols. I–XI edited by E. B. O'Callaghan. Vols. XII–XV edited by B. Fernow. 15 vols. Albany: Weed, Parsons and Co. [etc.], 1856–1887.
Ecclesiastical Records of the State of New York. Edited by Edward T. Corwin. 7 vols. Albany: James B. Lyon Co., 1901–1916.
Edmundson, George. "The Dutch in Western Guiana," *English Historical Review* XVI (1901), pp. 640–75.
————. "The Dutch on the Amazon and Negro in the Seventeenth Century," *English Historical Review*, XVIII (1903), pp. 642–63; and XIX (1904), pp. 1–25.
Eekhof, Albert. *Bastiaen Jansz. Krol, krankenbezoeker, kommies en kommandeur van Nieuw-Nederland (1595–1645); nieuwe gegevens voor de kennis der vestiging van ons kerkelijk en koloniaal gezag in Noord-Amerika*. The Hague: Martinus Nijhoff, 1910.
————. *Jonas Michaëlius, Founder of the Church in New Netherland; His Life and Work*. Leiden: A. W. Sijthoff, 1926.
"Een memorie over den toestand der West-Indische Compagnie in het jaar 1633," edited by M. G. de Boer, *Bijdragen en mededeelingen van het Historisch Genootschap*, XXI (1900), pp. 343–62.
Elias, Johan E. *De Vroedschap van Amsterdam, 1578–1795*. 2 vols. Haarlem: Vincent Loosjes, 1903–1905.
Examen over het Vertoogh tegen het ongefundeerde en schadelijcke sluyten der vryen handel in Brasil. [n. p.], 1637.
Fisher, Raymond H. *The Russian Fur Trade, 1550–1700*. University of California Publications in History XXXI. Berkeley and Los Angeles: University of California Press, 1943.
Forest, Mrs. Robert W. de. *A Walloon Family in America; Lockwood de Forest and His Forbears 1500–1848, . . . ; together with A Voyage to Guiana, Being the Journal of Jesse de Forest and His Colonists 1623–1625*. 2 vols. Boston and New York: Houghton Mifflin Co., 1914.
Gemeente Archief van Amsterdam. Samuel Blommaert. Memorie-boeck van ons geslachten.
————. Notarieel Archief.
————. Rechterlijke Archieven.
Grol, G. J. van. *Grondpolitiek in het West-Indische domein der Generaliteit; een historische studie*. 3 vols. The Hague: Algemeen Landsdrukkerij, 1934–1947.

Groot placaet-boeck, vervattende de placaten, ordonnantien ende edicten vande Doorluchtige, Hoogh Mog. Heeren Staten Generael der Vereenighde Nederlanden: ende vande Ed: Groot-Mog. Heeren Staten van Hollandt en West-Vrieslandt; mitsgaders vande Ed:Mog: Heeren Staten van Zeelandt. Waer by noch ghevoeght zijn eenige placaten vande voorgaende Graven ende Princen der selver landen, voor soo veel de selve als noch in gebruyck zijn. Edited by Cornelis Cau et al. 9 vols. The Hague: Weduwe ende erfgenamen van wylen Hillebrandt Iacobsz van Wouw [etc.], 1658–1770. Amsterdam: J. Allart, 1795–1796.

Hamelberg, J. H. J. *De Nederlanders op de West Indische eilanden.* Bijdrage tot de jaarverslagen van het Geschied-, Taal-, Land- en Volkenkundig Genootschap der Nederlandsche Antillen. Amsterdam: J. H. de Bussy, 1901.

———. *Documenten behoorende bij " Nederlanders op de West-Indische Eilanden."* Amsterdam: J. H. de Bussy, 1901.

Hart, Simon. *The Prehistory of the New Netherland Company; Amsterdam Notarial Records of the First Dutch Voyages to the Hudson.* Amsterdam: City of Amsterdam Press, 1959.

Historical Society of Pennsylvania. Dutch West India Company papers, 1626–1834.

History of the State of New York. Edited by Alexander C. Flick. 10 vols. Published under the auspices of the New York State Historical Association. New York: Columbia University Press, 1933–1937.

Hoboken, W. J. van. " The Dutch West India Company; The Political Background of Its Rise and Decline." *Britain and the Netherlands. Papers delivered to the Oxford-Netherlands Historical Conference,* pp. 41–61. London: Chatto & Windus, 1959.

Hunt, George T. *The Wars of the Iroquois: A Study in Intertribal Relations.* Madison: University of Wisconsin Press, 1940.

Jameson, J. Franklin. " Willem Usselinx, Founder of the Dutch and Swedish West India Companies," *Papers of the American Historical Association* II (1887).

Jessurun, J. Spinoza Catella. *Kiliaen van Rensselaer van 1623 tot 1636.* The Hague: Martinus Nijhoff, 1917.

Journael van de reis naar Zuid-Amerika (1598–1601) door Hendrik Ottsen. Edited by J. W. Ijzerman. Werken uitgegeven door de Linschoten-vereeniging, XVI. The Hague: Martinus Nijhoff, 1918.

" Koopmansadviezen aangaande het plan tot oprichting eener compagnie van assurantie, 1629–1635," edited by P. J. Blok, *Bijdragen en mededeelingen van het Historisch Genootschap,* XXI (1900), pp. 1–160.

Laet, Ioannes de. *Historie ofte Iaerlijck Verhael van de verrichtinghen der Geoctroyeerde West-Indische Compagnie, zedert haer begin, tot het eynde van 't jaer sesthien-hondert ses-en-dertich; begrepen in derthien boecken, ende met verscheyden koperen platen verciert.* Leyden: Bonaventuere ende Abraham Elzevier, 1644.

———. *Iaerlijck Verhael van de verrichtinghen der Geoctroyeerde West-Indische Compagnie in derthien boecken.* Edited by S. P. L'Honoré Naber. 4 vols. Werken uitgegeven door de Linschoten-vereeniging, XXXIV, XXXV, XXXVII, and XL. The Hague: Martinus Nijhoff, 1931–37. (A new edition of the preceding.)

———. *Nieuwe Wereldt ofte beschrijvinghe van West-Indien, wt veelerhande schriften ende aen-teekeningen van verscheyden natien by een versamelt door Joannes de Laet, ende met noodige kaerten en tafels voorsien.* Leyden: Isaack Elzevier, 1625.

Lambrechtsen, N. C. " A history of the New Netherlands," translated by Francis Adrian van der Kemp, *Collections of the New York Historical Society,* 2d series, I (1841), pp. 75–122. (The original, entitled *Korte beschrijving van de ontdekking en der verdere lotgevallen van Nieuw-Nederland*, was published at Middelburg by S. van Benthem, 1818.)

Lane, Frederic C. "Tonnages, Medieval and Modern," *Economic History Review*, 2d ser., XVII (1964), pp. 213–33.

Lannoy, Charles de, and Linden, Herman van der. *Histoire de l'expansion coloniale des peuples européens.* 3 vols. Bruxelles: Henri Lamerton; and Paris: Félix Alcan, 1907–1921.

Lescarbot, Marc. *History of New France.* Translated and edited by W. L. Grant, with an introduction by H. P. Biggar. 3 vols. Translation of the third edition (Paris, 1618). Publications of the Champlain Society. Toronto: Champlain Society, 1907–1914.

"Letters of Wouter van Twiller and the Director General and Council of New Netherland to the Amsterdam Chamber of the Dutch West India Company, August 14, 1636," edited by A. J. F. van Laer. *New York State Historical Association Quarterly Journal* I (1919): 44–50.

Levendich discovrs vant ghemeyne lants welvaert/ voor desen de Oost/ ende nu oock de West-Indische generale Compaignie aenghevanghen/ seer notabel om te lesen. [n. p.]: Broer Iansz., 1622.

Ligtenberg, Catharina. *Willem Usselinx.* Utrecht: A. Oosthoek, 1914.

Lintum, O. te. "De Kamer der West-Indische Compagnie te Delft." *Bijdragen tot de Taal-, Land- en Volkenkunde van Nederlandsch-Indië* LXIII (1910), pp. 93–108.

Menkman, W. R. *De West-Indische Compagnie.* Patria; vaderlandsche cultuur-geschiedenis in monografieën, onder redactie van Dr. J. H. Kernkamp, XLII. Amsterdam: P. N. van Kampen, 1947.

"Minutes of the Amsterdam Chamber of the Dutch West India Company, 1635–1636," edited by A. J. F. van Laer, *New York Genealogical and Biographical Record* XLIX (1918), pp. 217–28.

Missive daer in kortelijck en grondigh wert verthoont/ hoe veel de Vereenighde Nederlanden gelegen is aen de Oost ende West-Indische navigatie. Mitsgaders 't profijt dat men van de Oost-Indische Compagnie/ geduyrende den tijdt van 24. jaren herwaerts/ daer uyt heeft ghetrocken. Ende met fondamentale redenen werd bewesen/ dat door de gheoctroyeerde West-Indische navigatie/ meer voordeel voor de participanten met meerder dienste voor de Nederlantsche Provintien/ grooter schade ende afbreuck voor den Coninck van Spaengien zij te verwachten. Amsterdam: Broer Jansz., 1621.

Moerbeeck, Jan Andries. *Redenen/ waeromme de West-Indische Compagnie dient te trachten het landt van Brasilia den Coninck van Spangien te ontmachtigen, en dat ten eersten. Wesende een ghedeelte der proposities ghedaen door Ian Andries Moerbeeck aen zijn Vorstelijcke Ghenade Mauritio Prince van Orange/ etc. ende eenighe andere Heeren Ghecommitteerden van de Hooghe ende Groot-moghende Heeren de Staten Generael der Vereenichde Nederlanden/ in 's Graven Haghe den 4. 5. ende 6. April/ Anno 1623.* Amsterdam: Cornelis Lodewijcksz vander Plasse, 1624.

Muller, S. *Geschiedenis der Noordsche Compagnie.* Utrecht: Gebr. van der Post, 1874.

Murphy, Henry Cruse. *Henry Hudson in Holland: An Inquiry into the Origin and Objects of the Voyage which Led to the Discovery of the Hudson River.* 2d ed. The Hague: Martinus Nijhoff, 1909.

Narratives of New Netherland, 1609–1664. Edited by J. Franklin Jameson. Original Narratives of Early American History. New York: Charles Scribner's Sons, 1909.

Nassau-Siegen, Johan Maurits van. "Memorie van Prins Maurits van Nassau van 16 Jan. 1638, waarbij deze op vrijen handel aandringt en het monopolie der West-Indische Compagnie bestrijdt," *Kronijk van het Historisch Genootschap* XI (1855), pp. 60–70.

Netscher, P. M. *Geschiedenis van de kolonien Essequibo, Demerary, en Berbice, van de vestiging der Nederlanders aldaar tot op onzen tijd.* The Hague: Martinus Nijhoff, 1888.

New York State Library. New York Colonial Manuscripts.

N. G. *Reys-boeck van het rijcke Brasilien, Rio de la Plata ende Magallanes, daer in te sien is/ de ghelegentheydt van hare landen ende steden/ haren handel ende wandel/ met de vruchten ende vruchtbaerheyt der selver: alles met copere platen uytghebeelt. Als oock de leste reyse van den Heer van Dort, met het ver-overen van de Baeye de Todos los Santos, t'samen ghestelt door N. G.* [n. p.]: Ian Canin, 1624.

Nissenson, Samuel George. *The Patroon's Domain.* New York State Historical Association Series, No. V. New York: Columbia University Press, 1937.

O'Callaghan, E. B. *History of New Netherland; or New York under the Dutch.* 2d edition. New York: D. Appleton & Co., 1855.

Ooghen-Salve tot verlichtinghe, van alle participanten, so vande Oost, ende West-Indische Compagnien, mitsgaders verscheyden notabele consideratien, aengaende de vereeninghe van de Oost- ende- West-Indische Compaignien, met malkanderen. The Hague: Lieven de Lange, 1644.

Oost ende West-Indische spieghel waer in beschreven werden de twee laetste navigatien/ ghedaen inde jaeren 1614. 1615. 1616. 1617. ende 1618. De eene door den vermaerden zee-heldt Ioris van Spilbergen door de Strate van Magellanes, ende soo rondt om den gantschen aerdt-cloot/met alle de bataellien soo te water als te lande gheschiet. Hier syn meede by ghevoecht twee historien, de eene vande Oost ende de andere vande West-Indien, met het ghetal der schepen, forten, soldaten ende geschut. De andere ghedaen by Iacob Le Maire, de welcke in 't Zuyden de Straet Magellanes, een nieuwe straet ontdeckt heeft/ met de beschrijvinghe aller landen/ volcken ende natien. Alles verciert met schoone caerten ende figueren hier toe dienstelijck. Zutphen: Andries Janssz van Aelst, 1621.

Oud-archief van Deventer. Letters of P. Blauhaen and Others, Memoranda, etc., Concerning Deventer's Participation in the West India Company.

Paltsits, Victor Hugo. "The founding of New Amsterdam in 1626," *Proceedings of the American Antiquarian Society, Worcester, Mass.*, new series, XXXIV (1925), pp. 39–65.

Posthumus, N. W. *Inquiry into the History of Prices in Holland.* Publications of the International Scientific Committee on Price History. 2 vols. Leiden: E. J. Brill, 1946.

Purchas, Samuel. *Hakluytus posthumus or Purchas his pilgrimes contayning a history of the world in sea voyages and land travells by Englishmen and others.* 20 vols. Reprint of 1625 edition. Glasgow: James MacLehose and Sons, 1905–1907.

Rees, O. van. *Geschiedenis der staathuishoudkunde in Nederland tot het einde der achttiende eeuw.* 2 vols. Utrecht: Kemink en Zoon, 1865–1868.

Roever, Nicolaas de. "Kiliaen van Rensselaer en zijne kolonie Rensselaerswyck," *Oud Holland*, VIII (1890), pp. 29–74, 241–96.

Ruiters, Dierick. *Toortse der zee-vaert door Dierick Ruiters (1623). Samuel Brun's Schiffarten (1624).* Edited by S. P. L'Honoré Naber. Werken uitgegeven door de Linschoten-vereeniging, VI. The Hague: Martinus Nijhoff, 1913. Originally published in Vlissingen by Marten Abrahamsz. van der Nolck, 1623.

Savary des Bruslons, Jacques. *Dictionnaire Universal de Commerce.* 3 vols. Paris: Jacques Estienne, 1723–1730.

Schreiner, Johan. *Nederland og Norge 1625–1650. Trelastutførsel og handelspolitikk.* Skrifter utgitt av det Norske Videnskaps-Akademi i Oslo. II. Hist.-Filos. klasse 1933 no. 3. Oslo: Jacob Dybwab, 1933.

Sir Ferdinando Gorges and his province of Maine. Including the Brief Narration, his Defence, the Charter granted to him, his will, and his letters. Edited by James Phinney Baxter. 3 vols. Publications of the Prince Society. Boston: The Prince Society, 1890.

Sombart, Werner. *Luxus und Kapitalismus.* Studien zur Entwicklungsgeschichte des modernen Kapitalismus. Munich and Leipzig: Verlag von Duncker & Humblot, 1913.

" Some Early Dutch manuscripts. Letters to Adriaen Gerritsen Papendorp," edited by A. J. F. van Laer. *New York Historical Association Quarterly Journal,* III (1922), pp. 221–33.

Stokes, I. N. Phelps. *The Iconography of Manhattan Island.* 6 vols. New York: Robert H. Dodd, 1915–1928.

" Stukken betreffende den vrijen handel op Brazilië, 1637." *Kroniek van het Historisch Genootschap* XXV (1869): 191–205.

Trelease, Allen W. *Indian Affairs in Colonial New York: The Seventeenth Century.* Ithaca, New York: Cornell University Press, 1960.

United States Commission to Investigate and Report upon the True Divisional Line between Venezuela and British Guiana. *Report and Accompanying Papers.* 2 vols. Washington: Government Printing Office, 1897.

University of Minnesota, James Ford Bell Collection. Copije vande misiue aende Camer van Zeelandt van Jan Adriaensz vander Goes:en Johannes Beverlandt In datto den 30 September 1627 vuijten Riuier Isequebe.

Van Rensselaer Bowier Manuscripts, Being the Letters of Kiliaen van Rensselaer, 1630–1643, and other Documents Relating to the Colony of Rensselaerswyck.... With an introductory essay by Nicolaas de Roever, late archivist of the City of Amsterdam, translated by Mrs. Alan H. Strong. Translated and edited by A. J. F. van Laer. Albany: University of the State of New York, 1908.

Velius, Theodorus. *Chronijk van Hoorn, daar in het begin, aanwasch, en tegenwoordige staat dier stad verhaalt worden. Als mede de gedenkwaardige geschiedenissen die, zo voor, in, als na den trubbel, in of omtrent dezelve en door geheel West-Vriesland gebeurt zyn, tot het jaar 1630.* 4th printing, edited by Sebastiaan Centen. Hoorn: Jacob Duyn, 1740.

Versteeg, Dingman. *Manhattan in 1628 as Described in the Recently Discovered Autograph Letter of Jonas Michaëlius Written from the Settlement on the 8th of August of That Year, and Now First Published; With a Review of the Letter and an Historical Sketch of New Netherland to 1628.* New York: Dodd, Mead, and Company, 1904.

Vertoogh, over den toestant der West-Indische Compagnie, in haer begin, midden, ende eynde, met een remedie tot redres van deselve. Rotterdam: Iohannes van Roon, 1651.

Vosburgh, Royden Woodward. " The settlement of New Netherland, 1624–1626." *New York Genealogical and Biographical Record* LV (1924), pp. 3–15, 211–13.

Vries, David Pietersz. de. *Korte historiael, ende journaels-aenteyckeninge van verscheyden voyagiens in de vier deelen des wereldts-ronde, als Europa, Africa, Asia, ende Amerika gedaen.* Edited by H. T. Colenbrander. Werken uitgegeven door de Linschoten-vereeniging," III. Original published at Alckmaer by Symon Cornelisz. Brekegeest, 1655. The Hague: Martinus Nijhoff, 1911.

Wagenaar, Jan. *Vaderlandsche historie, vervattende de geschiedenissen der nu Vereenigde Nederlanden, inzonderheid die van Holland, van de vroegste tyden af: uit de geloofwaardige schryvers en egte gedenkstukken samengesteld.* 21 vols. Amsterdam: J. Allart, 1790–1796.

Walton, Gary M. " Sources of Productivity Change in American Colonial Shipping, 1675–1775." *Economic History Review,* 2nd series, XX (1967), pp. 67–78.

Wassenaer, Nicolaes van. *Historisch verhael alder ghedenck-weerdichste geschiedenissen die hier en daer in Europa, als in Duijtschlant, Vranckrijck, Enghelant, [Denemarcken,] Hungarijen, Polen, [Sweden, Moscovien,] Sevenbergen, Wallachien, Moldavien, Turckijen, [Zwitserland,] en Nederlant, [in Asia, . . . : in Africa, . . . : in America, . . . :] van den beginne des jaers 1621: [tot Octobri (1629)], voorgevallen syn.* 17 vols. Amsterdam: Jan Evertss. Cloppenburgh and Ian Iansz, 1622–1630.

West-Indische Compagnie. *Articulen, met approbatie vande Ho: Mog: Staten Generael der Vereenighde Nederlanden/ provisioneelijck beraemt by bewinthebberen vande Generale geoctroyeerde West-Indische Compagnie/ ter Vergaderinghe vande Neghenthiene/ over het open ende vry stellen vanden handel ende negotie op de stadt Olinda de Parnambuco, ende custen van Brasil.* Amstelredam: Paulus Aertsz van Ravensteyn, 1630.

Wieder, F. C. *Onderzoek naar de oudste kaarten van de omgeving van New York.* Overgedrukt uit het ' Tijdschrift van het Koninklijk Aardrijkskundig Genootschap,' 2d ser. vol. XXXV (1918), afl. 2. [Leiden]: Boekhandel en drukkerij voorheen E. J. Brill, 1918.

————. *De stichting van New York in juli 1625.* Werken uitgegeven door de Linschoten-vereeniging, XXVI. The Hague: Martinus Nijhoff, 1925.

Winkle, Edward Van. *Manhattan, 1624–1639.* New York: The author, 1916.

Winthrop, John. *Winthrop's Journal, 1630–1649.* Edited by James Kendall Hosmer. 2 vols. Original Narratives of Early American History. New York: Charles Scribner's Sons, 1908.

Witsen, Nicolaes. *Aeloude en hedendaegsche scheeps-bouw en bestier: waer in wijtloopigh wert verhandelt, de wijze van scheeps-timmeren, by Grieken en Romeynen: scheeps-oeffeningen, strijden, tucht, straffe, wetten en gewoonten. Beneffens evenmatige grootheden van schepen onses tijts, ontleet in alle hare deelen: verschil van bouwen tusschen uitheemschen en onzen landaert: Indisch vaertuygh: galey-bouw: hedendaegsche scheeps-plichten: verrijckt met een reex verklaerde zee-mans spreeck-woorden en benamingen.* Amsterdam: Casparus Commelijn; Broer en Jan Appelaer, 1671.

INDEX

Accoordt, 35–36

Africa. *See* West Africa

Agriculture in New Netherland: established, 83–85; experiments with, 83; judged unprofitable, 95–97, 100; and private enterprise, 95; problems of (*c.* 1628), 90; renewed interest in (1638), 153

Ahasimus, 136

Amazon River, 47, 98

Amsterdam, Chamber of: as administrator of New Netherland, 39, 83; capital invested in, 36, 37*n*; drafts plan for New Netherland (1638), 148, 149; *hoofdparticipanten* elect directors in, 34, 35; mentioned, 39*n*–43 *passim*, 133

Amsterdam, City of: and Brazil trade, 50, 145–46; *Kerckmisse*, 23

Angola, 70*n*

Archangel, Russia, 3, 63

Argijn, West Africa, 39*n*

Arnhem, Commissioner of States General, 138

Assembly of the Nineteen. *See* General Assembly of the Nineteen

Bahia, Brazil, 50–51, 54, 83, 88

Baltic lands: exports from, compared with New Netherland exports, 63–64, 68–69; shipping costs from, 64–69, 157–60

Baltic trade: shipping patterns of, 67

Barbados, West Indies, 162

Beaver pelts: trade in, relative to other furs, 20; traded in 1628–32, 131; traded in 1630, 129; traded in 1633, 130; traded in 1634–35, 131, 141. *See also* Furs; Fur trade

Berbice River, Guiana, 97, 101

Beverlant, Johannes, 98

Bewinthebberen. *See* Directors of West India Company

Bicker, Cornelis, 113, 114

Biscayan shallops, 19, 126. *See also* Sloops

Block, Adriaen, 5–8, 56

Blommaert, Samuel: commissioner for New Netherland, 112, 113; director, 162, 163; dishonesty of, 109, 117, 161–63; personal background, 161–62; patroon, 162; pools patroonship, 114, 162–63; purchases New Netherland, 106, 115

Blommaerts Vallei, 113*n*

Board of Audit, 39, 40

Bontenos, Jacob, 7*n*

Bout, Jan Evertsz, 136*n*

Bouwerijen of West India Company, 91, 95, 136*n*. *See also* Agriculture in New Netherland

Bradford, William, 96*n*

Brazil: Company's expenditures in, 145 and *n*; dispute over free trade with, 144–47; Dutch immigration to, 146–47; overseas trade of, 45, 50, 70*n*, 144–45; potential market for New Netherland grain, 70; situation in (*c.* 1624), 50–52; mentioned, 37. *See also* Amazon River; Bahia; Olinda; Pernambuco; Recife

Brazilwood, 51

Bremen, Germany, 63

Brouwer, Hendrick, 164*n*

Burgh, Albert Coenraets. *See* Coenraets, Albert

Cabo do Norte, Brazil, 98

Callao, Peru, 49

Cameren. *See* Chambers of West India Company

Canada, 3

Canary Islands, 45

Cannons, 126–27

Cape Hinlopen, 135

Cape May, 135

Cape Verde, West Africa, 39*n*, 49, 70*n*

Carib Indians, 98–99

Cartel agreement between *voorcompagnieën*, 8, 9

Castle Island, Hudson River, 83

Cattle. *See* Livestock

Cayenne River, Guiana, 98, 103

Ceulen, Mattias van, 121 and *n*

Chambers of West India Company: disobedience to Nineteen of, 39; dispute over Brazil trade, 144, 149; duties of, 39; purpose of, 28–29; rivalry between 40–41; subdivision of, 39–40. *See also* Amsterdam, Chamber of; Groningen-Friesland, Chamber of; Maes, Chamber of; Noorderquartier, Chamber of the; Zeeland, Chamber of
Champlain, Samuel de, 60, 76
Charter for Guiana. *See* Freedoms for Guiana
Charter of West India Company. *See* Octroy
Charter parties, 64–65
Chile, 46
Christiaensz, Hendrick, 5–7
Claesz, Hans, 7n
Coenraets, Albert: ambassadorial missions of, 165–66; and patroonship controversy, 138–39, 165; character of, 116–17, 166; commissioner for New Netherland, 113, 132, 143; director, 132, 164–66; draws *provisionele ordere*, 77; family connections, 164; in Amsterdam government, 164, 166; patroon, 113, 165; political convictions of, 164–65; pools patroonship, 114, 165
Coenraets Baij, 113n
Coloniërs: and fur trade, 79, 86; legal protections for, 81; obligations to Company, 80; ownership of land by, 77–78. *See also* Colonization of New Netherland
Colonization of New Netherland: abandonment of, considered, 124–25; arguments for and against, 59–60; Chamber Amsterdam's draft plan for (1638), 149–50; provisional arrangement of 1638/39 for, 151; undertaken (1624–25), 81–87. *See also* Coloniërs
Commissioners for New Netherland: and *Vryheden*, 109–10; identity of, 112; influence of, on New Netherland policy, 41; opinions of, concerning New Netherland's development, 100, 114; who were also patroons, 112
Connecticut River: Bloomaert's patroonship on, 162; Dutch colonists on, 82,

82n, 87; English encroachment on, 124n, 131, 141, 142; seasonal fur trading on, 93
Convoyen, 67, 105. *See also* Taxation
Cotton, 48, 49
Council for New England, 59n
Court of Amsterdam, 135
Courten, Pieter, 13, 52n
Crol, Bastiaen, 130
Curaçao. 39n, 43, 126n

Danzig: Dutch shipping to, 63, 66, 67, 157, 159. *See also* Baltic lands; Baltic trade
Defense of New Netherland, 108, 146, 149–50, 152. *See also* Munitions
De jure primae occupationis claims, 72, 82 and n, 96
Delaware Bay: climate of, 56–57; Coenraets patroonship on, 165; whales in, 93, 116. *See also* Delaware River; Swanendael
Delaware River: cost of trade on, 125; Dutch settlers on, 82–87 *passim*; permanent garrison on, needed, 141; probable seasonal trade on, 93; mentioned, 151n. *See also* Delaware Bay; Swanendael
Delft, Subchamber of, 34n, 40, 41
Dermer, Thomas, 13
Deventer, City of, 36
Dieterinck, Albert, 130n
Directors of West India Company, 29, 30–31, 40–41
Donck, Commissioner of States General, 138
Dordrecht (Dort), Subchamber of, 40, 41
Draft plan of Chamber Amsterdam (1638), 149
Dunkirk Privateers, 66, 85, 158
Dyes, 47, 48, 98, 99
Dying, 79

East India Company (Dutch): compared with West India Company, 25, 27, 29; corruption of directors, 32–33; directors banned from West India Company directorship, 36
Eelckens, Hendrick, 13, 22
Eelckens, Jacques or Jacob, 11n, 22, 131n
Eendracht, 82n, 130, 140, 141

El Dorado, 48

Elmina, Guinea Coast, 49, 88, 153

Enckhuysen, Subchamber of, 40, 41

Engel, Adriaen Jansz, 13

England: claims to New Netherland of, 13–14; detains *Orangen boom*, 84; threat to New Netherland from, 71–72, 96*n*. *See also* Englishmen

Englishmen: in New Netherland territory, 93, 131, 141, 142; on Essequibo River, 99. *See also* England

Essequibo River: colonies on, 47, 97, 98–99

Exports from New Netherland other than furs, 61–63, 70–71

Family: as colonizing unit, 75

Fire arms, 21, 151*n*, 152

Fish in New Netherland, 63, 92–93

Forest, Jesse de, 75*n*

Fort Amsterdam (Manhattan Island): cost of maintaining, 125–27; ruinous condition of, 142, 154; staked out, 86; mentioned, 80, 108, 141

Fort Good Hope (Connecticut River), 131, 151*n*

Fort Nassau (Amazon River), 47

Fort Nassau (Delaware River), 141, 142

Fort Nassau (Hudson River), 11–12, 83, 93

Fort Nassau (Mouree, West Africa), 49

Fort Orange (Amazon River), 47

Fort Orange (Hudson River): colonists withdrawn from, 87; construction of, 83; cost of maintaining, 125–27; importance of, 93, 110; trade at, 141, 142; mentioned, 91, 116, 141, 151*n*

Fort Wilhelmus (Hudson River), 82*n*

Fortuyn (of May), 8

Fortuyn (*spiegelship* of 55 lasts), 6, 8, 18

Fransz, Pieter, 8, 21*n*

Free trade in Brazil. *See* Brazil

Free trade in New Netherland, 148–52

Freedoms for Guiana; as precedent for New Netherland freedoms, 100–1, 108–9, 110; of 1627, 79, 101–3; of 1628, 79, 103, 104–5

Freedoms for New Netherland: in 1628, 103–104, 107, 108; in 1629. *See* *Vryheden*

Freight charges: on Brazilian exports, 145; paid by Guiana patroons, 104;

to Norway and New Netherland, compared, 66, 157–60; to New Netherland, 64, 65, 127; to Baltic ports and New Netherland, compared, 64–66, 157–60; to Baltic ports, 69

" French " Indians: and Iroquois, 94, 132, 141; at Fort Orange, 93; mentioned, 20

French traders, 3, 93, 96*n*

Fur market of Western Europe, 22–23. *See also* Fur trade

Fur monopoly in New Netherland, 104, 147, 149, 151. *See also* Fur trade

Fur smuggling, 94, 123*n*, 147

Fur trade: and *coloniërs*, 79, 86; and patroons, 104–12 *passim*, 122, 133; at Swanendael, 116; between Iroquois and " French " Indians, 132, 141; in competition with the French, 20, 93; of *voorcompagnieën*, 6, 7, 18–22, 58; profitability, 124–29; seasonality, 17; in 1624–28, 93–94, 111*n*, 128; in 1630, 128, 129; in 1633–36, 130–32, 141–42. *See also* Fur market; Fur monopoly; Fur smuggling; Furs; Trading truck

Furs: export duty on, 109, 111; in New Netherland, 18, 20–21; minor varieties traded, 3, 21; sources of, other than New Netherland, 3; winter pelts superior, 17. *See also* Beaver pelts; Fur market; Fur monopoly; Fur smuggling; Fur trade; Otter pelts

Generael Octroy (1614), 9–10

General Assembly of the Nineteen: approves patroon system, 95, 101–7 *passim*; composition of, 27, 29, 36; conciliatory policy toward patroons, 133–34; method of operation, 37–38; supervision by States General of, 27. *See also* West India Company

General Charter (1614), 9–10

General Charter for Guiana. *See* Freedoms for Guiana

General Insurance Company, 158, 159, 165

Gijsselingh, Johan, 121

Godijn, Samuel: commissioner for New Netherland, 112, 113; director, 56; draws up *provisionele ordere*, 77; patroon, 113, 116; pools patroonship, 114, 167; purchases land in New

Netherland, 106, 115; mentioned, 109–10. *See also* Patroons; Patroonships; Swanendael
Godijns Punt, 113*n*
Goeree, West Africa, 49
Goes, Jan van der, 98, 99
Gold, 47, 48, 49, 62*n*, 99
Gold Coast. *See* Guinea
Gorges, Sir Ferdinando, 13
Governors Island, 82 and *n*, 113*n*
Grain: Dutch imports of, from Baltic, 63; possible New Netherland export, 61*n*, 68–70, 153; price of, in Amsterdam, 68; shipping charges for, 68–69
Grape products, 62*n*, 92. *See also* Wine
Griffioen, 84*n*
Groningen-Friesland, Chamber of, 36
Guiana: administration of, 39*n*; agriculture in, 99; colonies in, 47, 97–99; state of, 1623, 47–48. *See also* Amazon River; Essequibo River; Freedoms for Guiana
Guinea, 49, 70*n*, 153

Hamburg, 63
Hamel, Hendrick, 113, 114, 116, 132
Hamels Hoofden, 113*n*
Handicrafts: forbidden to *coloniërs*, 79
Haringh, 143, 144, 154, 155
Havana, Cuba, 45, 50
Hendricksz, Cornelis, 19
Hermite, Jakob L', 53
Heyn, Piet, 26, 89, 106, 110
Hirelings: sent to New Netherland, 74, 84, 85; unsatisfactoriness of, 90, 129, 142
Hoboken, 136
Holscher, Jan, 6*n*, 7*n*
Hongers, Hans, 7*n*
Hoofdparticipanten: accoordt with directors, 35–36; defined, 30; influence of, in Company affairs, 42–43; permitted to nominate directors, 34; safeguards for, 35–36
Hoogcamers Eylandt, *see* Governors Island
Hooghkamer, Jacob Pietersz, 113, 114
Hoope, 4
Hoorn, Subchamber of, 34*n*, 40–41
Hoorn partnership for New Netherland trade, 8, 13
Housatonic River, 21
Houttuyn, 158*n*
Hudson, Henry, 3, 4*n*, 56

Hudson River: climate of, 59*n*; settlement on, 82; trade on, 5, 8; mentioned, 12, 85
Hulft, Pieter Evertsz, 84
Hulst, Willem van, 83
Huntum, Hans, 130–32

Immigrants to New Netherland: concessions to, 77–81, 149–50, 151–52; means of attracting, 146–47
Indians. *See* Carib Indians; "French" Indians; Indians in New Netherland; Iroquois; Mahicans; Mohawks; Quiripeys; Sickenames
Indians in New Netherland: commercialization of, 18, 20, 21; Company's respect for, 87; and fire arms, 87, 151*n*, 152; as labor, 69; terms of trade with, 128; trade at English posts, 93; trade provisions to Dutch, 61, 88
Indian War, 1643–44, 152
Insurance rates: of proposed General Insurance Company, 159; on Baltic voyages, 66–67, 158; on New Netherland voyages, 64, 66–67, 128, 158
Iroquois, 132, 141

Jamestown, 75
Jews, 50
Jorisz, Adriaen, 56

Kieft, Willem, 143, 154
Königsberg: Dutch shipping to, 63, 66, 67, 157, 159; exports timber, 63. *See also* Baltic lands; Baltic trade

Labor: cost of, 68, 69, 71. *See also* Hirelings
Laet, Johannes [de]: character of, 117; commissioner for New Netherland, 112, 113; director, 166, 167; draws *provisionele ordere*, 77; pools patroonship, 167; member National Synod of Dordrecht, 166; patroon, 113–14, 167; scholarly achievements, 166–67; mentioned, 109
Lampo, Johan, 81
Last (a ship's measurement), 18*n*
Lastetold, 67
Legal proceedings in New Netherland, 81
Leipzig, Germany, 23

Letterhout, 98
Leyden, 166
Liebergen, Arnout van, 7*n*
Liefde, 151
Lima, Peru, 49
Livestock: bought by Van Rensselaer, 124*n*; killed by Indians, 132*n*; sent to New Netherland, 84–85, 86; shortage of, in New Netherland, 90; sold by Company, 95; mentioned, 159
Lübeck, Germany, 63

Maeckereel, 52
Maes, Chamber of, 34–39 *passim*
Maire, Isaac Le, 162
Maire, Jacques Le, 162
Mahicans, 87, 91, 94
Manatus maps, 136*n*
Manhattan Island: *bouwerijen* on, 85, 91; purchased, 86; settlement on, 85, 87; mentioned, 61
Martsen, Jacob, 101, 102, 103
Masts, 68
Mau, Sijmen Lambertsz, 4
May, Cornelis Jacobsz, 8, 56, 81
Meeuwken, 16*n*
Memorial of Four New Netherland Patroons (1634), 106
Metals, 50, 62 and *n. See also* Gold; Mines in New Netherland
Mexico, 45, 50
Michaëlius, Jonas, 90, 130*n*
Middelburg, City of, 40
Mines in New Netherland, 79–80, 92. *See also* Metals
Minuit, Pieter, 130*n*
Mohawk River, 12
Mohawks, 91, 94, 131
Moor, Jan de, 47, 97, 101, 103
Morgen: defined, 89*n*
Mossel, Thijs, 6–11 *passim*
Mouree, West Africa, 49
Munitions, 126–27. *See also Defense of New Netherland*
Murderers Island, 82*n*

Naval stores in New Netherland, 126
Negro slaves, 45, 48, 69, 99
New England, 16*n*, 70, 153
Newfoundland, 5, 76
New France, 3
New Netherland: abandonment considered, 148, 152–53; administration,

39; climate, 57; compared to Guiana, 97–98; disagreement over colonization, 57–58; discovery, 3; duration of voyages to, 17*n*, 158–59; colonizing expedition, 81–83; as investment alternative for Company, 54, 71; potential export products, 61–71, 153; prospects in 1638, 153; provisioning role of, 60–61, 70; routes to, 15–16; in 1628, 89–93; in 1635, 142; in 1638, 154
New Netherland Commission. *See* Commissioners for New Netherland
New Netherland Company, 9–13, 14, 15. *See also Voorcompagnieën*
New Plymouth, 131
"New Project," 1638, 150
New Sweden, 117, 163
Nieu Nederlandt (130 lasts), 81, 82*n*
Nieu Nederlandt (400 lasts), 82*n*, 92
Nineteen, The. *See* General Assembly of the Nineteen
Nooms, Simon, 8, 9
Noorderquartier, Chamber of the, 34, 36, 39
Norway, 63, 67, 159, 160
Noten Eylandt, 82 and *n,* 113*n*

Octroy: amplification of, 33, 35–36; bias towards warfare of, 26, 27; geographical limits of, 25; privileges granted by, 25–26
Olinda, Brazil, 120, 144
Omvallende Nooteboom, 20*n,* 126*n*
Onrust, 19*n*
Orangen boom, 83, 85
Otter pelts, 20, 129, 130, 131, 141
Ouwevaer, 106*n*
Oxensterna, Swedish Chancellor, 163

Paauw, Michiel, 114, 136, 138. *See also* Pavonia
Panama, 45
Paraiba, Brazil, 145
Paraquit, 126*n*
Patroons in Caribbean and Guiana. *See* Freedoms for Guiana; Martsen, Jacob; Moor, Jan de; Pere, Abraham van
Patroons in New Netherland: activities to 1632, 115–16; and fur trade, 110–12, 122, 133–34; Company harassment of, 123; sell patroonships, 138–39; state grievances to Nineteen, 133;

supposed deception by, 109–19; mentioned, 102. *See also* Blommaert, Samuel; Ceulen, Mattias van; Coenraets, Albert; Freedoms for New Netherland in 1628; Godijn, Samuel; Hamel, Hendrick; Laet, Johannes de; Paauw, Michiel; Patroonships in New Netherland; Patroon system in New Netherland; Rensselaer, Killiaen van; Vries, David de; *Vryheden*

Patroonships in New Netherland: Company purchase of, 138–39. *See also* Blommaert, Samuel; Coenraets, Albert; Pavonia; Rennsselaerswyck; Swanendael

Patroon system in Caribbean and Guiana. *See* Freedoms for Guiana

Patroon system in New Netherland: background of, 89–94; opponents of, 109, 117–18; precedents for, 100, 102; proposed by commissioners for New Netherland, 100. *See also* Freedoms for Guiana; Freedoms for New Netherland in 1628; Patroons in New Netherland; Patroonships in New Netherland; *Vryheden*

Pavonia, 121, 136–37

Pearls, 63

Pelgrom, Francoijs, 5, 7n, 56

Pelgrom, Leonnaert, 5, 56

Pelgrom, Pauels, 7n, 56

Peltries. *See* Furs

Pere, Abraham van, 97, 101, 103

Pernambuco, Brazil, 45, 50–51, 145, 146

Peru, 49

Pilgrims, 14, 61n, 72, 93, 131. *See also* Bradford, William; Plymouth Adventurers

Plague, 84

Plancius, Petrus, 7

Plantages, 136n

Plymouth Adventurers, 74

Poincten van beschrijvinge, 38

Political constitution of New Netherland, 80–81

Porto, Brazil, 50

Porto Rico, 88

Port Royal, 75, 76

Portuguese, 45, 70n, 98

Pos, Sijmen Dircxz, 129

Price, Jan, 52n

Princes Island, 82n

Prins Willem, 154

Private enterprise, 74–75, 85. *See also* Coloniërs; Freedoms for Guiana; Freedoms for New Netherland in 1628; Patroons in New Netherland; *Provisionele ordere; Vryheden*

Privateering, 44–46, 88, 105

Provisional arrangement of 1638/39, 151–52

Provisionele ordere, 77–81

Provisions: bought from Indians, 61, 88; estimated cost of, for New Netherland staff, 126

Puncto del Rey, Venezuela, 25, 33, 48, 55

Quebec, 75

Quiripeys (Indian tribe), 21

Raleigh, Sir Walter, 48

Ranst, Pieter, 84

Rapaille, Catalijna Trico, 82n

Rasieres, Isaac de, 23, 90, 91, 93

Recife, Brazil, 120

Reijnst, Gerrit, 162

Religion in New Netherland, 80–81

Rensselaer, Kiliaen van: and fur trade, 115, 116; colonizing efforts of, 106, 115, 116, 123n; commissioner for New Netherland, 112, 113; Memorial to the Nineteen, 106; mentioned, 109–10, 116; pools patroonship, 114; registers patroonship, 113. *See also* Rensselaerswyck

Rensselaers Hoeck, 113n

Rensselaerswyck, Colony of, 105, 116, 137. *See also* Rensselaer, Kilian van

Rensselaerswyck, (a ship), 17, 158n

Reval, shipping charges from, 66, 67–68, 159

Riga, 63, 67, 159

Romonde, Jan, 129

Rooduyf, 20n

Rotterdam, Subchamber of, 39n, 40, 41

Russian furs, 3, 22

Ruyl, Albert Gerritsz, 10

Ruyll, Gerrit Allertsz, 6n

Ruyter, 85n, 65

Ryser, Cornelis, 5

Sagadahoc, 75

St. Lawrence River, 3

St. Martin, West Indies, 162

St. Pieter, 5

St. Vincent, West Indies, 165
Salt: at Puncto del Rey, 25, 48; proposed New Netherland production of, 63, 92; mentioned, 159
Sandy Hook, 113n
Sandy Hook Bay, 113n
San Juan de Porto Rico, 88
Scandinavia, 63
Schenck, Wessel, 7n
Schiltpadde, 18
Seven Ster, 142, 143
Sewan, 22, 93, 111
Shallops, 19, 126. See also Sloops
Shipbuilding in New Netherland, 56, 92
Shipping costs: New Netherland vs. Baltic, 64–69
Ships: as mobile trading posts, 18–19; size used by Dutch in Baltic, 18; size used by voorcompagnieën, 18
Siberia, 3
Sickenames (an Indian tribe), 22
Sierra Leone, 39n
Silver Fleet, 26, 45, 106, 117, 120
Sloops, 19, 93, 126. See also Shallops
Snellen, Willem, 15
Sound toll, 67
Southberch, 123n, 130
Spain, 44, 45, 48
Spiegelschip, 6 and n
Spilbergen, Jaris van, 49
Spranger, Gommer, 113, 114
Staten Island, 136
States General: and accoordt, 35; amplifies Octroy, 33; approves Company monopoly in Brazil, 146; demands free trade in New Netherland, 148, 150; influence on West India Company of, 27, 43, 53, 55; investment of, in West India Company, 36, 37; issues Generael Octroy, 9; medicates Company-patroon dispute, 134, 138; and subscription drive, 31–33, 35
States of Holland, 33, 34
Stettin, Germany, 63
Subchambers, 34n, 39–41
Sugar, 45, 47, 50, 51
Sulfur, 62 and n
Swanendael: agricultural efforts, 116; exterminated by Indians, 135; fur trade, 116, 122; hopes for whaling, 116; location of, 116, 135; purchase of, by Company, 121, 135; mentioned, 57, 132. See also Delaware

Bay; Delaware River; Godijn, Samuel
Swarte Paert, 84n
Sweerts, Barent, 7n
Sweden, 117, 163–64
Swol, 127n

Taxation: in Brazil, 51, 149; in Guiana, 104, 105; in New Netherland, 105, 148n, 149, 151–52. See also Convoyen; Lastetold
Timber: as New Netherland export, 61, 68, 91–92; cost of, 68n; European sources of, 63. See also Masts; Wood Extracts
Tithes. See Taxation
Tobacco, 47, 48, 63, 97, 99
Tobago, 101, 103
Tolls, 67
Trading goods. See Trading truck
Trading posts: advantages of, 19–21, 58; on Essequibo River, 99. See also Fort Amsterdam (Hudson River); Fort Good Hope (Connecticut River); Fort Nassau (Delaware River); Fort Nassau (Hudson River)
Trading truck: and patroons, 115–16, 122; kind used, 7, 21, 93; value of, 94, 128. See also Fur trade
Tweenhuysen, Lambrecht van, 7n, 56
Twelve Years Truce, 50
Twiller, Wouter van, 130, 131, 140, 141, 143

Usselincx, Willem, 28n, 31, 46, 52

Veere, 40
Verhulst, Willem, 83
Viana, Brazil, 50
Viniculture, 92
Virginia Company of London, 54, 74, 77, 80
Vlissingen, 40
Vogelaer, Marcus de, 120, 133, 138
Vogels, Arnout, 3–7 passim, 22, 56, 77
Vogels partnership, 7n
Voorcompagnieën: defined, 14; goods traded by, 20, 21, 22; market for furs of, 22–23; competition between, 6–9, 13, 58–59; sailing patterns of, 16n, 17 and n; ships and boats of, 18, 19; trading posts of, 19, 20, 21. See also New Netherland Company
Vorst, Cornelis van, 136n

Vos, 8–9
Voyages to New Netherland: duration of, 16, 158–59; seasonality of, 17–18
Voyages to the Baltic, 159–60
Vries, David de, 19*n*, 57, 112, 122*n*, 123*n*
Vryheden, 79, 104–19 *passim*

Wages for New Netherland staff, 126
Walvisch, 19*n*, 122*n*
Walloons, 71, 75 and *n*, 76
Wapen van Amsterdam, 21*n*, 61*n*
Weaving, 79
Weede, Commissioner of States General, 138
West Africa: Company's expedition to, 1626, 88; potential market for New Netherland grain, 70; trade in, 45, 48–49, 55*n*. *See also* Argijn; Canary Islands; Cape Verde; Elmina; Goeree; Guinea; Mouree
West India Company: and fur trade, 86, 122, 133–34, 141, 155; and patroons, 109, 121, 122, 133–37; and *voorcompagnieën*, 15; cameral organization of, 28–29, 39–41; capital of, 36, 37, 88, 101, 120, 144; decline of, 37; in Brazil, 120, 144–47; Indian policy of, 83, 87; in Guiana, 97–105; investment needs and alternatives of, 44–52, 71; operational efficiency of, 37–43; opposes private investment within *Octroy*, 101; purpose of, 26, 43, 53; subscription drive, 31–37. *See also* Board of Audit; Chambers of West India Company; Commissioners for New Netherland; Directors of West India Company; General Assembly of the Nineteen; *Hoofdparticipanten; Octroy; Poincten van bescrijvingen*; Subchambers
West Indies, 44–45
Whales and whaling, 93, 116, 135
Wiapoco River, Guiana, 98
Wine, 45, 63. *See also* Grape products
Wit, de, early voyager to New Netherland, 21*n*
Witsen, Gerrit Jacobsz, 12
Witsen, Jonas, 8, 9, 12, 56
Witte Duyf, 16*n*, 18
Wood extracts, 61*n*, 63, 92

Yachts, 19, 93, 126

Zeeland, Chamber of, 34–43 *passim*, 98, 101, 145
Zeeland, Province of, 40, 47
Zeepaert, 126*n*
Zuylen, Philips van, 44*n*